DRAWN
WITH THE
SWORD

DRAWN

WITH THE

SWORD

James M. McPherson

REFLECTIONS ON THE AMERICAN CIVIL WAR

New York   Oxford

OXFORD UNIVERSITY PRESS

1996

Oxford University Press

Oxford   New York
Athens   Auckland   Bangkok   Bombay
Calcutta   Cape Town   Dar es Salaam   Delhi
Florence   Hong Kong   Istanbul   Karachi
Kuala Lumpur   Madras   Madrid   Melbourne
Mexico City   Nairobi   Paris   Singapore
Taipei   Tokyo   Toronto

and associated companies in
Berlin   Ibadan

Copyright © 1996 by James M. McPherson

Published by Oxford University Press, Inc.,
198 Madison Avenue, New York, New York 10016

Oxford is a registered trademark of Oxford University Press

Library of Congress Cataloging-in-Publication Data
McPherson, James M.
Drawn with the sword : reflections on the American Civil War /
James M. McPherson.
p. cm.   ISBN 0-19-509679-7
1. United States—History—Civil War, 1861–1865.   I. Title.
E468.M228   1996
973.7—dc20   95-38107

1 3 5 7 9 8 6 4 2

Printed in the United States of America
on acid-free paper

To My Father

and the

memory of

My Mother

Fondly do we hope—fervently do we pray—that this mighty scourge of war may speedily pass away. Yet, if God wills that it continue, until all the wealth piled by the bond-man's two hundred and fifty years of unrequited toil shall be sunk, and until every drop of blood drawn with the lash, shall be paid by another drawn with the sword, as was said three thousand years ago, so still it must be said "the judgments of the Lord, are true and righteous altogether."

Abraham Lincoln
second inaugural address
March 4, 1865

PREFACE

IN 1976 A DELEGATION OF HISTORIANS FROM THE SOVIET UNION visited the United States to participate in commemorations of the bicentennial of the American Revolution. Upon their arrival, a local host asked them which sites they would like to visit first. He assumed that they would want to see Independence Hall, or perhaps Lexington and Concord, or Williamsburg and Yorktown. But the answer was none of the above. They wished to go first to Gettysburg. The host—a historian of the Revolution and the early republic—was dumfounded. Why Gettysburg? he asked. Because, they replied, it is the American Stalingrad—the battlefield in America's Great Patriotic War where so many gave the last full measure of devotion that the United States might not perish from the earth.

Some historians might question whether the battle of Gettysburg was as crucial a turning point in the Civil War as the battle of Stalingrad was in World War II. And many might challenge the implied comparison of the Confederacy to Nazi Germany. But few would gainsay the importance of the Civil War as a defining experience in American history equal to and perhaps even greater than the Revolution itself. The war of 1861–1865 resolved two fundamental questions left unresolved by the war of 1776–1783: whether the United States would endure as one nation, indivisible; and whether slavery would continue to mock the ideals of liberty on which the republic was founded.

Little wonder, then, that popular interest in the Civil War eclipses interest in any other aspect of American history—a phenomenon analyzed in chapter 4 of this book. One reason for our fascination with the Civil War is that momentous issues were at stake: slavery and freedom; racism and equality; sectionalism and nationalism; self-government and democracy; life and death. The crucible of armed conflict called forth leaders who have acquired almost mythical stature in the American pantheon. These issues and leaders are the subjects of the essays that follow. Several themes tie the essays together: slavery as a polarizing issue that split the country and brought war (part 1); the evolution of the conflict from a limited war for restoration of the old Union to a "total war" for a new birth of freedom (parts 2 and 4); the role of blacks in the war (parts 2 and 4); the reasons for Northern victory (part 3); political and military leadership (parts 3 and 4); the enduring impact of the war on consciousness and institutions abroad as well as at home (parts 2, 4, and 5).

All of the essays in this volume except chapter 15 have been previously published as independent articles, lectures, or review essays, but each has been modified and updated for publication here. Each is complete in itself, but if I have done the job right, they also fit together in a cohesive pattern of chapters that can be read consecutively from beginning to end. Although the essays are grounded in many years of reading and research, they are more interpretive than monographic and I have therefore confined the footnotes mainly to citations for quotations.

The essays were written for all three of the "audiences" described in chapter 15. I hope that they may contain insights of value to professional historians, Civil War "buffs," and "general readers" alike. In 1873, as noted in chapter 5, Mark Twain wrote that the Civil

War had "uprooted institutions that were centuries old, changed the politics of a people, transformed the social life of half the country, and wrought so profoundly upon the entire national character that the influence cannot be measured short of two or three generations." If readers will take away from this book a greater understanding of how and why it did so, I will have accomplished my purpose.

Princeton, N.J.   J. M. M.
July 1995

PROVENANCE OF
THE CONTENTS

ALL BUT THE FINAL ESSAY IN THIS VOLUME HAVE BEEN PRE-
viously published. In most cases, however, I have updated and
slightly revised the essays in order to give the volume thematic coherence. I am indebted to the publications that own the copyrights
to previously published articles for permission to reprint them here
in their modified form. In some cases the original essay was published under a different title, as indicated below.

1. "Antebellum Southern Exceptionalism: A New Look at an Old
Question," *Civil War History* 29 (1983), 230–44.
2. "Tom on the Cross," published originally as the Introduction
to Harriet Beecher Stowe, *Uncle Tom's Cabin* (New York: Vintage
Books, 1991), xi–xx.
3. "The War of Southern Aggression," *New York Review of Books*,
19 January 1989, 16–20.
4. "The War that Never Goes Away," first published as "A War
That Never Goes Away," *American Heritage* 41 (1990), 41–49.
5. "From Limited to Total War, 1861–1865," first published as

"From Limited to Total War: Missouri and the Nation, 1862–1865," *Gateway Heritage: Magazine of the Missouri Historical Society* 12 (1992), 4–19.

6. "Race and Class in the Crucible of War," first published as "Wartime," *New York Review of Books,* 12 April 1990, 33–35.

7. "The *Glory* Story," first published as "The 'Glory Story': The 54th Massachusetts and the Civil War," *New Republic,* 8 and 15 January 1990, 22–27.

8. "Why Did the Confederacy Lose?" first published as "American Victory, American Defeat," in Gabor S. Boritt, ed., *Why the Confederacy Lost* (New York: Oxford University Press, 1992), 15–42.

9. "How the Confederacy Almost Won," first published as "How the North Nearly Lost," *New York Review of Books,* 12 October 1989, 43–46.

10. "Lee Dissected," first published as "How Noble Was Robert E. Lee?" *New York Review of Books,* 7 November 1991, 10–14.

11. "Grant's Final Victory," first published as "Ulysses S. Grant's Final Victory," *MHQ: The Quarterly Journal of Military History* 2 (1990), 96–103.

12. "A New Birth of Freedom," first published as "Liberating Lincoln," *New York Review of Books,* 21 April 1994, 7–10, and "The Art of Abraham Lincoln," *New York Review of Books,* 16 July 1992, 3–5.

13. "Who Freed the Slaves?" *Reconstruction* 2 (1994), 35–40.

14. " 'The Whole Family Man': Lincoln and the Last Best Hope Abroad," in Robert E. May, ed., *The Union, the Confederacy, and the Atlantic Rim* (West Lafayette: Purdue University Press, 1995), 131–58.

15. "What's the Matter with History?" first delivered as a paper at a conference entitled "The State of Historical Writing in North America," at the University of San Marino, Republic of San Marino, 6 June 1995.

CONTENTS

I

ORIGINS
OF THE
CIVIL WAR

1

ANTEBELLUM SOUTHERN
EXCEPTIONALISM

A New Look at an Old Question

THE THEME OF AMERICAN EXCEPTIONALISM PERMEATED WRITING
about the United States from its beginning but has come under
attack in recent years. Ever since Hector St. John Crèvecoeur asked
his famous question in 1782, "What Is the American, This New
Man?" native and foreign commentators alike have sought to define
what supposedly makes the United States exceptional, indeed unique,
among peoples of the world. Reaching the height of its influence in
the 1950s, the exceptionalist school argued that something special
about the American experience—whether it was abundance, free
land on the frontier, the absence of a feudal past, exceptional mobility and the relative lack of class conflict, or the pragmatic and con-
sensual liberalism of our politics—set the American people apart
from the rest of humankind. During the last three decades, however,
the dominant trends in American historiography have challenged
and perhaps crippled the exceptionalist thesis. Historians have demonstrated the existence of class and class conflict, ideological politics,
land speculation, and patterns of economic and social development
similar to those of western Europe which placed the United States

in the mainstream of modern North Atlantic history, not on a special and privileged fringe.[1]

While the notion of American exceptionalism has suffered considerable damage, another exceptionalist interpretation remains apparently live and well. Even though America may not be as different from the rest of the world as we thought, the South seems to have been different from the rest of America. In this essay, "Southern exceptionalism" refers to the belief that the South has "possessed a separate and unique identity . . . which appeared to be out of the mainstream of American experience."[2] Or as Quentin Compson (in William Faulkner's *Absalom, Absalom!*) expressed it in reply to his Canadian-born college roommate's question about what made Southerners tick: "You can't understand it. You would have to be born there."

The idea of Southern exceptionalism, however, has also come under challenge. The questions whether the South was indeed out of the mainstream and, if so, whether it has recently been swept into it have become lively issues in Southern historiography. The clash of viewpoints can be illustrated by a sampling of titles or subtitles of books that have appeared in recent decades. On one side we have *The Enduring South, The Everlasting South, The Idea of the South, The Lasting South, The Continuity of Southern Distinctiveness,* and *What*

---

1. For the pros and cons of the exceptionalism thesis, the following are valuable: Laurence Veysey, "The Autonomy of American History Reconsidered," *American Quarterly* 31 (1979), 455–77; Sean Wilentz, "Against Exceptionalism: Class Consciousness and the American Labor Movement," *International Labor and Working Class History* 26 (1984), 1–24; Byron E. Shafer, ed., *Is America Different? A New Look at American Exceptionalism* (Oxford, 1991); Ian Tyrrell, "American Exceptionalism in an Age of International History," *American Historical Review* 96 (1991), 1031–55, 1068–72; Michael McGerr, "The Price of the 'New Transnational History,'" *American Historical Review* 96 (1991), 1056–67; and Michael Kammen, "The Problem of American Exceptionalism: A Reconsideration," *American Quarterly* 45 (1993), 1–43.

2. Monroe L. Billington, ed., *The South: A Central Theme?* (Huntington, N.Y., 1976), p. 1.

Made the South Different?—all arguing, in one way or another, that the South was and continues to be different. On the other side we have *The Southerner as American, The Americanization of Dixie, Epitaph for Dixie, Southerners and Other Americans, The Vanishing South,* and *Into the Mainstream.* Some of these books insist that "the traditional emphasis on the South's differentness . . . is wrong historically."[3] Others concede that while the South may once have been different, it has ceased to be or is ceasing to be so. There is no unanimity among this latter group of scholars about precisely when or how the South joined the mainstream. Some emphasize the civil rights revolution of the 1960s; others the bulldozer revolution of the 1950s; still others the chamber of commerce Babbittry of the 1920s; and some the New South crusade of the 1880s. As far back as 1869 the Yankee novelist John William De Forest wrote of the South: "We shall do well to study this peculiar people, which will soon lose it peculiarities." As George Tindall has wryly remarked, the Vanishing South has "staged one of the most prolonged disappearing acts since the decline and fall of Rome."[4]

Some historians, however, would quarrel with the concept of a Vanishing South because they believe that the South as a separate, exceptional entity never existed—with of course the ephemeral exception of the Confederacy. A good many other historians insist not only that a unique South did exist before the Civil War, but also that its sense of being under siege by an alien North was the underlying cause of secession. A few paired quotations will illustrate these conflicting interpretations.

In 1960 one Southern historian maintained that "no picture of the Old South as a section confident and united in its dedication to a neo-feudal social order, and no explanation of the Civil War as a conflict between 'two civilizations,' can encompass the complexity

3. Charles Grier Sellers, ed., *The Southerner as American* (Chapel Hill, 1960), pp. v–vi.
4. George Brown Tindall, *The Ethnic Southerners* (Baton Rouge, 1976), p. ix.

and pathos of the antebellum reality." But later in the decade another historian insisted that slavery created "a ruling class with economic interests, political ideals, and moral sentiments" that included an "aristocratic, antibourgeois spirit with values and mores emphasizing family and status, a strong code of honor, and aspirations to luxury, ease, and accomplishment" that "set it apart from the mainstream of capitalist development." This ruling class possessed "the political and economic power to impose their values on [Southern] society as a whole." Since submission to the hegemony of Northern free-soilers would have meant "moral and political suicide" for this "special civilization" of the South, a "final struggle [was] so probable that we may safely call it inevitable." The first historian is Charles Sellers; the second, Eugene Genovese.[5]

Or let us examine another pair of quotations, the first published in 1973 by a Southern historian who asserted that the thesis of a "basically divergent and antagonistic" North and South in 1861 is "one of the great myths of American history." Almost as if in reply, a historian wrote a few years later that such an assertion "belies common sense and the nearly universal observation of contemporaries. We submit a single figure that . . . attests to the irrelevance of all [statistical manipulations] purporting to show similarities between North and South. The figure is 600,000—the number of Civil War graves." The first of these quotations is from Grady McWhiney. The second is from—Grady McWhiney.[6]

Finally, let us look at another pair of statements, the first from one of the South's most eminent historians writing in 1958: "The

5. Charles Grier Sellers, "The Travail of Slavery," in Sellers, ed., *The Southerner as American*, p. 40; Eugene D. Genovese, *The Political Economy of Slavery* (New York, 1965), pp. 7–8, 28–29, 247, 270; Genovese, *The World the Slaveholders Made* (New York, 1969), p. 33.

6. Grady McWhiney, *Southerners and Other Americans* (New York, 1973), p. 3; McWhiney and Forrest McDonald, "Communication," *American Historical Review* 86 (1981), 244. In *Cracker Culture: Celtic Ways in the Old South* (Tuscaloosa, Ala., 1988), McWhiney offers the provocative hypothesis that the Celtic heritage of many white Southerners accounts for Southern distinctiveness.

South was American a long time before it was Southern in any self-conscious or distinctive way. It remains more American by far than anything else, and has all along." The second is from an equally eminent historian writing in 1969: "A great slave society . . . had grown up and miraculously flourished in the heart of a thoroughly bourgeois and partly puritanical republic. It had renounced its bourgeois origins and elaborated and painfully rationalized its institutional, legal, metaphysical, and religious defenses. . . . When the crisis came [it] chose to fight. It proved to be the death struggle of a society." The first historian was C. Vann Woodward. The second—it should come as no surprise by now—was C. Vann Woodward.[7]

If given the opportunity, McWhiney and Woodward might be able to reconcile the apparent inconsistencies in these statements. Or perhaps they really changed their minds. After all, as Ralph Waldo Emerson told us more than a century ago, "a foolish consistency is the hobgoblin of little minds." In any case, the more recent vintage of both McWhiney and Woodward has a fuller, more robust, and truer flavor.

Many antebellum Americans certainly thought that North and South had evolved separate societies with institutions, interests, values, and ideologies so incompatible, so much in deadly conflict that they could no longer live together in the same nation. Traveling through the South in the spring of 1861, London *Times* correspondent William Howard Russell encountered this "conflict of civilizations" theme everywhere he went. "The tone in which [Southerners] alluded to the whole of the Northern people indicated the clear conviction that trade, commerce, the pursuit of gain, manufacture, and

---

7. C. Vann Woodward, *The Burden of Southern History* (Baton Rouge, 1960), p. 25; Woodward, *American Counterpoint: Slavery and Racism in the North-South Dialogue* (Boston, 1971), p. 281. Woodward subsequently noted that the English-born Northern journalist Edwin L. Godkin indulged in only "some exaggeration" when he wrote in 1880 that the South "differs nearly as much from the North as Ireland does, or Hungary or Turkey." Woodward, *Thinking Back: The Perils of Writing History* (Baton Rouge, 1986), p. 123.

the base mechanical arts, had so degraded the whole race" that Southerners could no longer tolerate association with them, wrote Russell. "There is a degree of something like ferocity in the Southern mind [especially] toward New England which exceeds belief." A South Carolinian told Russell: "We are an agricultural people, pursuing our own system, and working out our own destiny, breeding up women and men with some other purpose than to make them vulgar, fanatical, cheating Yankees." Louis Wigfall of Texas, a former U.S. senator, told Russell:

> We are a peculiar people, sir! . . . We are an agricultural people.
> . . . We have no cities—we don't want them. . . . We want no man-
> ufactures: we desire no trading, no mechanical or manufacturing
> classes. . . . As long as we have our rice, our sugar, our tobacco, and
> our cotton, we can command wealth to purchase all we want. . . .
> But with the Yankees we will never trade—never. Not one pound of
> cotton shall ever go from the South to their accursed cities.[8]

Such opinions were not universal in the South, of course, but in the fevered atmosphere of the late 1850s they were widely shared. "Free Society!" exclaimed a Georgia newspaper. "We sicken at the name. What is it but a conglomeration of greasy mechanics, filthy operatives, small-fisted farmers, and moon-struck theorists . . . hardly fit for association with a southern gentleman's body servant." In 1861 the *Southern Literary Messenger* explained to its readers: "It is not a question of slavery alone that we are called upon to decide. It is free society which we must shun or embrace." In the same year Charles Colcock Jones, Jr., a native of Georgia who had graduated from Princeton and from Harvard Law School, spoke of the development of antagonistic cultures in North and South: "In this country have arisen two races [i.e., Northerners and Southerners] which, although claiming a common parentage, have been so entirely sepa-

8. William Howard Russell, *My Diary North and South*, ed. Fletcher Pratt (New York, 1954), pp. 38, 78, 99.

rated by climate, by morals, by religion, and by estimates so totally opposite to all that constitutes honor, truth, and manliness, that they cannot longer exist under the same government."[9]

Spokesmen for the free-labor ideology, which was the dominant political force in the North by 1860, reciprocated these sentiments. The South, said Theodore Parker, was "the foe to Northern Industry—to our mines, our manufactures, and our commerce. . . . She is the foe to our institutions—to our democratic politics in the State, our democratic culture in the school, our democratic work in the community, our democratic equality in the family."[10] Slavery, said William H. Seward, undermined "intelligence, vigor, and energy" in both blacks and whites. It produced "an exhausted soil, old and decaying towns, wretchedly-neglected roads . . . an absence of enterprise and improvement." Slavery was therefore "incompatible with all . . . the elements of the security, welfare, and greatness of nations." The struggle between free labor and slavery, between North and South, said Seward in his most famous speech, was "an irrepressible conflict between two opposing and enduring forces." The United States was therefore two nations, but it could not remain forever so: it "must and will, sooner or later, become either entirely a slaveholding nation, or entirely a free-labor nation." Abraham Lincoln expressed exactly the same theme in his "house divided" speech. Many other Republicans echoed this argument that the struggle, in the words of an Ohio congressman, was "between systems, between civilizations."[11]

These sentiments were no more confined to fire-breathing Northern radicals than were Southern exceptionalist viewpoints confined

9. *Muscogee Herald,* quoted in *New York Tribune,* Sept. 10, 1856; *Southern Literary Messenger* 32 (Feb. 1861), 152; Robert Manson Myers, ed., *Children of Pride: A True Story of Georgia and the Civil War* (New Haven, 1972), p. 648.

10. Parker, "The Nebraska Question" (1854), in John L. Thomas, ed., *Slavery Attacked: The Abolitionist Crusade* (Englewood Cliffs, N.J., 1965), p. 149.

11. Quoted in Eric Foner, *Free Soil, Free Labor, Free Men: The Ideology of the Republican Party before the Civil War* (New York, 1970), 41, 68–70.

to fire-eaters. Lincoln represented the mainstream of his party, which commanded a majority of votes in the North by 1860. The dominant elements in the North and in the lower South believed the United States to be composed of two incompatible civilizations. Southerners believed that survival of their special civilization could be assured only in a separate nation. The creation of the Confederacy was merely a political ratification of an irrevocable separation that had already taken place in the hearts and minds of the people.

The proponents of an assimilationist rather than exceptionalist interpretation of Southern history maintain that this concept of a separate and unique South existed *only* in hearts and minds. It was a subjective reality, they argue, not an objective one. Objectively, they insist, North and South were one people. They shared the same language, the same Constitution, the same legal system, the same commitment to republican political institutions and a capitalist economy intertwined with that of the North, the same predominantly Protestant religion and British ethnic heritage, the same history, the same shared memories of a common struggle for nationhood.[12]

Two proponents of the objective similarity thesis were the late Edward Pessen and David Potter. In a long article entitled "How Different from Each Other Were the Antebellum North and South?" Pessen concludes that they "were far more alike than the conventional scholarly wisdom has led us to believe."[13] His evidence for this conclusion consists mainly of quantitative measures of the distribution of wealth and of the socioeconomic status of political officeholders in North and South. He finds that wealth was distributed in a similarly unequal fashion in both sections, voting requirements were similar, and voters in both sections elected a similarly disproportionate number of men from the upper economic strata to office. The problem with this argument is that it could be used to

12. This is the central thesis of F. N. Boney, *Southerners All* (Macon, Ga., 1984). See also James Oakes, *Slavery and Freedom: An Interpretation of the Old South* (New York, 1990), esp. pp. 40–42.

13. *American Historical Review* 86 (1980), 1119–49; quotation from p. 1147.

prove many obviously different and mutually hostile societies to be similar. France and Germany in 1914 and in 1932 had about the same distribution of wealth and similar habits of electing men from the upper strata to the Assembly or the Reichstag. England and France had a comparable distribution of wealth during most of the eighteenth century. Turkey and Russia were not dissimilar in these respects in the nineteenth century. And so on.

David Potter's contention that commonalities of language, religion, law, and political system outweighed differences in other areas is more persuasive than the Pessen argument. But the Potter thesis nevertheless begs some important questions. The same similarities prevailed between England and her North American colonies in 1776, but they did not prevent the development of a separate nationalism in the latter. It is not language or law alone that is important, but the uses to which either is put. In the United States of the 1850s, Northerners and Southerners spoke the same language, to be sure, but they were increasingly using this language to revile each other. Language became an instrument of division, not unity. The same was true of the political system. So also of the law: Northern states passed personal liberty laws to defy a national Fugitive Slave Law supported by the South; a Southern-dominated Supreme Court denied the right of Congress to exclude slavery from the territories, a ruling that most Northerners considered an infamous distortion of the Constitution. As for a shared commitment to Protestantism, this too had become a divisive rather than unifying factor, with the two largest denominations—Methodist and Baptist—having split into hostile Southern and Northern churches over the question of slavery, and the third largest—Presbyterian—having split partly along sectional lines and partly on the question of slavery. As for a shared historical commitment to republicanism, by the 1850s this too was more divisive than unifying. Northern Republicans interpreted this commitment in a free-soil context, while most Southern whites continued to insist that one of the most cherished tenets of republican liberty was the right of property—including property in slaves.

There is another dimension of the Potter thesis—or perhaps it would be more accurate to call it a separate Potter thesis—that might put us on the right track to solve the puzzle of Southern exceptionalism. After challenging most notions of Southern distinctiveness, Potter concluded that the principal characteristic distinguishing the South from the rest of the country was the persistence of a "folk culture" in the South.[14] This gemeinschaft culture, with its emphasis on tradition, rural life, close kinship ties, a hierarchical social structure, ascribed status, patterns of deference, and masculine codes of honor and chivalry, persisted in the South long after the North began moving toward a gesellschaft culture with its impersonal, bureaucratic, meritocratic, urbanizing, commercial, industrializing, mobile, and rootless characteristics. Above all, the South's folk culture valued tradition and stability and felt threatened by change; the North's modernizing culture enshrined change as progress and condemned the South as backward.

A variety of statistics undergird the gemeinschaft-gesellschaft contrast. The North was more urban than the South and was urbanizing at a faster rate. In 1820, 10 percent of the free-state residents lived in urban areas (defined by the census as towns or cities with a population of 2,500 or more) compared with 5 percent in the slave

14. This brief summary of and gloss upon Potter's writings necessarily oversimplifies arguments that are complex, subtle, and at times ambivalent. Potter's emphasis on the commonalities of Northern and Southern culture can be found in his essay "The Historian's Use of Nationalism and Vice Versa," in Potter, *The South and the Sectional Conflict* (Baton Rouge, 1968), pp. 68–78, and Potter, *The Impending Crisis 1848–1861* (New York, 1976), pp. 8–14, 29–34, 449–50, 469–74. The brief explication of his "folk culture" argument can be found in *ibid.,* 451, 456–57, and in *The South and the Sectional Conflict,* pp. 15–16. The notion of a persistent folk culture in the South is associated mainly with the work of the Southern sociologist Howard Odum; for an analysis of this concept in the context of Odum's work, see Daniel T. Rodgers, "Regionalism and the Burdens of Progress," in J. Morgan Kousser and James M. McPherson, eds., *Region, Race, and Reconstruction: Essays in Honor of C. Vann Woodward* (New York, 1982), pp. 3–26.

states. By 1860 the figures were 26 percent and 10 percent, respectively.[15] More striking was the growing contrast between farm and nonfarm occupations in the two sections. In 1800, 82 percent of the Southern labor force worked in agriculture compared with 68 percent in the free states. By 1860 the Northern share had dropped to 40 percent, while the Southern proportion had actually increased slightly, to 84 percent.[16] Southern agriculture remained traditionally labor-intensive while Northern farming became increasingly capital-intensive and mechanized. By 1860 the free states had nearly twice the value of farm machinery per acre and per farmworker as the slave states. And the pace of industrialization in the North far outstripped that in the South. In 1810 the slave states had an estimated 31 percent of the capital invested in manufacturing in the United States; by 1860 this had declined to 16 percent.

A critic of the inferences drawn from these data might point out that in many respects the differences between the free states east and west of the Appalachians were nearly or virtually as great as those between North and South, yet these differences did not produce a sense of separate nationality in East and West. This point is true—as far as it goes. While the western free states at midcentury did have a higher proportion of workers employed in nonfarm occupations than the South, they had about the same percentage of urban population and the same amount per capita invested in manufacturing. But the crucial factor was *the rate of change.* The West was urbanizing and industrializing more rapidly than either the Northeast or the South. Therefore while North and South as a whole were growing relatively farther apart, the eastern and western free states were drawing closer together. This process frustrated Southern hopes for an alliance with the Old Northwest on grounds of similarity of

15. Unless otherwise specified, the data presented here and in following paragraphs are from the published tables of the U.S. census.

16. Stanley Lebergott, "Labor Force and Employment, 1800–1960," in *Output, Employment, and Productivity in the United States after 1800, Studies in Income and Wealth,* vol. 30 (New York, 1966), p. 131.

agrarian interests. From 1840 to 1860 the rate of urbanization in the West was three times greater than in the Northeast and four times greater than in the South. The amount of capital invested in manufacturing grew twice as fast in the West as in the Northeast and nearly three times as fast as in the South. The same was true of employment in nonfarm occupations. The railroad-building boom of the 1850s tied the Northwest to the Northeast with links of iron and shifted the dominant pattern of inland trade from a North-South to an East-West orientation. The remarkable growth of cities like Chicago, Cincinnati, Cleveland, and Detroit with their farm-machinery, food-processing, machine-tool, and railroad-equipment industries foreshadowed the emergence of the industrial Midwest and helped to assure that when the crisis of the Union came in 1861 the West joined the East instead of the South.

According to a thorough study of antebellum Southern industry, the Southern lag in this category of development resulted not from any inherent economic disadvantages—not shortage of capital, nor low rates of return, nor nonadaptability of slave labor—but from the choices of Southerners to invest more of their money in agriculture and slaves than in manufacturing.[17] In the 1780s Thomas Jefferson had praised farmers as the "peculiar deposit for substantial and genuine virtue" and warned against the industrial classes in cities as sores on the body politic. In 1860 many Southern leaders still felt the same way; as Louis Wigfall put it in the passage quoted earlier, "We want no manufactures; we desire no trading, no mechanical or manufacturing classes."

Partly as a consequence of this attitude, the South received only a trickle of the great antebellum stream of immigration. Fewer than one-eighth of the immigrants settled in slave states, where the foreign-born percentage of the population was less than a fourth of

17. Fred Bateman and Thomas Weiss, *A Deplorable Scarcity: The Failure of Industrialization in the Slave Economy* (Chapel Hill, 1981), esp. pp. 15, 103, 121, 127, 160–62.

the North's percentage. The South's white population was ethnically more homogeneous and less cosmopolitan than the North's. The traditional patriarchal family and tight kinship networks typical of gemeinschaft societies, reinforced in the South by a relatively high rate of cousin marriages, also persisted much more strongly in the nineteenth-century South than in the North.[18]

The greater volume of immigration to the free states contributed to the faster rate of population growth there than in the South. Another factor in this differential growth rate was out-migration from the South. During the middle decades of the nineteenth century, twice as many whites left the South for the North as vice versa. These facts did not go unnoticed at the time; indeed, they formed the topic of much public comment. Northerners cited the differential in population growth as evidence for the superiority of the free-labor system; Southerners perceived it with alarm as evidence of their declining minority status in the nation. These perceptions became important factors in the growing sectional self-consciousness that led to secession.

The most crucial demographic difference between North and South resulted from slavery. Ninety-five percent of the country's black people lived in the slave states, where blacks constituted one-third of the population in contrast to their 1 percent of the Northern population. The implications of this for the economy and social structure of the two sections, not to mention their ideologies and politics, are obvious and require little elaboration here. Two brief points are worth emphasizing, however. First, historians in the last generation have discovered the viability of African-American culture under slavery. They have noted that black music, folklore, speech patterns, religion, and other manifestations of this culture influenced white society in the South. Since the African-American culture was

---

18. Bertram Wyatt-Brown, *Southern Honor: Ethics and Behavior in the Old South* (New York, 1982), esp. chap. 5; Robert C. Kenzer, *Kinship and Neighborhood in a Southern Community* (Knoxville, 1987).

preeminently a folk culture with an emphasis on oral tradition and other nonliterate forms of ritual and communication, it reinforced the persistence of a traditional, gemeinschaft, folk-oriented society in the South.

Second, many historians have maintained that Northerners were as committed to white supremacy as Southerners. This may have been true, but the scale of concern with this matter in the South was so much greater as to constitute a different order of magnitude and to contribute more than any other factor to the difference between North and South. And of course slavery was more than an institution of racial control. Its centrality to many aspects of life focused Southern politics almost exclusively on defense of the institution—to the point that, in the words of the *Charleston Mercury* in 1858, "on the subject of slavery . . . the North and South . . . are not only two Peoples, but they are rival, hostile Peoples."[19]

The fear that slavery was being hemmed in and threatened with destruction contributed to the defensive-aggressive style of Southern political behavior. This aggressiveness sometimes took physical form. Southern whites were more likely to carry weapons and to use them against other human beings than Northerners were. The homicide rate was higher in the South. The phenomenon of dueling persisted longer there. Bertram Wyatt-Brown attributes this to the Southern code of honor based on traditional patriarchal values of courtesy, status, courage, family, and the symbiosis of shame and pride.[20] The enforcement of order through the threat and practice of violence also resulted from the felt need to control a large slave population.

Martial values and practices were more pervasive in the South than in the North. Marcus Cunliffe has argued to the contrary, but

19. Quoted in John McCardell, *The Idea of a Southern Nation* (New York, 1979), pp. 270–71.

20. Dickson D. Bruce, *Violence and Culture in the Antebellum South* (Austin, Tex., 1979); Edward L. Ayers, *Vengeance and Justice: Crime and Punishment in the 19th-Century American South* (New York, 1984); Wyatt-Brown, *Southern Honor,* part 3.

the evidence confutes him. Cunliffe's argument is grounded mainly in two sets of data: the prevalence of militia and volunteer military companies in the free as well as in the slave states; and the proportion of West Pointers and regular army officers from the two sections. Yet the first set of data do not support his thesis, and the second contradict it. Cunliffe does present evidence on the popularity of military companies in the North, but nowhere does he estimate the comparative numbers of such companies in North and South or the number of men in proportion to population who belonged to them. If such comparative evidence could be assembled, it would probably support the traditional view of a higher concentration of such companies in the South. What Northern city, for example, could compare with Charleston, which had no fewer than twenty-two military companies in the late 1850s—one for every two hundred white men of military age? Another important quasi-military institution in the South with no Northern counterpart escaped Cunliffe's attention—the slave patrol, which gave tens of thousands of Southern whites a more practical form of military experience than the often ceremonial functions of volunteer drill companies could do.[21]

As for the West Point alumni and regular army officers, it is true, as Cunliffe points out, that about 60 percent of these were from the North and only 40 percent from the South in the late antebellum decades. What he fails to note is that the South had only about 30 percent of the nation's white population during this era, so that on a proportional basis the South was overrepresented in these categories. Moreover, from 1849 to 1861 all of the secretaries of war were Southerners, as were the general in chief of the army, two of the three brigadier generals, all but one commander of the army's geographical

21. Marcus Cunliffe, *Soldiers and Civilians: The Martial Spirit in America 1775–1865* (Boston, 1968), esp. chap. 10; Rollin G. Osterweis, *Romanticism and Nationalism in the Old South* (New Haven, 1949), p. 127. For other evidence of Southern bellicosity, see John Hope Franklin, *The Militant South 1800–1861* (Cambridge, Mass., 1956).

departments on the eve of the Civil War, the authors of the two manuals on infantry tactics and the artillery manual used at West Point, and the professor who taught tactics and strategy at the military academy.

Other evidence supports the thesis of a significant martial tradition in the South contrasted with a concentration in different professions in the North. More than three-fifths of the volunteer soldiers in the Mexican War came from the slave states—on a per capita basis, four times the proportion of free-state volunteers. Seven of the eight military "colleges" (not including West Point and Annapolis) listed in the 1860 census were in the slave states. A study of the occupations of antebellum men chronicled in the *Dictionary of American Biography* found that the military profession claimed twice the percentage of Southerners as of Northerners, while this ratio was reversed for men distinguished in literature, art, medicine, and education. In business the per capita proportion of Yankees was three times as great, and among engineers and inventors it was six times as large.[22] When Southerners labeled themselves a nation of warriors and Yankees a nation of shopkeepers—a common comparison in 1860—or when Jefferson Davis told a London *Times* correspondent in 1861 that "we are a military people," they were not just whistling Dixie.[23]

One final comparison is in order—a comparison of education and literacy in North and South. Contemporaries considered this a matter of importance. The South's perceived backwardness in schooling and its large numbers of illiterates framed one of the principal free-soil indictments of slavery. This was one area in which a good many Southerners admitted inferiority and tried to do something about it.

22. Rupert B. Vance, "The Geography of Distinction: The Nation and Its Regions, 1790–1927," *Social Forces* 18 (1939), 175–76.

23. Osterweis, *Romanticism and Nationalism,* esp. pp. 90–91, 105; Grady McWhiney and Perry D. Jamieson, *Attack and Die: Civil War Military Tactics and the Southern Heritage* (University, Ala., 1982), esp. p. 171; Russell, *My Diary North and South,* p. 94.

But in 1860, after a decade of school reform in the South, the slave states still had only half the North's proportion of white children enrolled in school, and the length of the annual school term in the South was little more than half as long as in the North.[24] Of course education did not take place solely in school. But other forms of education—in the home, at church, through lyceums and public lectures, by apprenticeship, and so on—were also more active in North than South. According to the census of 1860, per capita newspaper circulation was three times greater in the North, and the number of library volumes per white person was nearly twice as large.

The proportion of illiterate white people was three times greater in the South than in the North. If the black population is included, as indeed it should be, the percentage of illiterates was seven or eight times as high in the South. In the free states, what two historians have termed an "ideology of literacy" prevailed—a commitment to education as an instrument of social mobility, economic prosperity, progress, and freedom.[25] While this ideology also existed in the South, especially in the 1850s, it was much weaker there and made slow headway against the inertia of a rural folk culture. "The Creator did not intend that every individual human being should be highly cultivated," wrote William Harper of South Carolina. "It is better that a part should be fully and highly educated and the rest utterly ignorant." Commenting on a demand by Northern workingmen for universal public education, the *Southern Review* asked: "Is this the way to produce producers? To make every child in the state a literary character would not be a good qualification for those who must live by manual labor."[26]

24. Albert Fishlow, "The Common School Revival: Fact or Fancy," in Henry Rosovsky, ed., *Industrialization in Two Systems* (New York, 1966), esp. p. 62.

25. Lee Soltow and Edward Stevens, *The Rise of Literacy and the Common School in the United States: A Socioeconomic Analysis to 1870* (Chicago, 1981), esp. p. 61.

26. Quoted in Carl Kaestle, *Pillars of the Republic: Common Schooling and American Society, 1780–1860* (New York, 1983), pp. 206–7.

The ideology of literacy in the North was part of a larger ferment which produced an astonishing number of reform movements that aroused both contempt and fear in the South. Southern whites viewed the most dynamic of these movements—abolitionism—as a threat to their very existence. Southerners came to distrust the whole concept of "progress" as it seemed to be understood in the North. *De Bow's Review* declared in 1851: "Southern life, habits, thoughts, and aims, are so essentially different from those of the North, that here a different character of books . . . and training is required." A Richmond newspaper warned in 1855 that Southerners must stop reading Northern newspapers and books and stop sending their sons to colleges in the North, where "every village has its press and its lecture room, and each lecturer and editor, unchecked by a healthy public opinion, opens up for discussion all the received dogmas of faith," where unwary youth are "exposed to the danger of imbibing doctrines subversive of all old institutions." Young men should be educated instead in the South"where their training would be moral, religious, and conservative, and they would never learn, or read a word in school or out of school, inconsistent with orthodox Christianity, pure morality, the right of property, and sacredness of marriage."[27]

In all of the areas discussed above—urbanization, industrialization, labor force, demographic structure, violence and martial values, education, and attitudes toward change—contemporaries accurately perceived significant differences between North and South, contrasts that in most respects were increasing over time. The question remains: Were these disparities crucial enough to make the South an exception to generalizations about antebellum America?

This essay concludes by suggesting a tentative answer to that

27. *De Bow's Review,* quoted in McCardell, *The Idea of a Southern Nation,* p. 205; Richmond newspaper quoted in Avery Craven, *The Coming of the Civil War* (New York, 1942), pp. 301–2.

question. Perhaps it was the *North* that was "different," that departed from the mainstream of historical development; and perhaps therefore we should speak not of Southern exceptionalism but of Northern exceptionalism. This idea is borrowed shamelessly from C. Vann Woodward, who applied it, however, to the post–Civil War United States. In essays written during the 1950s on "The Irony of Southern History" and "The Search for Southern Identity," Woodward suggested that, unlike other Americans but like most people in the rest of the world, Southerners had known poverty, failure, defeat, and thus had a skeptical attitude toward "progress." The South shared a bond with the rest of humankind that other Americans did not share.[28] This theme of Northern exceptionalism might well be applied also to the antebellum United States—not for Woodward's categories of defeat, poverty, and failure, but for the categories of a persistent folk culture discussed in this essay.

At the beginning of the republic the North and South were less different in most of these categories than they became later. Nearly all Northern states had slavery in 1776, and the institution persisted in some of them for decades thereafter. The ethnic homogeneity of Northern and Southern whites was quite similar before 1830. The proportion of urban dwellers was similarly small and the percentage of the labor force employed in agriculture similarly large in 1800. The Northern predominance in commerce and manufacturing was not so great as it later became. Nor was the contrast in education and literacy as large as it subsequently became. A belief in progress and commitments to reform or radicalism were no more prevalent in the North than in the South in 1800—indeed, they may have been less so. In 1776, in 1800, even as late as 1820, similarity in values and institutions was the salient fact. Within the next generation, difference and conflict became prominent. This happened primarily because of developments in the North. The South changed relatively

28. Woodward, *The Burden of Southern History*, pp. 3–26, 167–91.

little, and because so many Northern changes seemed threatening, the South developed a defensive ideology that resisted change.

In most of these respects the South resembled a majority of the societies in the world more than the changing North did. Despite the abolition of legal slavery or serfdom throughout most of the Western Hemisphere and western Europe, much of the world—like the South—had an unfree or quasi-free labor force. Most societies in the world remained predominantly rural, agricultural, and labor-intensive; most, including even several European countries, had illiteracy rates as high or higher than the South's 45 percent; most like the South remained bound by traditional values and networks of family, kinship, hierarchy, and patriarchy. The North—along with a few countries in northwestern Europe—hurtled forward eagerly toward a future of industrial capitalism that many Southerners found distasteful if not frightening; the South remained proudly and even defiantly rooted in the past.

Thus when secessionists protested in 1861 that they were acting to preserve traditional rights and values, they were correct. They fought to protect their constitutional liberties against the perceived Northern threat to overthrow them. The South's concept of republicanism had not changed in three-quarters of a century; the North's had. With complete sincerity the South fought to preserve its version of the republic of the Founding Fathers—a government of limited powers that protected the rights of property, including slave property, and whose constituency comprised an independent gentry and yeomanry of the white race undisturbed by large cities, heartless factories, restless free workers, and class conflict. The accession to power of the Republican party, with its ideology of competitive, egalitarian, free-labor capitalism, was a signal to the South that the Northern majority had turned irrevocably toward this frightening future. Indeed, the Black Republican party appeared to the eyes of many Southern whites as "essentially a revolutionary party" composed of "a motley throng of Sans culottes . . . Infidels and freelovers, interspersed by Bloomer women, fugitive slaves, and amalgamationists."[29] Therefore secession was a preemptive counterrevolut to prevent the Black Republican revolution from engulfing th South. "*We* are not revolutionists," insisted James D. B. De Bow and Jefferson Davis during the Civil War. "We are resisting revolution. . . . We are not engaged in a Quixotic fight for the rights of man; our struggle is for inherited rights. . . . We are upholding the true doctrines of the Federal Constitution. We are conservative."[30]

Union victory in the war destroyed the Southern vision of America and ensured that the Northern vision would become the American vision. Until 1861, however, it was the North that was out of the mainstream, not the South. Of course the Northern states, along with Britain and a few countries in northwestern Europe, were cutting a new channel in world history that would doubtless have become the mainstream even if the American Civil War had not happened. But for Americans the Civil War marked the turning point. A Louisiana planter who returned home sadly after the war wrote in 1865: "Society has been completely changed by the war. The [French] revolution of '89 did not produce a greater change in the 'Ancien Régime' than has this in our social life." And four years later George Ticknor, a retired Harvard professor, concluded that the Civil War had created a "great gulf between what happened before in our century and what has happened since. . . . It does not seem to me as if I were living in the country in which I was born."[31] From the war sprang the great flood that wrenched the stream of American history into a new channel and transferred the burden of exceptionalism from North to South.

29. *New Orleans Daily Delta,* Nov. 3, 1860; Steven A. Channing, *Crisis of Fear: Secession in South Carolina* (New York, 1970), p. 287.

30. *De Bow's Review* 33 (1862), 44; Dunbar Rowland, ed., *Jefferson Davis, Constitutionalist: His Letters, Papers, and Speeches,* 10 vols. (Jackson, Miss., 1923), VI, 357.

31. Richard Taylor to Samuel L. M. Barlow, Dec. 13, 1865, Barlow Papers, Huntington Library; Ticknor quoted in Morton Keller, *Affairs of State: Public Life in Late Nineteenth Century America* (Cambridge, Mass., 1977), p. 2.

2

TOM ON THE CROSS

"So you're the little woman who wrote the book that made this great war," said Abraham Lincoln to Harriet Beecher Stowe when they met at the White House in the fall of 1862.[1] Lincoln's remark was far from facetious. The extraordinary impact of *Uncle Tom's Cabin* may have done more to arouse antislavery sentiments in the North and to provoke angry rebuttals in the South than any other event of the antebellum era—certainly more than any other literary event.

When first published in weekly installments in the antislavery newspaper *National Era* from the summer of 1851 to the spring of 1852, the story attracted little attention outside antislavery circles. But when it appeared between hard covers in 1852, *Uncle Tom's Cabin* suddenly became the publishing phenomenon of all time. With little advance notice and no reviews, it sold three thousand copies the first

---

1. Raymond Weaver, introduction to *Uncle Tom's Cabin* (New York: Modern Library edition, 1948), p. xi.

day, twenty thousand in the first three weeks. Then sales really took off. Three mills ran full tilt just to supply paper for the book. Within a year it had sold three hundred thousand copies in the United States and three million the world over. By the time Lincoln met Stowe, *Uncle Tom's Cabin* had been translated into over twenty languages and had sold more than two million copies in the United States alone. This is equivalent to almost twenty-five million in the more populous America of today.[2]

The only thing remotely comparable has been the popularity of *Gone with the Wind*. It is no coincidence that both books focus on the great American trauma that led to civil war. Yet while *Gone with the Wind* glamorized the Old South and romanticized the Confederacy, *Uncle Tom's Cabin* helped shape attitudes that would compass the destruction of both. Although Margaret Mitchell's novel influenced views of the South, of African-Americans, and of the past, those views are now in eclipse, and *Gone with the Wind* is read today mainly for entertainment.

Uncle Tom's Cabin has its moments of drama, comedy, and pathos that enthrall the reader, but its engrossing power lies more in the message than in the medium. It is a morality play, a contest between good and evil, a clarion call for readers to buckle on their righteous armor to battle for the oppressed slave. "That triumphant work," wrote Henry James who had been moved by *Uncle Tom's Cabin* in his youth, was "much less a book than a state of vision." When Lincoln was wrestling with the problem of slavery in the summer of 1862, he borrowed from the Library of Congress *A Key to Uncle Tom's Cabin,* a book put together by Stowe in 1853 containing some of the documentation for scenes in the novel. In England Lord Palmerston, who as prime minister during the American Civil War faced the decision whether to recognize and support the Confederacy, had

---

2. Moira Davison Reynolds, *Uncle Tom's Cabin and Mid-Nineteenth Century United States* (Jefferson, N.C., 1985), pp. 11–12.

read *Uncle Tom's Cabin* three times and admired it "not only for the story but for the statesmanship of it."[3]

No, Lincoln's remark to Stowe was hardly facetious; her book did shape history. That is one reason why it is still read today, nearly 150 years after it first appeared. *Uncle Tom's Cabin* is one of the crucial documents of the American past; to read it is to deepen and broaden one's understanding of the coming of the Civil War.

The Fugitive Slave Law, enacted as part of the Compromise of 1850, sparked the writing of the book. As one element of a complicated effort to resolve various slavery issues with concessions to both sides, the Fugitive Slave Law gave the national government unprecedented powers to reach into free states and help slaveowners recover their human property that had escaped to freedom. In some ways, though, the law boomeranged on the South. Although federal marshals helped slave owners recover 332 fugitives during the 1850s, this achievement paled beside the anger and resistance it kindled in the North among those who had not previously been noted for opposition to slavery. For most Yankees, the peculiar institution had been distant and abstract. The plight of freedom-seeking men and women being manacled and returned to slavery at gunpoint made this abstraction a flesh-and-blood reality. Many Northerners both black and white participated in several dramatic rescues of fugitives during 1851–1852, the very time at which *Uncle Tom's Cabin* was appearing serially in the *National Era*.[4]

Soon after passage of the Fugitive Slave Law, Harriet Beecher Stowe's sister-in-law had written to her: "Hattie, if I could use a pen as you can, I would write something that will make this whole na-

3. James quoted in Charles H. Foster, *The Rungless Ladder: Harriet Beecher Stowe and New England Puritanism* (Durham, N.C., 1954), pp. 28–29; Earl Schenk Miers, ed., *Lincoln Day by Day: A Chronology 1809–1865*, 3 vols. (Washington, 1960), III, 121; Palmerston quoted in James Ford Rhodes, *History of the United States*, 8 vols. (New York, 1920), I, 282.

4. Stanley W. Campbell, *The Slave Catchers: Enforcement of the Fugitive Slave Law, 1850–1860* (Chapel Hill, 1970).

tion feel what a cursed thing slavery is." Stowe's reputation as a writer existed at that time mainly among her family. The mother of six living children in 1850, she had nevertheless found time over the years to write several short stories and sketches for small-circulation weekly newspapers and religious periodicals. Most of these had moralistic, pious themes. Stowe was the daughter, sister, and wife of Congregationalist clergymen and theologians, two of whom—her father, Lyman, and brother, Henry Ward—were among the foremost American divines of the nineteenth century. She had breathed the doctrinal air of sin, guilt, atonement, and salvation since childhood. These seemed unpromising ingredients for a best-selling novel. In addition, Stowe was overwhelmed with the duties of child care and the establishment of a new household in Brunswick, Maine, where her husband Calvin Stowe had just taken a chair in theology at Bowdoin College. Nevertheless, to her sister-in-law's entreaty she responded: "I will if I live."[5]

Stowe later said that a vision of Uncle Tom's death came to her during Communion one Sunday, and she rushed home to write it down as if in a trance. In this recountal lay the origin, perhaps, of her later assertion that she did not write *Uncle Tom's Cabin;* God wrote it, and she served merely as His amanuensis. But after Stowe became world famous, she gave different and contradictory answers to the flood of queries about how she wrote the novel, where she got ideas for the plot and models for the characters, and similar kinds of questions that bedevil renowned authors. What can be known with certainty is that in the spring of 1851 Stowe wrote to the editor of the *National Era,* offering a "series of sketches" titled *Uncle Tom's Cabin* to run for "three or four" installments. Like one of her most celebrated characters, the sketches just "growed"—to some forty installments, subsequently reorganized into forty-five chapters for the book.[6]

5. Joan D. Hedrick, *Harriet Beecher Stowe: A Life* (New York, 1994), pp. 206–7.

6. *Ibid.,* p. 208.

Echoes of the fugitive slave controversy dominate the earlier, more tightly written chapters of the book. This section is climaxed by one of the most memorable images in all literature, Eliza's flight with her infant son across ice floes on the Ohio River. In Ohio she is reunited with her husband, George, who has also escaped from Kentucky. Aided by friendly Quakers as well as by a politician whose previous support for the Fugitive Slave Law is melted by higher-law Samaritanism, they make it to Canada along the Underground Railroad after outwitting pursuing slave catchers in a series of derring-do adventures.

Up to this point, about one-third of the way through the novel, the narrative of Eliza's escape has alternated with the second, contrapuntal plot: Tom's sale to a slaveowner farther south. With Eliza and George safely on their way, Tom's story takes over, and the focus shifts from escape northward to descent southward, more deeply into the tragedy of slavery. Here the narrative threatens to get out of hand in the multiplication of episodes to meet the inexorable deadlines of weekly installments. But if Eliza crossing the ice is the most dramatic scene in the novel, Tom's experiences in the South provide the sheer emotional power that literally caused grown men to cry. These chapters also furnish the novel's unforgettable characters: Tom himself; the cynical but sympathetic Augustine St. Clare; his hateful neurasthenic wife, Marie; their saintly daughter, Little Eva; Augustine's quintessentially Yankee cousin, Miss Ophelia; the incomparable Topsy; and, of course, the embodiment of evil, Simon Legree.

It is these characters and the dramatic themes they illustrate that make this novel as readable and meaningful today as when it first appeared. Stowe had a remarkable ability to portray character, mainly through dialogue and behavior. Her imagination and writing style are pictorial rather than cerebral; she imagined these characters as a three-dimensional picture—or a vision, as she would have put it—and somehow managed to transfer the picture to the reader's imagination. These visual images, like the musical leitmotiv in an opera, become associated with themes of love, suffering, loss, death, power, subordination, courage, salvation.

The dominant theme, which links the specific evil of slavery with a universal sentiment, is the tragedy of forcible separation of families. This theme had an especially poignant impact in antebellum America. During the previous two generations, profound changes had occurred in both the nature and the ideal of the family. In the overwhelmingly rural population of eighteenth-century America, families were large and functioned as economic units of production. Children received little if any schooling and went to work early on the farm, which produced most of the necessities of life. But with the rapid development of commercial agriculture, industry, and towns after 1815, the middle-class family became increasingly a unit of consumption instead of production. The ideal of romantic love rather than economic advantage increasingly governed the choice of a marriage partner. The father went *away* from home to office, factory, or field to produce goods or services for the market. The mother stayed home to nurture children, who were no longer an economic asset as workers. Childhood emerged as a separate stage of life, motherhood as a sacred ideal; affection and suasion replaced repression and corporal punishment as the means of disciplining children. The birthrate dropped as parents lavished more love on fewer children and devoted more resources to their education. A "cult of domesticity" emerged to describe the ideal of middle-class America centered on the sacredness of home and family.

This domesticity became the focus of a genre of sentimental popular novels. The expanded literacy and leisure of middle-class women made them the chief readers as well as authors of such books. It was within this tradition that Harriet Beecher Stowe wrote. She aimed *Uncle Tom's Cabin* at the heart of middle-class, Protestant, family-centered America. And she hit her mark. The social and political importance of her subject—slavery—as well as her genius at creating character lifted this novel far above the sentimental clichés of the genre. Stowe wrung every possible drop of pathos out of Eliza's desperate flight to avoid separation from her child, Tom's tearful fare-well to his family when he was sold south, Lucy's suicide when her ten-month-old son was sold from her, Cassy's murder of her two-week-old baby rather than see him grow up to be sold, and other harrowing incidents of forced family separation. As Tom holds his infant daughter and says good-bye to his sons preparatory to leaving with the slave trader, his wife, Chloe, cries out in anguish to the unwitting, chortling child: "Ay, crow away, poor crittur! . . . ye'll have to come to it, too! ye'll live to see yer husband sold, or mebbe be sold yerself; and these yer boys, they's to be sold, I s'pose, too, jest like as not, when dey gets good for somethin'; an't no use in niggers havin' nothin'!"[7]

In case readers missed the point, Stowe sometimes stepped outside the story to deliver a homily, or put in the mouth of a minor charac-ter the moral, as with a white woman on the steamboat carrying Tom south, who says: "The most dreadful part of slavery, to my mind, it its outrages on the feelings and affections,—the separating of families, for example."[8] Stowe herself had lost a child to cholera in 1849, a searing experience that remained with her as she wrote the novel. "It was at his dying bed and at his grave that I learned what a poor slave mother may feel when her child is torn from her. . . . Much that is in that book had its roots in the awful scenes and sorrows of that summer."[9] Again, in case any obtuse reader of *Uncle Tom's Cabin* missed the point, Stowe supplied it explicitly in the dialogue. "Ma'am," says Eliza to Mrs. Bird, to whose home the es-caping slave mother had been taken after crossing the ice, "have you ever lost a child?" Mrs. Bird breaks down in tears. "Why do you ask

7. There have been many editions of *Uncle Tom's Cabin,* all with different paginations. Unless otherwise indicated, citations in this essay will be to the Vintage Books/the Library of America edition (New York, 1991). This quotation is from pp. 119–20.

8. *Ibid.,* p. 150.

9. Quoted in Reynolds, *Uncle Tom's Cabin and Mid-Nineteenth Century United States,* p. 145.

that? I have lost a little one." Eliza replies: "Then you will feel for me. I have lost two, one after another,—left 'em buried there when I came away; and I had only this one left . . . and, ma'am, they were going to take him away from me,—to *sell* him,—sell him down south, ma'am, to go all alone,—a baby that had never been away from his mother in his life! I could n't stand it, ma'am."[10]

Nor could Stowe's readers in the 1850s stand it. By the first half the twentieth century, though, tastes had changed, and many potential readers could not stand what they considered the mawkish sentimentality and didacticism of *Uncle Tom's Cabin*. The deathbed scenes of Little Eva, Tom's pious homilies, the sprawling plot with its contrived coincidences, the author's preachy asides, and other conventional devices of Victorian popular fiction turned off literary critics and readers alike. After remaining continuously in print for seventy years, the novel went out of print until republished in a Modern Library edition in 1948. Its image, meanwhile, had been smirched by the ubiquitous "Tom Shows" on stage and in vaudeville, which caricatured Stowe's original plot and characters.

During the first half of the twentieth century the climate of scholarly and popular opinion toward the history of slavery, abolition, and the South also tended to discredit the novel. Historians as well as novelists and filmmakers portrayed slavery as a benign institution, abolitionists as irresponsible fanatics who provoked an unnecessary war, and the Old South as a stately civilization unjustly victimized and destroyed by the Civil War. Harriet Beecher Stowe was said to have known nothing of slavery, never to have visited the South, and to have drawn her scenes and characters entirely from her fevered abolitionist imagination. *Birth of a Nation* and *Gone with the Wind* replaced *Uncle Tom's Cabin* as America's paradigmatic image of the Civil War era.

All this has changed since the 1950s. Slavery is now seen as oppressive, exploitative, the tragic flaw in American society; the ante-

10. *Uncle Tom's Cabin,* p. 105.

bellum South pursued a defensive-aggressive political strategy that led to secession and war; the abolitionists were courageous progressives; the North's cause in the Civil War was just; the abolition of slavery and destruction of the Old South were the great positive results of that war. In this changed climate of opinion, *Uncle Tom's Cabin* has blossomed again as a work of great social importance and even of literary merit.

Having read and enjoyed the novel as a high school student in the 1950s, I experienced the disillusionment of a hypercritical college student whose professors convinced me that *Uncle Tom's Cabin* was maudlin pulp and that I should concentrate on Hawthorne and Melville and other *real* novelists of that era. I can still recall the thrill of rediscovery, a half-dozen years later in the mid-1960s, when I read Edmund Wilson's penetrating and appreciative essay on Harriet Beecher Stowe in *Patriotic Gore: Studies in the Literature of the American Civil War:* "To expose oneself in maturity to *Uncle Tom* may therefore prove a startling experience. It is a much more impressive work than one has ever been allowed to suspect."[11] My initial instinct had not been wrong after all! I returned to the book in my own "maturity" and found it as exciting and meaningful as Wilson did.

Since then a whole army of literary critics have reevaluated *Uncle Tom's Cabin.* A half-dozen books of serious and balanced criticism, several new biographies of Stowe, many articles, and numerous modern editions of the novel have appeared during the past thirty years. It is now clear that Stowe knew more about slavery than earlier critics allowed. Eighteen years' residence in Cincinnati had brought her into contact with many fugitives who had fled across the river from Kentucky; she had visited a Kentucky plantation herself; one of her brothers had lived in Louisiana, and he furnished Stowe with material that provided the basis for Simon Legree and his plantation. Although, like all novelists, she drew on a fertile imagination for incidents and characters, many of these—including Topsy, whose

11. (New York, 1962), p. 5.

whimsical personality was similar to that of a black girl Stowe taught in Sunday school—were also drawn from real events and people.[12]

There has been a countervailing trend to these positive reevaluations of *Uncle Tom's Cabin.* Many modern readers, especially blacks, are put off by the overtones of racism in Stowe's portrayal of black characteristics. Most important, they are angered by Uncle Tom himself, whose apparent fawning servility toward white oppressors has made the phrase "Uncle Tom" a hissing byword among African-Americans.[13]

It is true that Stowe shared the racial preconceptions common among many whites and even some blacks of her time, an attitude that historian George Fredrickson has labeled "romantic racialism." She depicted the "Anglo-Saxon race" as "hard and dominant," an unemotional, aggressive, enterprising people whose technological and economic skills enabled them to dominate nonwhite races. The African, by contrast, was an "imaginative and impassioned" race, "not naturally daring and enterprising, but home-loving and affectionate," a "kindly race" with an appreciation of music and beauty. The Caucasian was, in a word, a "masculine" race, the Negro a "feminine" and childlike people.[14]

Little wonder that blacks today find this unpalatable. But Stowe's romantic racialism had another dimension. These "African" traits of

12. In addition to works already cited, see E. Bruce Kirkham, *The Building of Uncle Tom's Cabin* (Knoxville, 1977); Elizabeth Ammons, ed., *Critical Essays on Harriet Beecher Stowe* (Boston, 1980); Thomas F. Gossett, *Uncle Tom's Cabin and American Culture* (Dallas, 1985); Eric J. Sundquist, ed., *New Essays on Uncle Tom's Cabin* (New York, 1986); Josephine Donovan, *Uncle Tom's Cabin: Evil, Affliction, and Redemptive Love* (Boston, 1991); Johanna Johnston, *Runaway to Heaven: The Story of Harriet Beecher Stowe* (New York, 1963); Edward C. Wagenknecht, *Harriet Beecher Stowe: The Known and the Unknown* (New York, 1965).

13. Howard C. Furnas, *Goodbye to Uncle Tom* (New York, 1956).

14. George M. Fredrickson, *The Black Image in the White Mind: The Debate on Afro-American Character and Destiny, 1817–1914* (New York, 1971), chap. 4; *Uncle Tom's Cabin,* pp. 42, 93, 118, 176.

"childlike simplicity of affection, and facility of forgiveness," she wrote, "exhibit the highest form of the peculiarly *Christian* life." For Stowe and many of her readers, Christian virtues were the highest virtues. The meek shall inherit the earth. A little child shall lead them. In the better world to come, the African traits would prove *superior* to those of the Anglo-Saxon. In what really counted for Stowe and the Christian culture of which she was a part, African-Americans were a finer race than white Americans, just as women and children had a finer nature than men. "The African race has peculiarities," says one of Stowe's characters, who speaks for the author, "yet to be unfolded in the light of civilization and Christianity, which, if not the same with those of the Anglo-Saxon, may prove to be, morally, of even a higher type." [15]

This idea is the key to Uncle Tom's character. He was not the obsequious bootlicker of prevailing image, which in any case derives mostly from the vulgarization of Tom by eighty years of Tom Shows on stage and vaudeville. The common opprobrium of Uncle Tom-ism, it seems safe to say, is expressed by people who have not read the book—or at least have not understood it. In Christian terms, Tom is by far the strongest character in the novel. Indeed, he is a Christ figure. Tom forgives his oppressors; so did Jesus. Tom turns the other cheek to blows; so did Jesus. Tom blesses those who curse him; so did Jesus. Tom prays for those who sin against him; so did Jesus. In Christian theology, Christ gave his life to save humankind; in Stowe's novel, Tom gives his life to save his people.

At the very outset, we learn that Tom's owner must sell him to satisfy debts that would otherwise sink the plantation and cause the sale of all the slaves. When his wife urges Tom, like Eliza, to flee north instead of waiting to be sold south, he replies: "If I must be sold, or all the people on the place, and everything go to rack, why, let me be sold. . . . It's better for me alone to go, than to break up the place and sell all. Mas'r an't to blame, Chloe." At the climax of

15. *Uncle Tom's Cabin,* pp. 213, 503.

the novel, when Legree literally beats Tom to death because he refuses to tell what he knows of Cassy and Emmy's hiding place, the
parallel between Christ's crucifixion and Tom's death must be clear
to all but the most obtuse reader:

> Tom opened his eyes, and looked upon his master. "Ye poor misera-
> ble critter!" he said, "there an't no more ye can do! I forgive ye, with
> all my soul!" and he fainted entirely away. . . . Tom stood perfectly
> submissive; and yet Legree could not hide from himself that his
> power over his bond thrall was somehow gone. . . . He understood
> full well that it was GOD who was standing, between him and his
> victim. . . . That submissive and silent man, whom no taunts, nor
> threats, nor stripes, nor cruelties, could disturb, roused a voice within
> him, such as of old his Master roused in the demoniac soul, saying,
> "What have we to do with thee, thou Jesus of Nazareth?"[16]

Stowe's readers lived in an age that understood this message better than ours does. But the triumph of another nonviolent Christian
movement a century later caused a modern commentator, Howard
Mumford Jones, to compare Uncle Tom, "this splendid black Christian Prometheus," to "the Christianity of Martin Luther King, Jr."
Jones also compared Uncle Tom as a classic figure in literature to
Victor Hugo's Jean Valjean: "The important difference between *Les
Misérables* and *Uncle Tom's Cabin* is not one between a white hero
and a black hero; it is that in Hugo's novel we witness the conversion of the hero to Christian selflessness, whereas in Mrs. Stowe's,
the conversion having already been made, we witness a series of tests
whether the hero can endure until he dies."[17]

Readers must decide for themselves whether *Uncle Tom's Cabin*
equals *Les Misérables* as a work of literature. Most will probably decide that it does not. But as a work of social reform, its success was

16. *Ibid.,* pp. 55, 459, 481.
17. Jones, introduction to *Uncle Tom's Cabin* (Columbus, Ohio, 1969), pp.
vi–vii.

greater. A decade later, many young men who had read *Uncle Tom's Cabin* marched off to war with the words written by another Yankee woman ringing in their ears:

> *As He died to make men holy,*
> *Let us die to make men free.*

3

THE WAR OF
SOUTHERN AGGRESSION

"SOUTH CAROLINA," WROTE ONE OF THE STATE'S FEW OPPONENTS of secession in 1860, "is too small for a republic, but too large for an insane asylum."[1] In earlier years most Southerners outside the Palmetto State would have agreed. In 1832 no other state joined South Carolina in its "nullification" of a national tariff law that Carolina planters viewed as discriminatory against plantation agriculture. On that occasion the Carolina planters and their allies backed down rather than face the wrath of President Andrew Jackson, who vowed to send in the army and hang the ringleaders of nullification. Again in 1851 they had to contain their zeal for a separate slaveholding republic when other Southern states refused to secede in protest against the Compromise of 1850, which had admitted California as a free state. But on their third try, in 1860, South Carolina's Southern Rights radicals pulled ten other slave states into secession.

The catalyst that turned what some called the Palmetto insane

1. James L. Petrigru to Benjamin F. Perry, December 8, 1860, quoted in Lacy K. Ford, Jr., *Origins of Southern Radicalism: The South Carolina Upcountry, 1800–1860* (New York, 1988), p. 371.

asylum into the Confederate States of America was the election of Abraham Lincoln to the presidency. This "Black Republican" had pronounced slavery "a moral wrong and injustice," and had called upon Americans to restrict its further expansion as a first step toward its "ultimate extinction" sometime in the twentieth century. To escape this fate, the South declared its independence and fired on American soldiers at Fort Sumter in Charleston Bay, thereby provoking a war that cost more American lives, soldier and civilian, than all of the country's other wars combined.

To a good many Southerners the events of 1861–1865 have been known as "the War of Northern Aggression." Never mind that the South took the initiative by seceding in defiance of an election of a president by a constitutional majority. Never mind that the Confederacy started the war by firing on the American flag. These were seen as preemptive acts of defense against Northern aggression. The election of Lincoln by Northern votes was *a deliberate, cold-blooded insult and outrage* to Southern honor, a New Orleans newspaper declared, while a committee of the Virginia legislature declared that "the very existence of such a party [Republican] is an offense to the whole South."[2] As for the firing on Sumter, it was merely a response to provocation by the Lincoln administration, which kept Union troops there after the Confederacy had warned them to leave. "The *aggressor* in a war," explained Confederate Vice President Alexander Stephens, "is not he who strikes the first blow . . . but the first who renders force *necessary*."[3]

Secession and the firing on Sumter were, in Southern eyes, the culmination of decades of aggression by a growing Northern majority that was becoming increasingly antislavery. But Southern leaders knew that the best defense was a good offense. When Yankee citi-

2. *New Orleans Crescent,* Nov. 9, 1860; *Report of the Joint Committee of the General Assembly of Virginia on the Harper's Ferry Outrage,* Jan. 26, 1860, Virginia State Papers (1859–1860), Doc. 31.

3. Alexander H. Stephens, *A Constitutional View of the Late War between the States,* 2 vols. (Chicago, 1868–1870), II, 35. Italics in original.

zens harbored fugitive slaves, Southerners in Congress passed a Fugitive Slave Law that gave the national government greater powers than it had ever before possessed to reach into Northern states and capture the fugitives (so much for Southern commitment to states' rights). When Republicans called for the exclusion of slavery from new territories, the Southern majority on the Supreme Court ruled, in the *Dred Scott* case, that Congress had no power to prevent slaveholders from taking their human property into any territory they wished. When the antislavery majority of settlers in Kansas territory made bondage insecure there, Southerners demanded a federal slave code enforced by the U.S. Army to protect their "rights" in such territories. When Northern Democrats refused to endorse this demand, Southerners in 1860 split the party in two, thereby ensuring the election of Lincoln, which in turn provoked secession.

Not all of the architects of this offensive-defensive strategy were South Carolinians. But the large number who were made the Palmetto State a hotbed of Southern Rights radicalism. During the height of John C. Calhoun's power it was said that when Calhoun took snuff, South Carolina sneezed. It could also be said that when South Carolinians took snuff, the South sneezed. Calhoun led the Southern Rights wing of the Democratic party until he died in 1850. His theory of slavery as a "positive good" and his doctrine of state sovereignty as a buttress of slavery lived on as the rationale for secession. Consumed by ambition for the presidency, an office that for thirty years he sought in vain, Calhoun dedicated his career to constructing elaborate methods to sustain Southern political power despite the region's shrinking minority of the American population. These methods included at one time or another state "interposition" or nullification of federal laws, Southern control of the Democratic party, a Southern Rights party that would dominate a divided North, and a "concurrent majority" whereby either section would have a veto power over legislation passed by a national majority.

In the first full-scale biography of Calhoun to appear in almost forty years, John Niven describes these ideas as part of Calhoun's

"defensive posture" against the North's "aggressions and encroachments on our rights."[4] Calhoun's position had not always been defensive. Born during the final year of America's war of independence, Calhoun inherited the driving energy of his father, a pioneer
of Scots-Irish descent whose slaves had carved a two-thousand-acre
plantation out of the up-country South Carolina wilderness. Calhoun
graduated from Yale College and studied law with a leading Con-
necticut judge before returning home to marry his cousin, heiress of
a well-to-do low-country planter. Elected to Congress in 1810, Calhoun began a career of forty years in politics that included six years
in the House, eight as secretary of war, eight as vice president, one
as secretary of state, and fifteen as a senator. During the first decade
of this remarkable career, Calhoun was an expansive nationalist advocating government intervention to promote commercial and industrial growth. In the 1820s he reversed his views, fearful that all such
growth would benefit only the North, leaving his beloved South vulnerable to the Yankee colossus. Increasingly dour and sour, Calhoun
devoted himself to the long campaign to thwart Northern aggressions.

These aggressions consisted mainly of antislavery rhetoric and
economic policies favoring free-labor capitalism over slave-plantation
agriculture. But, as Niven shows, Calhoun's "defensive mode" could
become quite aggressive in its own right. He would deny First
Amendment rights to opponents of slavery by excluding their literature from the mails and refusing to receive their petitions to Congress. Calhoun's favorite tactic was to profess a desire to preserve the
Union but to predict disunion if the North refused concessions to
Southern rights, thus placing the blame on the North for imperiling
the Union.

Calhoun claimed to espy aggression from afar. In 1826, as vice

4. John Niven, *John C. Calhoun and the Price of Union: A Biography* (Baton
Rouge, 1988), pp. xv, 324.

president, he foresaw dire consequences if the government extended diplomatic recognition to Haiti. Such action "would in the present tone of feelings to the south lead to great mischief," he wrote.

> It is not so much recognition simply, as what must follow it. We must send and receive ministers, and what would be our social relations to a Black minister in Washington? . . . Must his daughters and sons participate in the society of our daughters and sons? . . . Small as these considerations appear to be they involve the peace and perhaps the union of the nation.[5]

To placate the South, the U.S. government refused to recognize Haiti until 1862—after the South had seceded.

Southern threats to secede served the section well in the crisis that led to the Compromise of 1850. If Congress insisted on admitting California with the free-state constitution written by gold rush settlers, Calhoun told the Senate, slave states could not "remain in the Union consistently with their honor and safety." To a friend Calhoun wrote: "You will see that I have made up the issue between North and South. If we flinch we are gone, but if we stand fast on it, we shall triumph either by compelling the North to yield to our terms, or declaring our independence of them."[6] Other Southern leaders were less subtle than Calhoun. "We ask you to give us our rights" in California, Congressman Albert G. Brown of Mississippi said. "If you refuse, I am for taking them by armed occupation." James H. Hammond of South Carolina told Calhoun that if the North got California, thereby robbing the South of equal representation in the Senate (fifteen free states and fifteen slave states before

5. *Ibid.,* p. 115.

6. *Congressional Globe,* 31st Congress, 1st Session, appendix, pp. 451–55; Calhoun to Henry W. Conner, Feb. 19, 1847, quoted in Chaplain W. Morrison, *Democratic Politics and Sectionalism: The Wilmot Proviso Controversy* (Chapel Hill, 1967), p. 35.

California came in), "we should . . . kick them out of the Capitol & set it on fire."[7]

These tactics did not prevent the admission of a free California, but they did win access for slavery to the rest of the region conquered from Mexico (the territories of New Mexico and Utah enacted slave codes, though few slaves were taken there). So the South pursued the same tactics throughout the 1850s, winning repeal of the Missouri Compromise ban on slavery north of 36°30′ in the Kansas-Nebraska Act of 1854, warning Northern conservatives not to vote for the first "Black Republican" presidential candidate, John C. Frémont, in 1856 (if Frémont won, said the governor of Virginia, slave states would "proceed at once to 'immediate, absolute and eternal separation' "), and forcing President James Buchanan in 1858 to support the admission of Kansas as a slave state—if he had refused, Buchanan explained, Southern states would "secede from the Union or take up arms."[8]

Congressman Preston Brooks of South Carolina showed that the South meant business. When Senator Charles Sumner of Massachusetts made unflattering remarks about Brooks's cousin Senator Andrew Butler in 1856, Brooks walked into the Senate and bludgeoned Sumner with a heavy cane until he fell unconscious. Censured by the House, Brooks was unanimously reelected by his constituents; from all over the South he received gifts of new canes bearing such inscriptions as "USE KNOCK-DOWN ARGUMENTS." During a bitter contest to elect a Speaker of the House in 1859, which pitted Northern and Southern representatives against each other, the governor of South Carolina wired one of the state's congressmen: "If you upon consul-

---

7. *Congressional Globe,* 31st Congress, 1st Session, p. 261; Hammond to Calhoun, March 6, 1850, quoted in Holman Hamilton, *Prologue to Conflict: The Crisis and Compromise of 1850* (Lexington, Ky., 1964), p. 74.

8. Governor Henry A. Wise quoted in Roy F. Nichols, *The Disruption of American Democracy* (New York, 1948), p. 44; Buchanan quoted in George Fort Milton, *The Eve of Conflict: Stephen A. Douglas and the Needless War* (Boston, 1934), p. 271.

tation decide to make the issue of force in Washington, write or telegraph me, and I will have a regiment in or near Washington in the shortest possible time."[9]

In 1860 Southerners again threatened to secede if a Republican was elected president. Lincoln was fed up with their protestations that they were merely trying to protect themselves from Northern aggression. "You say, you will destroy the Union," said Lincoln on February 27, 1860, in a speech at New York City intended to be read by Southerners; "and then, you say, the great crime of having destroyed it will be upon us! That is cool. A highwayman holds a pistol to my ear, and mutters through his teeth, 'Stand and deliver, or I shall kill you, and then you will be a murderer!'"[10] This time the South made good its threat. And Lincoln opposed the last-minute attempts to woo them back with the Crittenden Compromise, which opened future territories south of 36°30' to slavery. The South had long had an eye on annexation of Cuba, where slavery existed, and portions of Central America, where it could be introduced. "We have just carried an election on principles fairly stated," Lincoln wrote to a Republican congressman in January 1861.

> Now we are told . . . the government shall be broken up, unless we surrender to those we have beaten. . . . If we surrender, it is the end of us. . . . They will repeat the experiment upon us *ad libitum*. A year will not pass, till we shall have to take Cuba as a condition upon which they will stay in the Union. . . . The tug has to come & better now than later.[11]

The tug came on April 12, when Southern artillery sent shells crashing into Fort Sumter.

Southerners exhibited their sense of victimization in this matter.

9. Quoted in Allan Nevins, *The Emergence of Lincoln* (New York, 1950), II, 122.

10. Roy P. Basler, ed., *The Collected Works of Abraham Lincoln* (New Brunswick, N.J., 1953–1955), II, 546–47.

11. *Ibid.,* IV, 172, 150.

Lincoln tricked us into firing on Sumter, they declared. We acted in self-defense. The North was the aggressor. Everyone is against us and our institution of slavery. But we know we are right and we will fight for our rights.

Some insight into the Southern psychology is provided by the "secret and sacred" diaries of James H. Hammond. Like Calhoun a cotton planter and slaveholder in up-country South Carolina, Hammond possessed a large ego and insatiable political ambitions. But he also had insatiable sexual appetites, which threatened to cut short his political career and to destroy the marriage that had brought him his plantation and slaves. By his wife he fathered eight children. In 1839 he bought an eighteen-year-old slave, Sally, and her infant daughter Louisa. Hammond took Sally as a concubine and fathered several children by her; when Louisa reached the age of twelve, he transferred his desires to her and fathered more children. Hammond kept all of his dark-skinned progeny in slavery as "their happiest earthly condition." [12]

During the 1830s Hammond was elected to a term in Congress. There he earned some fame for a speech that thundered awesome threats if Congress should act on petitions for the abolition of slavery in the District of Columbia. If that day ever came, said Hammond, he was for "disunion, and civil war, if need be. A Revolution must ensue, and this Republic sink in blood." [13]

In 1842 Hammond won the governorship of South Carolina. During his term, and for more than a year before it, he engaged in frequent sexual play with the four teenage daughters of his brother-in-law, Wade Hampton II, the largest planter in South Carolina and reputedly one of the richest men in America. "Here were four lovely creatures from the tender but precocious girl of 13 to the mature but

---

12. James H. Hammond to James H. Hammond, Jr., Feb. 19, 1856, in Carol Bleser, ed., *Secret and Sacred: The Diaries of James Henry Hammond, a Southern Slaveholder* (New York, 1988), p. 19.

13. *Ibid.*, p. 11.

fresh and blooming woman nearly 19," wrote Hammond in his diary after their father had learned of the affair and put a stop to it,

> all of them rushing on every occasion into my arms and covering me with kisses . . . pressing their bodies almost into mine, wreathing their limbs with mine, encountering warmly every portion of my frame, and permitting my hands to stray unchecked over every part of them and to rest without the slightest shrinking from it, in the most secret and sacred regions.

These activities, Hammond continued,

> extended to every thing short of direct sexual intercourse [and] for two years were carried on not with one, but indiscriminately with all of them . . . and renewed every time or nearly every time we met at my house in Columbia, which was never less than once a week while I was there, and most usually much oftener. . . . Is it in flesh and blood to withstand this? Is there a man, with manhood in him and a heart susceptible of any emotions of tenderness, who could tear himself from such a cluster of lovely, loving, such amorous and devoted beings? Nay are there many who would have the self-control to stop where I did? Am I not after all entitled to some . . . credit for not going further? [14]

Hampton was restrained from challenging Hammond to a duel only by the need to shield his daughters from publicity (the inevitable rumors nevertheless seem to have repelled potential suitors, for none of the four girls ever married). But the powerful planter saw to it that Hammond's political career went into limbo. Not until Hampton was on his deathbed did Hammond win election to the Senate in 1857. By then he was reunited with his wife, who had stuck by him through the Hampton scandal and the liaison with Sally but had left him for several years when she learned about Louisa.

When Lincoln won the presidency Hammond resigned from the

---

14. *Ibid.,* pp. 172–73, 175.

Senate. Already in ill health, he did not survive the Confederacy he had done so much to create. Hammond died on November 13, 1864, at the age of fifty-seven, just as General Sherman was setting forth on his march from Atlanta to the sea. Hammond's wife and children, astonishingly, cherished his memory and kept his diaries intact except for two deletions, one of them concerning the Hampton scandal. For more than half a century the diaries remained under lock and key at the South Caroliniana Library of the University of South Carolina, available with restrictions to only a handful of scholars. Through the devotion to untrammeled scholarship of the library's director, Les Inabinet, and Carol Bleser's careful editing, the diaries became available for the edification of the reading public.

Hammond was scarcely a typical Southern planter or politician. Many others, of course, had slave concubines. The secession governor of South Carolina, Francis Pickens (Calhoun's cousin) had several slave mistresses and children by all of them. The Confederate general Jubal Early fathered both black and white illegitimate children. But nothing like the dalliance with the Hampton girls has come to light about any other planter or political leader, while the combination of self-pity and narcissism revealed in Hammond's diary seems uniquely pathological. Drought, floods, poor crops, debt, and the enmity of neighbors were all part of a conspiracy of the universe against him. "God hates *me*. . . . Every man's hand is against me. . . . Deserted by God, persecuted and robbed by man, what can I do?" Epidemics that took the lives of his slaves caused sorrow for his own loss but little sympathy for the slaves, whom Hammond lumped with his livestock:

> It crushes me to the earth to see every thing of mine so blasted around me. Negroes, cattle, mules, hogs, every thing that has life around me seems to labour under some fated malediction. . . . I have lost 89 negroes and at least 50 mules and horses in 11 years. Several of the

horses, blooded mares, costing me $1000 to 1500. . . . Great God what have I done. Never was a man so cursed![15]

When his wife left Hammond after she discovered his affair with the twelve-year-old Louisa, he expressed bitter astonishment at the pettiness of woman. After all, other men did the same; why should he be singled out for blame?

> What devils women are! How their jealousy blinds them. . . . Utterly forgetful of me and my prospects . . . my wife [has] paralysed me by her arrogance and violence. . . . My God! what have I done or omitted to do to deserve this fate? . . . I have been guilty in indiscretions—venial ones in the judgment of all history and in the practice of every social system until my case. . . . No one *not one,* exercises the slightest indulgence towards me. Nothing is overlooked, nothing forgiven.[16]

After Calhoun died, Hammond considered himself "the first man in SoCa . . . as a Statesman and man of intellect I could guide the State and the South through all their present difficulties" if only Wade Hampton had not destroyed his career for "frivolous causes, the occurrence of which were among the most common events. . . . If my career had not been so often cut short, I could and would have dissolved this Union. . . . Thus and thus only can the Great Revolution be . . . ultimately accomplished."[17]

It would push analogy too far to view Hammond's mentality as a microcosm of the mentality of the antebellum South. But the sense of victimization, the lashing out of aggrieved innocence toward one's persecutor, the aggression bred by frustration present in both cases are nevertheless suggestive.

In any event it is not hard to understand why slaveholders like

15. *Ibid.,* pp. 264, 107, 79, 101, 78.
16. *Ibid.,* pp. 269, 254, 255, 231.
17. *Ibid.,* pp. 210, 244, 245.

Hammond, Pickens, and the numerous other South Carolina planters in Lacy Ford's *Origins of Southern Radicalism* would regard the electoral victory of the antislavery Republican party as a mortal threat to their future. What is more difficult to comprehend is "why the plain folk of the Old South, the white majority, willingly joined the region's planter elite to fight a long and bloody war seemingly waged in defense of slavery." That is the question Ford seeks to answer in his penetrating study of South Carolina's up-country, which along with the rest of the state almost unanimously supported secession in 1860.[18]

James Hammond's most famous speech in the U.S. Senate provides clues to the answer. The speech had two equally notable parts. The first expressed the "King Cotton" thesis. "The slaveholding South is now the controlling power of the world," Hammond told the Senate in 1858. It supplied 80 percent of the world's cotton and covered 850,000 square miles,

> as large as Great Britain, France, Austria, Prussia, and Spain. Is that not territory enough to make an empire that shall rule the world? . . . Would any sane nation make war on us? Without firing a gun, without drawing a sword, should they make war on us we could bring the whole world to our feet. . . . No, you dare not make war on cotton. . . . Cotton *is* king.[19]

This attitude helps to explain why Southern states seceded in 1861 confident that the Yankees would not fight, or that if they did Britain would intervene in the Confederacy's favor to ensure the continued flow of cotton. *Origins of Southern Radicalism* helps us to understand this hubris by analyzing the cotton fiefdom and the psychology it generated in one corner of the South.

18. Lacy K. Ford, Jr., *Origins of Southern Radicalism: The South Carolina Upcountry, 1800–1860* (New York, 1988); quotation from p. vii.

19. *Selections from the Letters and Speeches of the Hon. James H. Hammond of South Carolina* (New York, 1866), pp. 316–17.

But Lacy Ford, who is descended from yeoman farmer stock in South Carolina, concentrates more on the questions raised by the second theme of Hammond's Senate speech. Northern exponents of free-labor capitalism had indicted plantation agriculture and slavery as economically backward and exploitative of both the slaves and white nonslaveholders. Hammond answered the first part of that indictment with his panegyric of King Cotton's economic prowess. He responded to the second with his notorious "mud-sill" metaphor portraying slavery as an institution that lifted all whites—yeomen, workers, and planters alike—to a level above that of the working classes in "free" societies. "Your whole hireling class of manual laborers and 'operatives,' as you call them, are essentially slaves," Hammond told Northern senators.

> In all social systems there must be a class to do the menial duties, to perform the drudgery of life. . . . It constitutes the very mud-sill of society. . . . Fortunately for the South, she found a race adapted to the purpose. . . . The difference between us is that our slaves are hired for life and well compensated. . . . Yours are hired by the day, not cared for, and scantily compensated.[20]

Hammond here reformulated the "country-republican" ideology, as Lacy Ford labels it, that eighteenth-century Jeffersonians handed down to succeeding generations. In this ideology an essential component of personal liberty was independence. The opposite of independence, of course, was dependence. A man who depended on another for his living was not truly free—he was subject to the dictation of the employer who paid his wages. Independence—and therefore liberty—was achieved by ownership of productive property. Only a society of farmers, artisans, and professionals who owned their means of production could sustain a republican government; the development of a class of dependent wage-earners would undermine liberty

20. *Ibid.*, pp. 317–19.

and destroy republican government. The Southern yeoman farmer, writes Ford in reaffirmation of recent scholarship on this class, "feared the fall from independent producer to dependent proletarian, a status he equated with enslavement."[21]

The existence of genuine black slavery gave a peculiar racial twist to this ideology. Whether or not they owned productive property, all Southern whites owned the most important property of all—a white skin. This enabled them to stand above the mudsill of black slavery and prevented them from sinking into the morass of inequality, as did wage workers and poor men in the North. John C. Calhoun expressed it well. "With us," he said to the Senate in 1848, "the two great divisions of society are not the rich and poor, but white and black; and all the former, the poor as well as the rich, belong to the upper class, and are respected and treated as equals."[22] Because the slave system was "of all others the best adapted to the freedom and equality of the whites," a South Carolina newspaper editor said, the election of Lincoln presented a mortal threat to the liberty of Southern yeomen. "If slaves are freed, whites will become menials," an up-country politician added. "We will lose every right and every liberty which belongs to the name of freemen."[23] Indeed, the Baptist clergyman James Furman warned after Lincoln's election, "If you are tame enough to submit, Abolition preachers will be at hand to consummate the marriage of your daughters to black husbands."[24]

Little wonder, then, that "the common people" of South Carolina, as a contemporary observer put it, were "the most resolute" opponents of "Northern aggression." With the slogan "Freedom is not possible without slavery" ringing in their ears, they went to war

21. Ford, *Origins of Southern Radicalism,* pp. 51–52, 84.
22. Quoted in Niven, *Calhoun,* p. 316.
23. Quoted in Ford, *Origins of Southern Radicalism,* pp. 360, 204, 369.
24. Quoted in Steven A. Channing, *Crisis of Fear: Secession in South Carolina* (New York, 1970), p. 287.

against the Yankees alongside their slave-owning neighbors to "perpetuate and diffuse the very liberty for which Washington bled, and which the heroes of the Revolution achieved."[25] George Orwell need not have created the fictional world of *1984* to describe Newspeak. He could have found it in the South Carolina of 1861.

25. Quoted in Ford, *Origins of Southern Radicalism,* pp. 368, 369; and in James Oakes, *The Ruling Race: A History of American Slaveholders* (New York, 1982), p. 141.

II

THE WAR
AND
AMERICAN
SOCIETY

4

THE WAR THAT NEVER
GOES AWAY

"AMERICANS JUST CAN'T GET ENOUGH OF THE CIVIL WAR." SO says a man who should know, Terry Winschel, historian of the Vicksburg National Military Park. Millions of visitors come to Vicksburg and a score of other Civil War battlefield parks every year. More than forty thousand Civil War reenactors spend hundreds of dollars each on replica weapons, uniforms, and equipment; many of them travel thousands of miles to help restage Civil War battles. They constituted the thousands of extras in the movies *Glory* and *Gettysburg*. Another 250,000 Americans describe themselves as Civil War buffs or "hobbyists" and belong to one of the hundreds of Civil War round tables or societies, subscribe to at least one of a half-dozen magazines devoted to Civil War history, or buy and sell Civil War memorabilia. Some forty million viewers are estimated to have watched Ken Burns's eleven-hour video documentary on the Civil War, first broadcast on PBS in 1990. Many of these same viewers tune in weekly to watch *Civil War Journal* on the Arts & Entertainment channel—a series that has run for fifty-two episodes from 1993 to 1995.

Above all, Americans buy books on the Civil War. This has always been true. More than fifty thousand separate books or pamphlets on the war have been published since the guns ceased firing more than a century and a quarter ago. In recent years some eight hundred titles, many of them reprints of out-of-print works, have come off the presses annually. Nearly every month a new Civil War book is offered by the History Book Club or the Book-of-the-Month Club, often as the main selection. Civil War books are the leading sellers for the History Book Club. Many bookstore owners echo the words of Jim Lawson, general manager of the Book 'N Card shop in Falls Church, Virginia. "For the last two years," he said in 1988, "Civil War books have been flying out of here. It's not [just] the buffs who buy; it's the general public, from high school kids to retired people." The pace has actually increased since 1988. Several publishers sustain their business by publishing Civil War books exclusively.[1]

What accounts for this intense interest in the fratricidal conflict that almost tore the country apart? There are several answers to this question. First, the human cost of the Civil War was for Americans by far the most devastating in our history. The 620,000 Union and Confederate soldiers who lost their lives almost equaled the 680,000 American soldiers who died in all the other wars this country has fought combined. When we add the unknown but probably substantial number of civilian deaths—from disease, malnutrition, exposure, or injury—among the hundreds of thousands of black and white refugees in the Confederacy, the toll of Civil War dead probably exceeds that of all other American wars put together. Consider two sobering facts about the battle of Antietam, America's single bloodiest day. The 23,000 casualties there were almost four times the num-

1. The information in these two paragraphs is drawn from the author's personal correspondence and experience, from the monthly periodical *Civil War News,* from the newsletters of several Civil War round tables and of an organization called Civil War Round Table Associates, and from Lew Lord, "Reliving the Civil War," *U.S. News & World Report,* Aug. 15, 1988, pp. 48–53, 56–61.

ber of American casualties on D day, June 6, 1944. The 6,300 men killed and mortally wounded in one day near Sharpsburg were nearly double the number of Americans killed and mortally wounded in combat in all the rest of the country's nineteenth-century wars combined—the War of 1812, the Mexican War, the Spanish-American War, and the Indian wars thrown in for good measure. Finally, mark an even more sobering fact. Two percent of the American population of 1860 were killed in the Civil War; if the United States suffered the same proportion of deaths in a war fought in the 1990s, the number of American war dead would exceed five million.

This ghastly toll gives the Civil War a kind of horrifying but hypnotic fascination. As Thomas Hardy once put it, "War makes rattling good history; but Peace is poor reading."[2] The sound of drum and trumpet, the call to arms, the clashing of armies have stirred the blood of nations throughout history. As the horrors and the seamy side of a war recede into the misty past, the romance and honor and glory forge into the foreground. Of no war has this been more true than of the Civil War, with its dashing cavaliers, its generals leading infantry charges, its diamond-stacked locomotives and paddle-wheeled steamboats, its larger-than-life figures like Lincoln, Lee, Grant, Jackson, and Sherman, its heroic and romantic women like Clara Barton and "Mother" Bickerdyke and Rose O'Neal Greenhow, its countless real-life heroines and knaves and heroes capable of transmutation into a Scarlett O'Hara, Rhett Butler, or Ashley Wilkes.

If romance is the other face of horror in our perception of the Civil War, the poignancy of a brothers' war is the other face of the tragedy of a civil war. In hundreds of individual cases the war did pit brother against brother, cousin against cousin, even father against son. This was especially true in border states like Kentucky, where the war divided such famous families as the Clays, Crittendens, and Breckinridges and where seven brothers and brothers-in-law of the

2. *The Oxford Dictionary of Quotations,* 2d ed. (Oxford, 1955), p. 236.

wife of the president of the United States fought for the Confederate States. But it was also true of states like Virginia, where Jeb Stuart's father-in-law commanded Union cavalry, and even of South Carolina, where Thomas F. Drayton became a brigadier general in the Confederate army and fought against his brother Percival, a captain in the Union navy, at the battle of Port Royal. Who can resist the painful human interest of stories like these—particularly when they are recounted in the letters and diaries of Civil War protagonists, preserved through generations and published for all to read as a part of the unending stream of Civil War books?

Indeed, the uncensored contemporary descriptions of that war by participants help explain its appeal to modern readers. There is nothing else in history to equal it. Civil War armies were the most literate that ever fought a war up to that time. Twentieth-century armies have censored soldiers' letters and discouraged diary keeping; Civil War armies did neither. Thus we have an unparalleled view of the Civil War by the people who experienced it. Many American families still possess the letters or diaries or other memorabilia of ancestors who fought in the war, which has helped keep its image alive in the minds and imaginations of millions of Americans today.

This consciousness of the Civil War, of the past as part of the present, continues to be more intense in the South than elsewhere. William Faulkner said of his native section that the past is not dead; it's not even past. As any reader of Faulkner's novels knows, the Civil War is central to that past that is present; it is the great watershed of Southern history; it is, as Mark Twain put it more than a century ago after a tour through the South, "what A.D. is elsewhere; they date from it."[3] The symbols of that past-in-present surround Southerners as they grow up, from the Robert E. Lee Elementary School or Jefferson Davis High School they attend and the Confederate battle flag that flies over their statehouse to the Confederate soldier enshrined in bronze or granite on the town square and the

3. *Life on the Mississippi* (New York: Heritage Press edition, 1944), p. 262.

family folklore about victimization by Sherman's bummers. Some of those symbols remain highly controversial and provoke as much passion today as in 1863: the song *Dixie,* for example, and the Confederate battle flag, which for many Southern whites continue to represent courage, honor, or defiance while to blacks they represent racism and oppression.

These symbols and the controversy they arouse suggest the most important reason for the enduring fascination with the Civil War: Great issues were at stake, issues about which Americans were willing to fight and die; issues whose resolution profoundly transformed and redefined the United States but at the same time are still alive and contested today. An exploration of some of these issues will help us understand the phenomenon of the war's vivid presence in our consciousness more than 130 years after the guns ceased firing.

The Civil War was fought mainly by volunteer soldiers who joined the colors before conscription went into effect. In fact, the Union and Confederate armies mobilized as volunteers a larger percentage of their societies' manpower than any other war in American history—perhaps in world history, with the possible exception of the French Revolution. And Civil War armies, like those of the French Revolution, were highly ideological in motivation. Most of the volunteers knew what they were fighting for, and why.[4] What were they fighting for? If asked to define it in a single word, many soldiers on both sides would have answered: liberty. They fought for the heritage of freedom bequeathed to them by the Founding Fathers. North and South alike wrapped themselves in the mantle of 1776. But the two sides interpreted that heritage in opposite ways, and at first neither side included the slaves in the vision of liberty for which it fought. The slaves did, however, and by the time of Lincoln's Gettysburg Address in 1863 the North also fought for "a new birth of freedom." These multiple meanings of freedom, and how they dis-

4. For a detailed discussion of this theme, see James M. McPherson, *What They Fought For, 1861–1865* (Baton Rouge, 1994).

solved and re-formed in kaleidoscopic patterns during the war, provide the central meaning of the war for the American experience.

When the "Black Republican" Abraham Lincoln won the presidency in 1860 on a platform of excluding slavery from the territories, Southerners compared him to George III and declared their independence from "oppressive Yankee rule." "The same spirit of freedom and independence that impelled our Fathers to the separation from the British Government," proclaimed secessionists, would impel the "liberty loving people of the South" to separation from the United States government. A Georgia secessionist declared that Southerners would be "either *slaves in the Union or freemen out of it.*"[5] Young men from Texas to Virginia rushed to enlist in this "Holy Cause of Liberty and Independence" and to raise "the standard of Liberty and Equality for white men" against "our Abolition enemies who are pledged to prostrate the white freemen of the South down to equality with negroes." From "the high and solemn motive of defending and protecting the rights which our fathers bequeathed to us," declared Jefferson Davis at the outset of war, let us "renew such sacrifices as our fathers made to the holy cause of constitutional liberty."[6]

But most Northerners ridiculed these Southern professions to be fighting for the ideals of 1776. That was "a libel upon the whole character and conduct of the men of '76," said the antislavery poet and journalist William Cullen Bryant. The Founding Fathers had fought "to establish the rights of man . . . and principles of universal liberty." The South, insisted Bryant, had seceded "not in the interest

5. Quotations from J. Mills Thornton III, *Politics and Power in a Slave Society: Alabama 1800–1860* (Baton Rouge, 1978), p. 216; and Michael P. Johnson, *Toward a Patriarchal Republic: The Secession of Georgia* (Baton Rouge, 1977), p. 36.

6. Henry Orr to his sister, Oct. 31, 1861, in John Q. Anderson, ed., *Campaigning with Parsons' Texas Cavalry Brigade, C.S.A.* (Hillsboro, Tex., 1967), p. 10; *LINCOLN ELECTED!* broadside from Bell County, Tex., Nov. 8, 1860, in McLelland Lincoln Collection, John Hay Library, Brown University; Dunbar Rowland, ed., *Jefferson Davis, Constitutionalist: His Letters, Papers, and Speeches,* 10 vols. (Jackson, Miss., 1923), V, 43, 202.

of general humanity, but of a domestic despotism. . . . Their motto is not liberty, but slavery." Northerners did not deny the right of revolution in principle; after all, the United States was founded on that right. But "the right of revolution," wrote Lincoln in 1861, "is never a legal right. . . . At most, it is but a moral right, when exercised for a morally justifiable cause. When exercised without such a cause revolution is no right, but simply a wicked exercise of physical power."[7] In Lincoln's judgment, secession was just such a wicked exercise. The event that precipitated it was Lincoln's election by a constitutional majority. As Northerners saw it, the Southern states, having controlled the national government for most of the previous two generations through their domination of the Democratic party, now decided to leave the Union just because they had lost an election.

For Lincoln and the Northern people, it was the Union that represented the ideals of 1776. The republic established by the Founding Fathers as a bulwark of liberty was a fragile experiment in a nineteenth-century world bestrode by kings, emperors, czars, and dictators. Most republics through history had eventually collapsed or were overthrown. Some Americans still alive in 1861 had seen French republics succumb twice to emperors and once to the restoration of the Bourbon monarchy. Republican governments in Latin America seemed to come and go with bewildering frequency. The United States in 1861 represented, in Lincoln's words, "the last best hope" for the survival of republican liberties in the world. Would that hope also collapse? "Our popular government has often been called an experiment," Lincoln told Congress on July 4, 1861. But if the Confederacy succeeded in splitting the country in two, it would set a fatal precedent that would destroy the experiment. By invoking this precedent, a minority in the future might secede from the Union whenever it did not like what the majority stood for, until the

---

7. *New York Evening Post,* Feb. 18, 1861; Roy P. Basler, ed., *The Collected Works of Abraham Lincoln,* 9 vols. (New Brunswick, N.J., 1953–1955), IV, 434n.

United States fragmented into a multitude of petty, squabbling auto-cracies. "The central idea pervading this struggle," said Lincoln, "is the necessity . . . of proving that popular government is not an ab-surdity. We must settle this question now, whether, in a free govern-ment, the minority have the right to break up the government when-ever they choose."[8]

Freedom for the slaves was not part of the liberty for which the North fought in 1861. That was not because the Lincoln administra-tion supported slavery; quite the contrary. Slavery was "an unquali-fied evil to the negro, to the white man . . . and to the State," said Lincoln on many occasions in words that expressed the sentiments of a Northern majority. "The monstrous injustice of slavery . . . de-prives our republican example of its just influence in the world—enables the enemies of free institutions, with plausibility, to taunt us as hypocrites." Yet in his first inaugural address, Lincoln declared that he had "no purpose, directly or indirectly, to interfere with . . . slavery in the States where it exists." He reiterated this pledge in his first message to Congress, on July 4, 1861, when the Civil War was nearly three months old.[9]

What explains this apparent inconsistency? The answer lies in the Constitution and in the Northern polity of 1861. Lincoln was bound by a Constitution that protected slavery in any state where citizens wanted it. The republic of liberty for whose preservation the North was fighting had been a republic in which slavery was legal every-where in 1776. That was the great American paradox—a land of freedom based on slavery. Even in 1861 four states that remained loyal to the Union were slave states, and the Democratic minority in free states opposed any move to make the war for the Union a war against slavery.

But as the conflict ground on, the slaves themselves took the first

8. Basler, ed., *Collected Works of Lincoln,* IV, 439; Tyler Dennett, ed., *Lincoln and the Civil War in the Diaries and Letters of John Hay* (New York, 1939), p. 19.
9. Basler, ed., *Collected Works of Lincoln,* III, 92, II, 255, IV, 250, 439.

step toward making it a war against slavery. Coming into Union lines by the thousands, they voted with their feet for freedom. As enemy property they could be confiscated by Union forces as "contraband of war." This was the thin edge of the wedge that finally broke apart the American paradox. By 1863 a series of congressional acts plus Lincoln's Emancipation Proclamation had radically enlarged Union war aims. The North henceforth fought not just to restore the old Union, not just to ensure that the nation born in 1776 "shall not perish from the earth," but also to give that nation "a new birth of freedom."

Northern victory in the Civil War resolved two fundamental, festering issues left unresolved by the Revolution of 1776: whether this fragile republican experiment called the United States would survive, and whether the house divided would continue to endure half slave and half free. Both of these issues remained open questions until 1865. Many Americans had doubted whether the republic would survive; many European conservatives had predicted its demise; some Americans advocated the right of secession and periodically threatened to invoke it; eleven states did invoke it in 1860 and 1861. But since 1865 no state or region has seriously threatened secession, not even during the "massive resistance" to desegregation from 1954 to 1964. Before 1865 the United States, land of liberty, was the largest slaveholding country in the world. Since 1865 that particular "monstrous injustice" and "hypocrisy" has existed no more.

In the process of preserving the Union of 1776 while purging it of slavery, the Civil War also transformed it. Before 1861 the words *United States* were a plural noun: "The United States *are* a large country." Since 1865 *United States* has been a singular noun. The North went to war to preserve the *Union;* it ended by creating a *nation.* This transformation can be traced in Lincoln's most important wartime addresses. The first inaugural address contained the word *Union* twenty times and the word *nation* not once. In Lincoln's first message to Congress, on July 4, 1861, he used *Union* forty-nine times and *nation* only three times. In his famous public letter to

Horace Greeley of August 22, 1862, concerning slavery and the war, Lincoln spoke of the Union nine times and the nation not at all. But in the Gettysburg Address fifteen months later, he did not refer to the Union at all but used the word *nation* five times. And in the second inaugural address, looking back over the past four years, Lincoln spoke of one side's seeking to dissolve the Union in 1861 and the other side's accepting the challenge of war to preserve the nation.

The old decentralized republic, in which the post office was the only agency of national government that touched the average citizen, was transformed by the crucible of war into a centralized polity that taxed people directly and created an internal revenue bureau to collect the taxes, expanded the jurisdiction of federal courts, created a national currency and a federally chartered banking system, drafted men into the army, and created the Freedmen's Bureau as the first national agency for social welfare. Eleven of the first twelve amendments to the Constitution had limited the powers of the national government; six of the next seven, starting with the Thirteenth Amendment in 1865, radically expanded those powers as the expense of the states. The first three of these amendments converted four million slaves into citizens and voters within five years, the most rapid and fundamental social transformation in American history—even if the nation did backslide on part of this commitment for three generations after 1877.

From 1789 to 1861 a Southern slaveholder was president of the United States two-thirds of the time, and two-thirds of the speakers of the House and presidents pro tem of the Senate had also been Southerners. Twenty of the thirty-five Supreme Court justices appointed during that half century were Southerners. The institutions and ideology of a plantation society and a caste system that had dominated half of the country before 1861 and sought to dominate more went down with a great crash in 1865 and were replaced by the institutions and ideology of free-labor entrepreneurial capitalism. For better or for worse, the flames of Civil War forged the framework of modern America.

So even if the veneer of romance and myth that has attracted so many of the current Civil War camp followers were stripped away, leaving only the trauma of violence and suffering, the Civil War would remain the most dramatic and crucial experience in American history. That fact will ensure the persistence of its popularity and its importance as an historical subject so long as there is a United States.

5

FROM LIMITED TO TOTAL WAR
1861–1865

A FEW YEARS AFTER THE CIVIL WAR, MARK TWAIN DESCRIBED
that great conflict as having "uprooted institutions that were centuries old, changed the politics of a people, transformed the social life
of half the country, and wrought so profoundly upon the entire national character that the influence cannot be measured short of two
or three generations."[1] This profound transformation was achieved
at enormous cost in lives and property. Fully one-quarter of the
white men of military age in the Confederacy lost their lives. And
that terrible toll does not include an unknown number of civilian
deaths in the South. Altogether nearly 4 percent of the Southern
people, black and white, civilians and soldiers, died as a consequence
of the war. This percentage exceeded the human cost of any country
in World War I and was outstripped only by the region between the
Rhine and the Volga in World War II. The amount of property and
resources destroyed in the Confederate States is almost incalculable.

1. Mark Twain and Charles Dudley Warner, *The Gilded Age* (New York:
New American Library edition, 1969), pp. 137–38.

It has been estimated at two-thirds of all assessed wealth, including the market value of slaves.[2]

This is the negative side of that radical transformation described by Mark Twain. The positive side included preservation of the United States as a unified nation, the liberation of four million slaves, and the abolition by constitutional amendment of the institution of bondage that had plagued the nation since the beginning, inhibited its progress, and made a mockery of the libertarian values on which it was founded. No other society in history freed so many slaves in so short a time—but also at such a cost in violence.

The Civil War mobilized human resources on a scale unmatched by any other event in American history except, perhaps, World War II. For actual combat duty the Civil War mustered a considerably larger proportion of American manpower than did World War II. And, in another comparison with that global conflict, the victorious power in the Civil War did all it could to devastate the enemy's economic resources as well as the morale of its home-front population, which was considered almost as important as enemy armies in the war effort. In World War II this was done by strategic bombing; in the Civil War it was done by cavalry and infantry penetrating deep into the Confederate heartland.

It is these factors—the devastation wrought by the war, the radical changes it accomplished, and the mobilization of the whole society to sustain the war effort that have caused many historians to label the Civil War a "total war." Recently, however, some analysts have questioned this terminology. They maintain that true total war—or in the words of Carl von Clausewitz, "absolute war"— makes no distinction between combatants and noncombatants, no discrimination between taking the lives of enemy soldiers and those

2. James L. Sellers, "The Economic Incidence of the Civil War in the South," *Mississippi Valley Historical Review* 14 (1927), 179–91; Stanley Engerman, "Some Economic Factors in Southern Backwardness in the Nineteenth Century," in John F. Kain and John R. Meyers, eds., *Essays in Regional Economics* (Cambridge, Mass., 1971), pp. 291, 300–302.

of enemy civilians; it is war "without any scruple or limitations," war in which combatants give no quarter and take no prisoners.[3]

Some wars have approached this totality—for example, World War II, in which Germany deliberately murdered millions of civilians in eastern Europe, Allied strategic bombing killed hundreds of thousands of German and Japanese civilians, and both sides sometimes refused to take prisoners and shot those who tried to surrender. In that sense of totality, the Civil War was not a total war. Although suffering and disease mortality were high among prisoners of war, and Confederates occasionally murdered captured black soldiers, there was no systematic effort to kill prisoners. And while soldiers on both sides in the Civil War pillaged and looted civilian property, and several Union commanders systematized this destruction into a policy, they did not deliberately kill civilians. Mark Neely, the chief critic of the notion of the Civil War as a total war, maintains that "the *essential* aspect of any definition of total war asserts that it breaks down the distinction between soldiers and civilians, combatants and noncombatants, and this no one in the Civil War did systematically."[4]

Even William T. Sherman, widely regarded as the progenitor of total war, was more bark than bite according to Neely. Sherman wrote and spoke in a nervous, rapid-fire, sometimes offhand manner; he said extreme things about "slaying millions" and "repopulating Georgia" if necessary to win the war. But this was rhetorical exaggeration. One of Sherman's most widely quoted statements—"We are not only fighting hostile armies, but a hostile people, and must

3. Mark E. Neely, Jr., "Was the Civil War a Total War?" *Civil War History* 37 (1991), 5–28; Eric T. Dean, Jr., "Rethinking the Civil War: Beyond 'Revolutions,' 'Reconstructions,' and the 'New Social History,'" *Southern Historian* 15 (1994), 28–50; "Civil War: Modern War or Not," session of the Society of Civil War Historians at the annual meeting of the Southern Historical Association in Louisville, Nov. 10, 1994; quotation from the definition of total war in *Oxford English Dictionary,* 2d ed., 18: 286–87.

4. Neely, "Was the Civil War a Total War?" p. 27.

make old and young, rich and poor, feel the hard hand of war"—
did not really erase the distinction between combatants and noncombatants, for Sherman did not mean it to justify killing civilians.[5]

To note the difference between rhetoric and substance in the Civil
War is to make a valid point. The rhetoric not only of Sherman but
also of many other people on both sides was far more ferocious than
anything that actually happened. Northerners had no monopoly on
such rhetoric. A Savannah newspaper proclaimed in 1863: "Let Yankee cities burn and their fields be laid waste," while a Richmond
editor echoed: "It surely must be made plain at last that this is to be
a war of extermination." A month after the firing on Fort Sumter, a
Nashville woman prayed that "God may be with us to give us
strength to conquer them, to exterminate them, to lay waste every
Northern city, town and village, to destroy them utterly."[6] Yankees
used similar language. In the first month of the war a Milwaukee
judge said that Northern armies should "restore New Orleans to its
native marshes, then march across the country, burn Montgomery to
ashes, and serve Charleston in the same way. . . . We must starve,
drown, burn, shoot the traitors."[7] In St. Louis the uneasy truce between Union and Confederate factions that had followed the riots
and fighting in May 1861 broke down a month later when the Union
commander Nathaniel Lyon rejected a compromise with pro-
Confederate elements, which included the governor, with these
words: "Rather than concede to the State of Missouri for one single
instant the right to dictate to my Government in any matter . . . I
would see you . . . and every man, woman, and child in the State,
dead and buried."[8]

5. *Ibid.,* pp. 14–15; John Bennett Walters, "General William T. Sherman
and Total War," *Journal of Southern History* 14 (1948), 463.

6. Charles Royster, *The Destructive War: William Tecumseh Sherman, Stonewall Jackson, and the Americans* (New York, 1991), pp. 35, 37–38, 211–12.

7. *Ibid.,* pp. 79–80.

8. Thomas L. Snead, *The Fight for Missouri from the Election of Lincoln to
the Death of Lyon* (New York, 1886), pp. 199–200.

These statements certainly sound like total war, war without limits or restraints. But of course none of the scenarios sketched out in these quotations literally came true—not even in Missouri, where reality came closer to rhetoric than anywhere else. Therefore, those who insist that the Civil War was not a total war appear to have won their case, at least semantically. Recognizing this, a few historians have sought different adjectives to describe the kind of conflict the Civil War became: One uses the phrase "destructive war"; another prefers "hard war."[9]

But these phrases, though accurate, do not convey the true dimensions of devastation in the Civil War. All wars are hard and destructive in some degree; what made the Civil War distinctive in the American experience? It *was* that overwhelming involvement of the whole population, the shocking loss of life, the wholesale devastation and radical social and political transformations that it wrought. In the experience of Americans, especially Southerners, this approached totality; it *seemed* total. Thus the concept, and label, of total war remains a useful one. It is what the sociologist Max Weber called an "ideal type"—a theoretical model used to measure a reality that never fully conforms to the model, but that nevertheless remains a useful tool for analyzing the reality.

That is the sense in which this essay will analyze the evolution of the Civil War from a limited to a total war. Despite that fierce rhetoric of destruction quoted earlier, the official war aims of both sides in 1861 were quite limited. In his first message to the Confederate Congress after the firing on Fort Sumter by his troops had provoked war, Jefferson Davis declared that "we seek no conquest, no aggrandizement, no concession of any kind from the States with which we were lately confederated; all we ask is to be let alone."[10] As for the Union government, its initial conception of the war was one of a

9. Royster, *The Destructive War;* Mark Grimsley, *The Hard Hand of War: Union Military Policy toward Southern Civilians, 1861–1865* (Cambridge, 1996).

10. Dunbar Rowland, ed., *Jefferson Davis, Constitutionalist: His Letters, Papers, and Speeches,* 10 vols. (Jackson, Miss., 1923), V, 84.

domestic insurrection, an uprising against national authority by certain lawless hotheads who had gained temporary sway over the otherwise law-abiding citizens of a few Southern states—or as Lincoln put it in his proclamation calling out seventy-five thousand state militia to put down the uprising, "combinations too powerful to be suppressed by the ordinary course of judicial proceedings." This was a strategy of limited war—indeed, so limited that it was scarcely seen as a war at all, but rather as a police action to quell a large riot. It was a strategy founded on an assumption of residual loyalty among the silent majority of Southerners. Once the national government demonstrated its firmness by regaining control of its forts and by blockading Southern ports, those presumed legions of Unionists would come to the fore and bring their states back into the Union. To cultivate this loyalty, and to temper firmness with restraint, Lincoln promised that the federalized ninety-day militia would avoid "any devastation, any destruction of, or interference with, property, or any disturbance of peaceful citizens."[11]

None other than William Tecumseh Sherman echoed these sentiments in the summer of 1861. Commander of a brigade that fought at Bull Run, Sherman deplored the marauding tendencies of his poorly disciplined soldiers. "No curse could be greater than invasion by a volunteer army," he wrote. "No Goths or Vandals ever had less respect for the lives and properties of friends and foes, and henceforth we should never hope for any friends in Virginia. . . . My only hope now is that a common sense of decency may be infused into this soldiery to respect life and property."[12]

The most important and vulnerable form of Southern property was slaves. The Lincoln administration went out of its way to reassure Southerners in 1861 that it had no designs on slavery. Congress

11. Roy P. Basler et al., eds., *The Collected Works of Abraham Lincoln,* 9 vols. (New Brunswick, N.J., 1953–1955), IV, 332.

12. Sherman to his wife, July 28, 1861, and undated, probably August 1861, in Mark A. DeWolfe Howe, ed., *Home Letters of General Sherman* (New York, 1909), 209, 214.

followed suit, passing by an overwhelming majority in July 1861 a resolution affirming that Union war aims included no intention "of overthrowing or interfering with the rights or established institutions of the States"—in plain words, slavery—but intended only "to defend and maintain the supremacy of the Constitution and to preserve the Union with all the dignity, equality, and rights of the several States unimpaired."[13]

There were, to be sure, murmurings in the North against this soft-war approach, this "kid-glove policy." Abolitionists and radical Republicans insisted that a rebellion sustained *by* slavery in defense *of* slavery could be crushed only by striking *against* slavery. As Frederick Douglass put it: "To fight against slaveholders, without fighting against slavery, is but a half-hearted business, and paralyzes the hands engaged in it. . . . Fire must be met with water. War for the destruction of liberty must be met with war for the destruction of slavery."[14] Several Union soldiers and their officers, some with no previous antislavery convictions, also began to grumble about protecting the property of traitors in arms against the United States.

The first practical manifestation of such sentiments came in Missouri. Thus began a pattern whereby events in that state set the pace for the transformation from a limited to a total war, radiating eastward and southward from Missouri. The commander of the Western Department of the Union army in the summer of 1861, with headquarters at St. Louis, was John C. Frémont, famed explorer of the West, first Republican presidential candidate (in 1856), and now ambitious for military glory. Handicapped by his own administrative incompetence, bedeviled by a Confederate invasion of southwest Missouri that defeated and killed Nathaniel Lyon at Wilson's Creek on August 10 and then marched northward to the Missouri River, and driven to distraction by Confederate guerrilla bands that sprang up almost everywhere, Frémont on August 30 took a bold step toward

13. *Congressional Globe,* 37th Congress, 1st Session, pp. 222–23.
14. *Douglass' Monthly,* May, September 1861.

total war. He placed the whole state of Missouri under martial law, announced the death penalty for guerrillas captured behind Union lines, and confiscated the property and emancipated the slaves of Confederate activists.[15]

Northern radicals applauded, but conservatives shuddered and border-state Unionists expressed outrage. Still pursuing a strategy of trying to cultivate Southern Unionists as the best way to restore the Union, Lincoln feared that the emancipation provision of Frémont's edict would

> alarm our Southern Union friends, and turn them against us—perhaps ruin our rather fair prospect for Kentucky. . . . To lose Kentucky is nearly the same as to lose the whole game. Kentucky gone, we can not hold Missouri, nor, as I think, Maryland. These all against us, and the job on our hands is too large for us. We would as well consent to separation at once, including the surrender of this capitol.[16]

Lincoln thus revoked the confiscation and emancipation provisions of Frémont's decree. He also ordered the general to execute no guerrillas without specific presidential approval. Lincoln feared that such a policy would only provoke reprisals whereby guerrillas would shoot captured Union soldiers "man for man, indefinitely." His apprehensions were well founded. One guerrilla leader in southeast Missouri had already issued a counterproclamation declaring that for every man executed under Frémont's order, he would "HANG, DRAW, and QUARTER a minion of said Abraham Lincoln."[17]

Lincoln probably had the Missouri situation in mind when he told Congress in his annual message of December 1861 that "in considering the policy to be adopted for suppressing the insurrection, I have

15. *War of the Rebellion . . . Official Records of the Union and Confederate Armies* (hereinafter *O.R.*), 128 vols. (Washington, 1880–1901), Ser. I, Vol. 3, pp. 466–67.

16. Basler, ed., *Collected Works of Lincoln*, IV, 506, 532.

17. *Ibid.*, p. 506; Jay Monaghan, *Civil War on the Western Border 1854–1865* (Boston, 1955), p. 185.

been anxious and careful that the inevitable conflict for this purpose shall not degenerate into a violent and remorseless revolutionary struggle."[18] But that was already happening. The momentum of a war that had already mobilized nearly a million men on both sides was becoming remorseless even as Lincoln spoke, and it would soon become revolutionary.

Nowhere was this more true than in Missouri. There occurred the tragedy of a civil war within the Civil War, of neighbor against neighbor and sometimes literally brother against brother, of an armed conflict along the Kansas border that went back to 1854 and had never really stopped, of ugly, vicious, no-holds-barred bush-whacking that constituted pretty much a total war in fact as well as in theory. Bands of Confederate guerrillas led by the notorious William Clarke Quantrill, Bloody Bill Anderson, and other pathological killers, and containing such famous desperadoes as the James and Younger brothers, ambushed, murdered, and burned out Missouri Unionists and tied down thousands of Union troops by hit-and-run raids. Union militia and Kansas Jayhawkers retaliated in kind. In contrapuntal disharmony guerrillas and Jayhawkers plundered and pillaged their way across the state, taking no prisoners, killing in cold blood, terrorizing the civilian population, leaving large parts of Missouri a scorched earth.

In 1863 Quantrill's band rode into Kansas to the hated Yankee settlement of Lawrence and murdered almost every adult male they found there, more than 150 in all. A year later Bloody Bill Anderson's gang took twenty-four unarmed Union soldiers from a train, shot them in the head, then turned on a posse of pursuing militia and slaughtered 127 of them including the wounded and captured. In April 1864 the Missourian John S. Marmaduke, a Confederate general (and later governor of Missouri), led an attack on Union supply wagons at Poison Springs, Arkansas, killing in cold blood almost as many black soldiers as Nathan Bedford Forrest's troops did

18. Basler, ed., *Collected Works of Lincoln*, V, 48–49.

at almost the same time in the more famous Fort Pillow massacre in Tennessee.[19]

Confederate guerrillas had no monopoly on atrocities and scorched-earth practices in Missouri. The Seventh Kansas Cavalry— "Jennison's Jayhawkers"—containing many abolitionists including a son of John Brown, seemed determined to exterminate rebellion and slaveholders in the most literal manner. The Union commander in western Missouri where guerrilla activity was most rife, Thomas Ewing, issued his notorious Order No. 11 after Quantrill's raid to Lawrence. Order No. 11 forcibly removed thousands of families from four Missouri counties along the Kansas border and burned their farms to deny the guerrillas the sanctuary they had enjoyed in this region. Interestingly, Ewing was William T. Sherman's brother-in-law. In fact, most of the Union commanders who subsequently became famous as practitioners of total war spent part of their early Civil War careers in Missouri—including Grant, Sherman, and Sheridan. This was more than coincidence. What they saw and experienced in that state helped to predispose them toward a conviction that, in Sherman's words, "we are not only fighting hostile armies, but a hostile people" and must make them "feel the hard hand of war."

That conviction took root and began to grow among the Northern people and their leaders in the summer of 1862. Before then, for several months in the winter and spring, Union forces had seemed on the verge of winning the war without resorting to such measures. The capture of Forts Henry and Donelson, the victories at Mill Springs in Kentucky, Pea Ridge in Arkansas, Shiloh in Tennessee, Roanoke Island and New Bern in North Carolina, the capture of

19. Monaghan, *Civil War on the Western Border;* Richard S. Brownlee, *Gray Ghosts of the Confederacy: Guerrilla Warfare in the West, 1861–1865* (Baton Rouge, 1958); Stephen Z. Starr, *Jennison's Jayhawkers: A Civil War Cavalry Regiment and Its Commander* (Baton Rouge, 1973); Albert E. Castel, *A Frontier State at War: Kansas, 1861–1865* (Ithaca, N.Y., 1958); Michael Fellman, *Inside War: The Guerrilla Conflict in Missouri during the American Civil War* (New York, 1989).

Nashville, New Orleans, and Memphis, the expulsion of organized Confederate armies from Missouri, Kentucky, and West Virginia, the Union occupation of much of the lower Mississippi Valley and a large part of the state of Tennessee, and the advance of the splendidly equipped Army of the Potomac to within five miles of Richmond in May 1862 seemed to herald the Confederacy's doom. But then came counteroffensives by Stonewall Jackson and Robert E. Lee in Virginia and by Braxton Bragg and Kirby Smith in Tennessee, which took Confederate armies almost to the Ohio River and across the Potomac River by September 1862.

Those deceptively easy Union advances and victories in early 1862 had apparently confirmed the validity of a limited-war strategy. Grant's capture of Forts Henry and Donelson, for example, had convinced him that the Confederacy was a hollow shell about to collapse. But when the rebels regrouped and counterpunched so hard at Shiloh that they nearly whipped him, Grant changed his mind. He now "gave up all idea," he later wrote, "of saving the Union except by complete conquest." Conmplete conquest meant not merely the occupation of territory, but also the crippling or destruction of Confederate armies. For if these armies remained intact they could reconquer territory, as they did in the summer of 1862. Grant's new conception of the war also included the seizure or destruction of any property or other resources used to sustain the Confederate war effort. Before those Southern counteroffensives, Grant said that he had been careful "to protect the property of the citizens whose territory was invaded"; afterwards his policy became to "consume everything that could be used to support or supply armies."[20]

"Everything" included slaves, whose labor was one of the principal resources used to support and supply Confederate armies. If the Confederacy "cannot be whipped in any other way than through a

20. *Personal Memoirs of U.S. Grant,* 2 vols. (New York, 1885–1886), I, 368–69.

war against slavery," wrote Grant, "let it come to that."[21] Union armies in the field as well as Republican leaders in Congress had been edging toward an emancipation policy ever since May 1861 when General Benjamin Butler had admitted three escaped slaves to his lines at Fort Monroe, labeled them contraband of war, and put them to work for wages to help support and supply *Union* forces. By the summer of 1862, tens of thousands of these contrabands had come within Union lines. Congress had forbidden army officers to return them. Legislation passed in July 1862 declared free all of those belonging to masters who supported the Confederacy. Frémont in Missouri turned out to have been not wrong, but a year ahead of his time.

By the summer of 1862 Lincoln too had come to the position enunciated a year earlier by Frederick Douglass: "To fight against slaveholders, without fighting against slavery, is but a half-hearted business." Acting in his capacity as commander in chief with power to seize property used to wage war against the United States, Lincoln decided to issue a proclamation freeing all slaves in those states engaged in rebellion. Emancipation, he told his cabinet in July 1862, had become "a military necessity, absolutely essential to the preservation of the Union. . . . We must free the slaves or be ourselves subdued. The slaves [are] undeniably an element of strength to those who [have] their service, and we must decide whether that element should be with us or against us. . . . Decisive and extensive measures must be adopted. . . . We [want] the army to strike more vigorous blows. The Administration must set an example, and strike at the heart of the rebellion."[22] After a wait of two months for a victory

21. Ulysses S. Grant to Jesse Root Grant, Nov. 27, 1861, in John Y. Simon, ed., *The Papers of Ulysses S. Grant,* 20 vols. to date (Carbondale, Ill., 1967–), III, 227.

22. Gideon Welles, "The History of Emancipation," *The Galaxy* 14 (1872), 842–43.

to give the proclamation credibility, Lincoln announced it on September 22, 1862, to go into effect on January 1, 1863.

With this action Lincoln embraced the idea of the Civil War as a revolutionary conflict. Things had changed a great deal since he had promised to avoid "any devastation, or destruction of, or interference with, property." The Emancipation Proclamation was just what the *Springfield Republican* pronounced it: "the greatest social and political revolution of the age." No less an authority on revolutions than Karl Marx exulted: "*Never* has such a gigantic transformation taken place so rapidly."[23] General Henry W. Halleck, who had been called from his headquarters in St. Louis (where he was commander of the Western Department) to Washington to become general in chief, made clear the practical import of the Emancipation Proclamation in a dispatch to Grant at Memphis in January 1863. "The character of the war has very much changed within the last year," he wrote. "There is now no possible hope of reconciliation with the rebels. . . . We must conquer the rebels or be conquered by them. . . . Every slave withdrawn from the enemy is the equivalent of a white man put *hors de combat*." One of Grant's field commanders explained that the new "policy is to be terrible on the enemy. I am using negroes all the time for my work as teamsters, and have 1,000 employed."[24]

The program of "being terrible on the enemy" soon went beyond emancipating slaves and using them as teamsters. In early 1863 the Lincoln administration committed itself to a policy that had first emerged, like other total-war practices, in the trans-Mississippi theater. The First Kansas Colored Volunteers, composed mostly of contrabands from Missouri, were the earliest black soldiers to see combat, in 1862, and along with the Louisiana Native Guards the first to take shape as organized units. Arms in the hands of slaves consti-

23. *Springfield Republican*, Sept. 24, 1862; Karl Marx, *On America and the Civil War,* ed. and trans. by Saul K. Padover (New York, 1972), p. 272.

24. Halleck in *O.R.,* Ser. I, Vol. 24, part 3, p. 157; Dodge quoted in Bruce Catton, *Grant Moves South* (Boston, 1960), p. 294.

tuted the South's ultimate revolutionary nightmare. After initial hesitation, Lincoln embraced this revolution as well. In March 1863 he wrote to Andrew Johnson, military governor of occupied Tennessee: "The bare sight of fifty thousand armed, and drilled black soldiers on the banks of the Mississippi, would end the rebellion at once. And who doubts that we can present that sight, if we but take hold in earnest?" By August 1863 Lincoln could declare in a public letter that "the emancipation policy, and the use of colored troops, constitute the heaviest blow yet dealt to the rebellion."[25]

Well before then the conflict had become remorseless as well as revolutionary, with Lincoln's approval. Two of the generals he brought to Washington from the West in the summer of 1862, John Pope and Henry W. Halleck, helped to define and enunciate the remorselessness. Both had spent the previous winter and spring in Missouri, where experience with guerrillas had shaped their hard-war approach. One of Pope's first actions upon becoming commander of the Army of Virginia was a series of orders authorizing his officers to seize Confederate property without compensation, to execute captured guerrillas who had fired on Union troops, and to expel from occupied territory any civilians who sheltered guerrillas or who refused to take an oath of allegiance to the United States. From Halleck's office as general in chief in August 1862 went orders to Grant, now commander of Union forces in western Tennessee and Mississippi. "Take up all active [rebel] sympathizers," wrote Halleck, "and either hold them as prisoners or put them beyond our lines. Handle that class without gloves, and take their property for public use. . . . It is time that they should begin to feel the presence of the war."[26]

With or without such orders, Union soldiers in the South were erasing the distinction between military and civilian property belong-

25. Basler, ed., *Collected Works of Lincoln,* VI, 149–50, 408–9.
26. *O.R.,* Ser. I, Vol. 12, part 2, pp. 50–52 (Pope's orders), Vol. 17, part 1, p. 150 (Halleck's dispatch).

ing to the enemy. A soldier from St. Louis with his regiment in west Tennessee wrote home that "this thing of guarding rebels' property has about 'played out.' " "The iron gauntlet," wrote another officer in the Mississippi Valley, "must be used more than the silken glove to crush this serpent."[27]

Inevitably, bitter protests against this harshness reached Lincoln from purported Southern Unionists. A few months earlier the president would have rebuked the harshness, as he had rebuked Frémont, for alienating potential Unionist friends in the South. But in July 1862 Lincoln rebuked the protesters instead. He asked one of them sarcastically if they expected him to fight the war "with elder-stalk squirts, charged with rose water?" Did they think he would "surrender the government to save them from losing all"? Lincoln had lost faith in those professed Unionists:

> The paralysis—the dead palsy—of the government in this whole struggle is, that this class of men will do nothing for the government . . . except [demand] that the government shall not strike its open enemies, lest they be struck by accident! . . . This government cannot much longer play a game in which it stakes all, and its enemies stake nothing. Those enemies must understand that they cannot experiment for ten years trying to destroy the government, and if they fail still come back into the Union unhurt.

Using one of his favorite metaphors, Lincoln warned Southern whites that "broken eggs cannot be mended." The rebels had already cracked the egg of slavery by their own rash behavior; the sooner they gave up and ceased the insurrection, "the smaller will be the amount of [eggs] which will be past mending."[28]

William Tecumseh Sherman eventually became the foremost mil-

27. A. Fisk Gore to sister Katie, Aug. 5, 1862, A. Fisk Gore Papers, Missouri Historical Society (St. Louis); officer quoted in Catton, *Grant Moves South,* p. 294.

28. Basler, ed., *Collected Works of Lincoln,* V, 344–46, 350.

itary spokesman for remorseless war and the most effective general in carrying it out. Sherman too had spent part of the winter of 1861–1862 in Missouri where he stored up impressions of guerrilla ferocity. Nonetheless, even as late as July 1862, as commander of Union occupation forces around Memphis, he complained of some Northern troops who took several mules and horses from farmers. Such "petty thieving and pillaging," he wrote, "does us infinite harm."[29] This scarcely sounds like the Sherman that Southerners love to hate. But his command problems in western Tennessee soon taught him what his brother-in-law Thomas Ewing was also learning about guerrillas and the civilian population that sheltered them across the river in Arkansas and Missouri. Nearly every white man, woman, and child in Sherman's district seemed to hate the Yankees and to abet the bushwhackers who fired into Union supply boats on the river, burned railroad bridges and ripped up the tracks, attacked Union picket outposts, ambushed Northern soldiers unless they moved in large groups, and generally raised hell behind Union lines. Some of the cavalry troopers who rode with Nathan Bedford Forrest and John Hunt Morgan on devastating raids behind Union lines also functioned in the manner of guerrillas, fading away to their homes and melting into the civilian population after a raid.

These operations convinced Sherman to take off the gloves. The distinction between enemy civilians and soldiers grew blurred. After fair warning, Sherman burned houses and sometimes whole villages in western Tennessee that he suspected of harboring snipers and guerrillas. The Union army, he now said, must act "on the proper rule that all in the South *are* enemies of all in the North. . . . The whole country is full of guerrilla bands. . . . The entire South, man, woman, and child, is against us, armed and determined."[30] This con-

29. *O.R.,* Ser. I, Vol. 17, part 2, pp. 88–89.

30. Quoted in John Bennett Walters, *Merchant of Terror: General Sherman and Total War* (Indianapolis, 1973), pp. 57–58, 59, 60.

viction governed Sherman's subsequent operations which left smol-
dering ruins in his track from Vicksburg to Meridian, from Atlanta
to the sea, and from the sea to Goldsboro, North Carolina.

When Mississippians protested, Sherman told them that they were
lucky to get off so lightly: A commander

> may take your house, your fields, your everything, and turn you all
> out, helpless, to starve. It may be wrong, but that don't alter the case.
> In war you can't help yourselves, and the only possible remedy is to
> stop the war. . . . Our duty is not to build up; it is rather to destroy
> both the rebel army and whatever of wealth or property it has
> founded its boasted strength upon.[31]

When Confederate General John Bell Hood charged him with
barbarism for expelling the civilian population from Atlanta, Sherman gave Hood a tongue-lashing. Accusations of barbarity, he said,
came with a fine irony from "you who, in the midst of peace and
prosperity, have plunged a nation into war . . . who dared and bad-
gered us to battle, insulted our flag . . . turned loose your privateers
to plunder unarmed ships, expelled Union families by the thousands
[and] burned their houses. . . . Talk thus to the marines, but not to
me, who have seen these things." Sherman vowed to "make Georgia
howl" in his march from Atlanta to Savannah, and afterwards expressed satisfaction with having done so. He estimated the damage
to Confederate resources "at $100,000,000; at least $20,000,000 of
which has inured to our advantage, and the remainder is simple
waste and destruction."[32] And this turned out to be mere child's play
compared with what awaited South Carolina.

Sherman was convinced that not only the economic resources but
also the will of Southern civilians sustained the Confederate war effort. His campaigns of devastation were intended to break that will

---

31. *O.R.,* Ser. I, Vol. 30, part 3, p. 403.
32. William T. Sherman, *Memoirs,* 2d ed. rev., 2 vols. (New York, 1886), II,
119–21, 125–27; *O.R.,* Ser. I, Vol. 44, p. 13.

as much as to destroy the resources. This is certainly a feature of
modern total war; Sherman was a pioneer in the concept of psychological warfare as part of a total war against the whole enemy population. Sherman was well aware of the fear that his soldiers inspired
among Southern whites. This terror "was a power," he wrote, "and
I intended to utilize it . . . to humble their pride, to follow them to
their inmost recesses, and to make them fear and dread us. . . . We
cannot change the hearts and minds of those people of the South,
but we can make war so terrible . . . [and] make them so sick of war
that generations would pass away before they would again appeal
to it."[33]

This strategy seemed to work; Sherman's destruction not only
deprived Confederate armies of desperately needed supplies; it also
crippled morale both on the home front and in the army. Numerous
soldiers deserted from Confederate armies in response to letters of
despair from home in the wake of Sherman's juggernaut. One
Southern soldier wrote after the march through Georgia: "I hev con-
ckludud that the dam fulishness uv tryin to lick shurmin Had better
be stoped, we have gettin nuthin but hell & lots uv it ever since we
saw the dam yankys & I am tirde uv it . . . thair thicker than lise
on a hen and a dam site ornraier." After the march through South
Carolina, a civilian in that state wrote: "All is gloom, despondency,
and inactivity. Our army is demoralized and the people panic
stricken. To fight longer seems to be madness."[34]

Philip Sheridan carried out a similar policy of scorched earth in
the Shenandoah Valley. Interestingly, Sheridan too had spent most
of the war's first year in Missouri. There as well as subsequently in
Tennessee and Virginia he saw the ravages of Confederate guerrillas,
and responded as Sherman did. If guerrilla operations and Union
counterinsurgency activities in Virginia during 1864 were slightly less

33. Sherman, *Memoirs*, I, 368, II, 249, 254.
34. Quotations in E. Merton Coulter, *The Confederate States of America* (Baton Rouge, 1950), pp. 549–50, and John G. Barrett, *Sherman's March through the
Carolinas* (Chapel Hill, 1956), p. 95.

vicious than in Missouri, it was perhaps only because the proximity of Washington and Richmond and of large field armies imposed some restraint. Nevertheless, plenty of atrocities piled up in John Singleton Mosby's Confederacy just east of the Blue Ridge and in the Shenandoah Valley to the west. In retaliation, and with a purpose similar to Sherman's to destroy the Valley's resources which helped supply Lee's army, Sheridan carried out a campaign of devastation that left nothing to sustain Confederate armies or even to enable the Valley's inhabitants to get through the winter. In little more than a week, wrote Sheridan in one of his reports, his army had "destroyed over 2,000 barns filled with wheat, hay, and farming implements; over seventy mills filled with flour and wheat; have driven in front of the army over 4,000 head of stock, and have killed and issued to the troops not less than 3,000 sheep." That was just the beginning, Sheridan promised. By the time he was through, "the Valley, from Winchester up to Staunton, ninety-two miles, will have little in it for man or beast."[35]

Several years later, while serving as an American observer at German headquarters during the Franco-Prussian War, Sheridan lectured his hosts on the correct way to wage war. The "proper strategy," said Sheridan, consisted first of "inflicting as telling blows as possible on the enemy's army, and then in causing the inhabitants so much suffering that they must long for peace, and force the government to demand it. The people must be left nothing but their eyes to weep with over the war."[36]

Abraham Lincoln is famed for his compassion; he issued many pardons and commuted many sentences of execution; the concluding passage of his second inaugural address, beginning "With malice toward none; with charity for all," is one of his most familiar utter-

---

35. *O.R.,* Ser. I, Vol. 43, part 1, pp. 30–31.

36. Michael Howard, *The Franco-Prussian War* (New York: Collier Books edition, 1969), p. 380.

ances. Lincoln regretted the devastation and suffering caused by the army's scorched-earth policy in the South. Yet he had warned Southerners in 1862 that the longer they fought, the more eggs would be broken. He would have agreed with Sherman's words to a Southerner: "You brought all this on yourselves." In 1864, after the march to the sea, Lincoln officially conveyed to Sherman's army the "grateful acknowledgments" of the nation; to Sheridan he offered the "thanks of the nation, and my own personal admiration, for [your] operations in the Shenandoah Valley." And while the words in the second inaugural about malice toward none and charity for all promised a generous peace, the victory that must precede that peace could be achieved only by hard war—indeed, by total war. Consider *these* words from the second inaugural:

> Fondly do we hope—fervently do we pray—that this mighty scourge of war may speedily pass away. Yet if God wills that it continue, until all the wealth piled by the bond-man's two hundred and fifty years of unrequited toil shall be sunk, and until every drop of blood drawn with the lash, shall be paid by another drawn with the sword, as was said three thousand years ago, so still it must be said "the judgments of the Lord, are true and righteous altogether."[37]

The kind of conflict the Civil War had become merits the label of total war. To be sure, Union soldiers did not set out to kill Southern civilians. Sherman's bummers destroyed property; Allied bombers in World War II destroyed hundreds of thousands of lives as well. But the strategic purpose of both was the same: to eliminate the resources and break the will of the people to sustain war. White people in large parts of the Confederacy were indeed left with "nothing but their eyes to weep with." This was not pretty; it was not glorious; it did not conform to the image of war held by most Americans in 1861 of flags waving, bands playing, and people cheer-

37. Basler, ed., *Collected Works of Lincoln*, VIII, 73–74, 182, 333.

ing on a spring afternoon. But as Sherman himself put it, in a speech to young men of a new generation fifteen years after the Civil War, the notion that war is glorious was nothing but moonshine. "When . . . you come down to the practical realities, boys," said Sherman, "war is all hell."[38]

38. Quoted in James Reston, Jr., *Sherman's March and Vietnam* (New York, 1984), p. xi.

6

RACE AND CLASS IN THE CRUCIBLE
OF WAR

SOCIAL HISTORY SINCE THE 1960s HAS BECOME THE LIVELIEST
field of American history. Historians have been using evidence about
class, race, ethnicity, and gender to gain insight into Americans' ev-
eryday lives—their work and leisure, their culture and ideology,
their relations with one another and with the political and economic
systems under which they have lived. From that research have come
new perspectives that have increased our understanding of the
American past—especially the past lives of blacks, women, ethnic
minorities, and blue-collar workers.

Until recently, warfare has been excepted from social history.
Narratives of campaigns and battles and of political leadership remained the dominant themes of histories about America's wars—
including its bloodiest and most consequential, the Civil War. But
military historians have finally discovered the value of social history,
while social historians have become aware of the enormous impact
of war on people and institutions.[1] The Civil War in particular mo-

1. Richard H. Kohn, "The Social History of the American Soldier: A Review and a Prospectus for Research," *American Historical Review* 86 (1981), 553–

bilized virtually the entire population in an all-out struggle for the survival of conflicting versions of Confederate or American nationalism, and for the preservation or destruction of slavery. It was a war fought by the most literate soldiers in history to that time, and in a society with a free and vigorous press. Millions of young men left their families for a prolonged absence, conscious of taking part in a great historical drama, which they recorded in diaries and in uncensored letters home.

Thus the American Civil War was in many ways the best-documented war in history. The letters and diaries of participants are an unparalleled source for the perceptions, ideas, and behavior of ordinary Americans in a conflict that transformed their society and altered the direction of the nation. The more imaginative social historians of warfare have used these sources recently to produce exciting work that tells us much about the impact of the Civil War on ordinary Americans who fought the war and in turn helped to shape its consequences.[2]

Three books published within a few months of each other provide excellent examples of these developments.[3] Joseph Glatthaar's *Forged*

67; Maris A. Vinovskis, ed., *Toward a Social History of the American Civil War: Exploratory Essays* (Cambridge, 1990); Catherine Clinton and Nina Silber, eds., *Divided Houses: Gender and the Civil War* (New York, 1992).

2. Joseph T. Glatthaar, *The March to the Sea and Beyond: Sherman's Troops in the Savannah and Carolinas Campaigns* (New York, 1985); Earl J. Hess, *Liberty, Virtue, and Progress: Northerners and Their War for the Union* (New York, 1988); Phillip Shaw Paludan, *"A People's Contest": The Union and Civil War* (New York, 1988); Randall C. Jimerson, *The Private Civil War: Popular Thought during the Sectional Conflict* (Baton Rouge, 1988); Reid Mitchell, *Civil War Soldiers: Their Expectations and Their Experiences* (New York, 1988); Reid Mitchell, *The Vacant Chair: The Northern Soldier Leaves Home* (New York, 1993); J. Matthew Gallman, *The North Fights the Civil War: The Home Front* (Chicago, 1994); George C. Rable, *Civil Wars: Women and the Crisis of Southern Nationalism* (Urbana, Ill., 1989).

3. Joseph T. Glatthaar, *Forged in Battle: The Civil War Alliance of Black Soldiers and White Officers* (New York, 1990); Iver Bernstein, *The New York City Draft Riots: Their Significance for American Society and Politics in the Age of the*

in Battle appeared at the same time and focused on the same subject as the movie *Glory*. Glatthaar drew on letters, diaries, and memoirs (mostly by white officers) as well as official documents for his account of the 179,000 black soldiers and their 7,000 white officers in the Union army. It is a story of the moral and physical courage of whites who risked social stigma in the North to become officers in "nigger regiments," and risked execution by Confederates for inciting slave insurrections. It is a story also of courage by black soldiers, most of them former slaves, who risked much to join the army and faced the same threat of execution if captured.

Glatthaar describes the government's unjust and discriminatory treatment of black soldiers in pay (until 1864 black soldiers were paid less than whites), promotion, medical care, and the disproportionate employment of black units as labor battalions and in other menial rear-echelon assignments. An important theme in the book (as in the film *Glory*) is the campaign by black soldiers and their officers to get the opportunity to fight. Only by proving themselves in combat could blacks overcome stereotypes of inferiority and prove their "manhood." They proved it in several battles when they got the chance, but that chance remained limited by army policies that kept most black units serving in garrisons and working on fatigue details. Thus their rate of death in combat was less than one-third that of white Union soldiers, while their mortality rate from disease was nearly twice as great.

Nevertheless, the courage and effectiveness of several black units in combat won increasing if sometimes grudging respect from initially skeptical or hostile whites. One white soldier wrote in 1864:

> The copperheads of the North need not complain of them being placed on an equal footing with the white soldiers, since the white soldier himself does not complain. After a man has fought two years he is willing that any thing shal[l] fight for the purpose of ending the

Civil War (New York, 1990); Michael Fellman, *Inside War: The Guerrilla Conflict in Missouri during the American Civil War* (New York, 1989).

war. We have become to[o] familiar with hardships to refuse to see men fight merely because their color is black.[4]

A white officer added: "The truth is they have fought their way into the respect of all the army." This was an exaggeration; many white soldiers retained their prejudices. But others were converted by what the *New York Times* described in 1864 as the "prodigious revolution which the public mind everywhere is experiencing."[5]

Forged in Battle is by no means the first study of black soldiers in the Civil War; several previous books have told important parts of that story. But it uses more of the soldiers' letters and diaries—including rare material from black soldiers—and concentrates more intensely on black-white relations within these regiments than any other study. Glatthaar's thesis is expressed by the title: loyalty, friendship, and respect among white officers and black soldiers were fostered by the mutual dangers they faced in combat. This was not universally true, to be sure. Some officers had gone into black units for promotion or other self-serving motives; many of these retained their racist attitudes toward the soldiers they commanded. But most officers probably shared the attitude articulated by a captain in a letter to his wife:

> A great many [white people] have the idea that the entire negro race are vastly their inferiors—a few weeks of calm unprejudiced life here would disabuse them I think—I have a more elevated opinion of their abilities than I ever had before. I *know* that many of them are vastly the *superiors* of those (many of those) who would condemn them to a life of brutal degradation.[6]

In trying to show that there was growing respect between blacks and whites, though, Glatthaar succumbs to the fashionable practice

4. L. Grim to Aunt Tillie, June 27, 1864, quoted in Glatthaar, *Forged in Battle*, p. 206.

5. Lewis Weld to mother, Aug. 17, 1864; *New York Times*, March 7, 1864; both quoted in Glatthaar, *Forged in Battle*, pp. 168, 142.

6. Charles Augustus Hill to wife, Oct. 13, 1863, quoted in *ibid.*, pp. 96–97.

of condemning all whites as racists. "Prior to the war," he writes of the men who became officers in black regiments, "virtually all of them held powerful racial prejudices" that were subsequently modified by experience.[7] Powerful racial prejudices? That was not true of Thomas Wentworth Higginson, or Norwood P. Hallowell, or George T. Garrison, or many other abolitionists and sons of abolitionists who became officers in black regiments.

Indeed, the contrary was true; they had spent much of their lives fighting the race prejudice endemic in American society, sometimes at the risk of their careers and even their lives. That is why they jumped at the chance to help launch an experiment with black soldiers which they hoped would help African-Americans achieve freedom and postwar civil equality. Perhaps by modern absolutist standards of racial egalitarianism (which few could meet today), these men harbored some mildly racist or paternalistic feelings. But to call these "powerful racial prejudices" is to indulge in what William Manchester has called "generational chauvinism—judging past eras by the standards of the present."[8]

Race is the analytical category that counts most for Glatthaar; in Iver Bernstein's study of the New York draft riots, the class feelings of the rioters are central while race and ethnicity are seen as less important. The worst mob violence in American history took place during the four days of rioting in New York City in 1863, although the death toll of 120 should be compared with the 11,000 soldiers killed and mortally wounded at Gettysburg two weeks earlier. The riots exposed severe stresses in Northern urban society, but, contrary to Bernstein's view, these stresses may have run along the lines of race and ethnicity more than along those of class. The rioters were mostly Irish Catholic immigrants (and their children); they mainly attacked the members of New York's small black population. For a year, Democratic leaders had been telling their Irish-American con-

7. *Ibid.,* p. 11.
8. *New York Times Book Review,* Feb. 4, 1990, p. 33.

stituents that the wicked Black Republicans were waging the war to free the slaves who would come North and take away the jobs of Irish workers. The use of black stevedores as scabs in a recent strike by Irish dockworkers made this charge seem plausible. The prospect of being drafted to fight to free the slaves made the Irish even more receptive to demogogic rhetoric.

The provisions in the Union conscription law that allowed a drafted man to avoid service by hiring a substitute or paying a three-hundred-dollar commutation fee gave an added edge of class bitterness to the controversy, producing the slogan of "RICH MAN'S WAR BUT POOR MAN'S FIGHT." In actual practice this slogan proved untrue. Unskilled workers and Irish-Americans were proportionately under-represented in the Union army. Draft insurance societies and appropriations by city councils or political machines to pay the commutation fees of drafted men who did not want to go enabled poor men to buy their way out of the draft almost as readily as rich men.

Nevertheless, the draft became a hated symbol of everything the working-class population of New York disliked about the war. In the riots they demolished draft offices and other federal property, burned black neighborhoods and the Colored Orphan Asylum; they lynched a dozen black men, attacked the premises of the *New York Times* and *New York Tribune* (both Republican), and sacked the homes of leading Republicans and abolitionists. In the end most of those killed were not blacks or abolitionists but rioters, shot down by police and by troops rushed to New York from Gettysburg.

Iver Bernstein tells the story of these awful events succinctly in the early pages of his book. But that is not his main purpose, and for a detailed account of the riots one must still read Adrian Cook's *The Armies of the Streets: The New York City Draft Riots of 1863.*[9] Bernstein's aim is to use the riots as a means to understand "the intricate and often obscure processes that gave rise to modern urban

9. (Lexington, Ky., 1974). .

America."[10] Unfortunately, his argument is also intricate and often obscure. It reaches back to the 1850s to analyze the workers' quest for security, status, and power in New York's economy and polity. Workers were divided by skill or craft, and sometimes by ethnicity, but according to Bernstein they sought consolidation and class unity in the face of the capitalist transformation that was eroding old skills and values.

The capitalist elite was also divided, partly between older merchants and bankers, with ties to the South and to foreign mercantile houses on one side and to the rising industrialists on the other. Most of the new industrialists were Republicans, with strong ties to the national administration during the Civil War. Many of the mercantile elite were Democrats. During the riots they took a "soft" position toward the mobs, hoping to calm the violence through persuasion and selective repression. The Republican industrialists—whose property was often the target of rioters—took a "hard" position, calling for martial law and a shoot-on-sight policy. Bernstein views the riots as a climactic moment in the contest between workers and the Republican industrialists. The war, the draft, and ethnic and racial hatreds were merely the catalyst that sparked the violence.

For Bernstein the main beneficiary of the efforts following the riots to resolve and reshape the class conflicts that had gotten out of control was the Tammany Hall faction of the Democratic party. Tammany supported the Union war effort with a flair for patriotic oratory and symbolism; after the war the Tammany machine ruled the city for a half-dozen years under Boss William Marcy Tweed. But the Tweed Ring collapsed under the weight of corruption and its inability to prevent another bloody riot in 1871, this one between Protestant Scots-Irish and Catholic Irish. The failure of several craft union strikes for the eight-hour day in 1872, Bernstein writes, shows that "industrialists emerged as the ultimate winners of the 1863 crisis, and their acquisitive individualism and repudiation of working-class

10. Bernstein, *New York City Draft Riots,* p. vii.

rule were not triumphant; workers in the draft riot trades met their final moment of defeat."[11]

Bernstein draws on studies of the "crowd" (not mobs) in early industrial Europe and America to develop his thesis of the class roots of the draft riots. Denied political power through existing elite institutions, crowds took to the streets to demonstrate against selected institutions of oppression. They acted in a "rational" manner in this selectivity, in contrast to the irrational mob frenzy depicted by earlier and more conservative historians. For Bernstein, the first day of the draft riots, in which skilled workers led selective and limited attacks on specific institutions they associated with class domination, conformed to this pattern. Only on the second day did the riots escalate into seemingly mindless, irrational large-scale violence committed by unskilled Irish workers who struck out savagely in all directions. Even then, though, a "rational" pattern can be discerned during the riot's second stage, whose targets were blacks (because they acted as strikebreakers) and Protestant antislavery Republican industrial leaders who served as hated symbols of the privileged middle class to the Irish population.

Bernstein's two stages are too schematic. The riots did grow in violence and viciousness as they went on, to be sure, but the mass participation and crazed bloodlust were there from the beginning. Rioters burned the Colored Orphan Asylum the first day and lynched blacks that day as on subsequent days. The frenzy of mob psychology would seem to offer a better basis for explanation than that of the rational crowd. And powerful ethnic or racial antagonisms seem to have been more salient than class consciousness.

After one reads about the clashes between Irish immigrants and blacks, Michael Fellman's account of guerrilla warfare in Missouri during the Civil War seems to take place in a different country. A border state of divided allegiances, Missouri suffered more than any other region from the internecine war of neighbor against neighbor

11. *Ibid.,* p. 239.

"inside" the larger Civil War of North against South. As in other guerrilla conflicts, the army controlled the towns and the daylight hours but the partisans controlled the countryside and the night. The guerrillas' need for sanctuary in rural districts and the army's search-and-destroy missions forced neutral civilians to choose sides or suffer the consequences—usually both.

The Confederate "bushwhackers" and Unionist "Jayhawkers" took no prisoners, killed in cold blood, plundered, and pillaged (but almost never raped or killed white women). Both sides committed atrocities that make the New York draft riots look like a Sunday-school picnic. Thousands of soldiers, guerrillas, and civilians lost their lives; whole counties were burned out and virtually depopulated. The hatreds and feuds of the war lingered for decades. The postwar outlaws Jesse and Frank James, Cole and Jim Younger, and others who darken the pages of Missouri history and myth got their start as Confederate guerrillas, riding with the notorious William Clarke Quantrill or the infamous Bloody Bill Anderson.

Fellman's is the best account of this "inside" war—in Missouri or in any of the other border regions where it flared with lesser but still powerful intensity. He has mined official archives and collections of letters from Union soldiers and from civilians (guerrillas left few letters) to get inside their minds. The analytical categories of ethnicity, gender, and class appear here, though at times in a marginal fashion. To a considerable degree, ethnic and cultural divisions defined the two sides in Missouri's civil war. German-Americans and Yankee settlers formed the core of Unionist strength in the region; Southern-born farmers (derisively labeled "Pukes" by adversaries) provided most of the guerrillas and their sympathizers. A chapter on women noncombatants, who were sometimes compelled to become auxiliaries to combat, shows sensitivity to the tensions between traditional female expectations and the exigencies of a society in wartime.

The issue of class in this conflict is more ambiguous. One school of interpretation has portrayed the guerrilla outlaws as defenders of a rural order of yeomen farmers against the encroachments of a capitalist market economy represented by Yankee soldiers and Unionists during the Civil War, and by banks and railroads afterward. Jesse James and his comrades were therefore not bloodthirsty killers but rather "social bandits" who fought a losing battle against the soulless forces of capitalist transformation. This thesis is roughly analogous to Iver Bernstein's portrait of many draft rioters as workers who attacked the institutions and symbols of industrial capitalism.

Such portraits reflect recent scholarship by social historians on American farmers and workers in the nineteenth century.[12] For Missouri, a romanticized version of this thesis emerged during the postwar decades in the form of a "noble guerrilla" tradition that fused with a "noble outlaw" legend to glamorize Jesse James, Cole Younger, and the others as Robin Hoods who took from the rich and gave to the poor. The same legend became incorporated in dozens of Hollywood movies.

Michael Fellman begins his book as if he were going to advance a similar interpretation. But he edges away from it and ultimately repudiates it:

> Journalists, pulp fiction writers, and Hollywood filmmakers, selling dreams to that huge audience which continues to enjoy the presence of the noble outlaw, have had every reason to perpetuate the legend rather than to realistically portray selfish bank robbers and cold-blooded bushwhackers.[13]

Fellman offers a psychological interpretation of the guerrillas and Jayhawkers. Many of the guerrillas were psychopathic killers, nihilistic lovers of violence. The war gave quasi-official sanction to their

12. See especially Steven Hahn and Jonathan Prude, eds., *The Countryside in the Age of Capitalist Transformation: Essays in the Social History of Rural America* (Chapel Hill, 1985); Bruce Laurie, *Artisans into Workers: Labor in Nineteenth-Century America* (New York, 1989); Grace Palladino, *Another Civil War: Labor, Capital, and the State in the Anthracite Regions of Pennsylvania* (Urbana, Ill., 1990); and, for Missouri, David Thelen, *Paths of Resistance: Tradition and Dignity in Industrializing Missouri* (New York, 1986).

13. Fellman, *Inside War*, p. 263.

atavistic impulses. The frustration of Union commanders with their failure to suppress the guerrillas, and the hair-trigger nerves of Union squads patrolling the menacing countryside where every innocent-looking farmer might be a bushwhacker, caused them to lash out with random violence that could only go on escalating. For many of the youthful guerrillas and soldiers, this violence was a rite of passage; to kill was to prove one's manhood. "It is useful," writes Fellman, "to employ the mytho-psychological language of oedipal rebellion in analyzing this process: displacement and destruction of the father's authority—replacement with the knightly, true young brotherhood." Fellman quotes with approval the postwar reflections of a Union officer who had discovered while fighting guerrillas in Missouri that

> there exists in the breasts of people of educated and christian communities wild and ferocious passions . . . which may be aroused and kindled by . . . war and injustice, and become more cruel and destructive than any that live in the breasts of savage and barbarous nations.[14]

True enough; the experience of the twentieth century has taught the same dispiriting lesson. But Fellman's psychological insights still do not answer the question of why Confederate guerrillas took to the bush in the first place. Did they fight just for the love of fighting? Partly. Were they defending traditional rural communities against alien Yankee capitalism? This seems doubtful.

Curiously, Fellman overlooks the most likely answer to the question. The fundamental cause of the Civil War was slavery. This institution was not as entrenched in Missouri as in the states that seceded. But it was the chief factor in determining the allegiance of those Missourians who cast their lot with the Confederacy. It also seems to have been an important factor for many guerrillas. A seminal study of the social origins of Missouri guerrillas by Don Bowen shows that they came from families that were three times more likely

14. *Ibid.,* pp. 148, 265–66.

to own slaves and had twice as much wealth as the average Missouri family. Cole and Jim Younger were the sons of Jackson County's richest slave owner. So much for the Robin Hood image. If there was a class or ideological dimension to Missouri's guerrilla warfare, it appears not to have been one of yeomen farmers versus capitalists, but of slave owners versus the advocates of free labor.[15]

A final observation is prompted by this account of terror and destruction in Missouri. Anyone who writes and lectures about the Civil War is asked frequently whether the Confederacy could have won if Southerners had resorted to guerrilla warfare on a large scale. An influential study has suggested that their failure to do so may have been "a major reason why the South lost the Civil War."[16] This seems improbable. Guerrilla tactics might have prolonged the war, perhaps for years, but the Confederacy would probably have lost in the end. The Union army would have turned loose the hard-bitten cavalry of Philip Sheridan and Judson Kilpatrick against the guerrillas. The entire South might then have become like Missouri.

Robert E. Lee was wiser than latter-day theorists who fantasize a Confederate victory through guerrilla warfare. When one of his subordinates suggested at Appomattox that Confederate soldiers could escape to the bush and become guerrillas rather than surrender, Lee said no. With Missouri perhaps in mind, he foresaw that the guerrillas "would become mere bands of marauders, and the enemy's cavalry would pursue them and overrun many sections they may never [otherwise] have occasion to visit. We would bring on a state of affairs it would take the country years to recover from."[17] Lee then rode off to meet General Grant.

15. Don R. Bowen, "Guerrilla War in Western Missouri, 1861–1865: Historical Extensions of the Relative Deprivation Hypothesis," *Comparative Studies in Society and History* 19 (1977), 30–51.

16. Richard E. Beringer, Herman Hattaway, Archer Jones, and William N. Still, Jr., *Why the South Lost the Civil War* (Athens, Ga., 1986), p. 342.

17. Douglas Southall Freeman, *R. E. Lee: A Biography,* 4 vols. (New York, 1934–1935), IV, 84.

7

THE *GLORY* STORY

"CAN MOVIES TEACH HISTORY?" ASKED THE TITLE OF A *New York Times* feature article.[1] The answer for *Glory* is yes. It is not only the first feature film to treat the role of black soldiers in the Civil War; it is also the most powerful movie about that war ever made, and one that strives for greater historical accuracy than we have come to expect from Hollywood. It does much to correct the distortions and romanticizations of such earlier blockbuster films as *Birth of a Nation* (1915) and *Gone with the Wind* (1939). It grapples more forthrightly with the issues of what the war was about than *Gettysburg* (1993). Approaching their sixtieth anniversary on the screen, Scarlett O'Hara and Rhett Butler are still teaching false and stereotyped lessons about slavery and the Civil War to millions of viewers. *Glory* throws a cold dash of realism over the "moonlight and magnolias" portrayal of the Confederacy. It also helps restore the courageous image of black soldiers and their white officers that prevailed in the North during the latter war years and early postwar

1. Nov. 26, 1989: Arts and Entertainment section.

decades, before the process of romanticizing the Old South obscured that image.

Glory tells the story of the Fifty-fourth Massachusetts Volunteer Infantry from its organization in the winter of 1863 to the climactic assault of July 18, 1863, against Fort Wagner, a massive earthwork guarding the approach to Charleston. The Union military and naval effort to capture Charleston failed in 1863. So did this assault on Fort Wagner led by the Fifty-fourth, which suffered nearly 50 percent casualties in the attack. One of them was Colonel Robert Gould Shaw, killed while leading his men over the parapet. But if in this narrow sense the attack was a failure, in a more profound sense it was a success of historic proportions. The unflinching behavior of the regiment in the face of an overwhelming hail of lead and iron answered the skeptic's question, "Will the Negro fight?" It demonstrated the manhood and courage of the race to millions of people in both North and South who had doubted whether black men would stand in combat against soldiers of the self-styled master race.

The events that led to this epochal moment in African-American history represented a radical evolution of the scope and purpose of the Civil War. The original war aims of Abraham Lincoln's administration had been to suppress an insurrection in eleven Southern states and to restore them to their old place in the Union. The North conceived of this as a limited war that would not fundamentally alter the American polity or society—including slavery. Four slave states had remained loyal to the Union. In 1861–1862 they would not have supported a war to abolish slavery. Neither would the Democrats, who constituted nearly half of the Northern electorate. And the Constitution that the North was fighting to defend guaranteed the protection of slavery in states that wanted it. Therefore, despite Lincoln's personal abhorrence of slavery, he could not willfully turn this war for the Union into a war against slavery. Nor could his War Department accept black volunteers in the Union army in 1861, for to do so would have sent a signal that this was to be an abolition war.

By 1862, though, it was becoming such a war by the actions of slaves themselves and of the Lincoln administration and Congress, and by the accelerating momentum of the conflict. Thousands of slaves flocked to Union army posts when Northern troops invaded portions of the South. Abolitionists and radical Republicans insisted that they must be granted freedom. The success of Confederate military offensives in 1862 convinced Republicans, including Lincoln, that the North could not win the war without mobilizing all its resources and striking against Southern resources used to sustain the Confederate war effort. The most important such resource was slavery, for slaves constituted the majority of the South's labor force. In the summer of 1862 Congress enacted legislation confiscating the property of Confederates, including slaves. Lincoln followed this action with the Emancipation Proclamation to free the slaves, invoking his power as commander in chief to seize enemy property used to wage war against the United States. The Proclamation also stated that blacks would be "received into the armed services of the United States."[2]

These events underlay the decision of Governor John Andrew of Massachusetts to organize a black regiment, which became the Fifty-fourth Massachusetts. A bold experiment, black soldiers could be made acceptable in the context of the time only if they were commanded by white officers. Andrew was determined to appoint officers "of firm antislavery principles . . . superior to a vulgar contempt for color."[3] In Robert Gould Shaw, son of a prominent abolitionist family, he found his man. As black volunteers came into training camp near Boston during the spring of 1863, Shaw helped shape them into a high-morale outfit eager to prove their mettle.

In May 1863 the Fifty-fourth completed its training and marched

2. Roy P. Basler et al., eds., *The Collected Works of Abraham Lincoln,* 9 vols. (New Brunswick, N.J., 1953–1955), VI, 28–30.

3. Andrew to Francis G. Shaw (Robert Gould Shaw's father), Jan. 30, 1863, in Henry Greenleaf Pearson, *The Life of John A. Andrew,* 2 vols. (Boston, 1904), II, 74–76.

through Boston to embark for the front (a scene depicted in stirring manner by *Glory*). About the same time the *New York Tribune,* the leading Northern newspaper and a supporter of arming blacks to fight for the Union and freedom, observed that most Yankees now endorsed that radical policy, but many still wondered whether blacks would make good soldiers. "Loyal whites have generally become willing that they should fight," declared a *Tribune* editorial, "but the great majority have no faith that they will do so. Many hope they will prove cowards and sneaks—others greatly fear it."[4]

The Fifty-fourth was not the first black regiment organized, or the first to see combat. To test the waters on this issue, the War Department had quietly allowed Union commanders of forces occupying portions of the lower Mississippi Valley, the Kansas-Missouri border, and the South Carolina sea islands to begin organizing black regiments in the fall of 1862. Four of these regiments fought in actions connected with the Vicksburg campaign during May and June 1863, winning plaudits for their performance. But these events had received little publicity in the Northern press.

The recruitment of black combat troops was still regarded as a risky experiment when the six hundred men of the Fifty-fourth moved out at dusk on July 18 to the attack on Fort Wagner. During the next few hours they more than justified the experiment. Forced by the ocean on one side and swamps on the other to approach the fort along several hundred yards of narrow beach, the regiment moved forward steadily through bursting shells and murderous musketry, losing men every step of the way but continuing right up the ramparts and breaching the parapet before the immense strength of the works stopped them. (The portrayal of this attack in *Glory* is the most realistic combat footage in any Civil War movie).

A war correspondent for the *New York Tribune* vividly described the battle to Northern newspaper readers. The Fifty-fourth's attack did more than prove that Fort Wagner was impregnable to infantry

4. *New York Tribune,* May 1, 1863.

assault; it disabused hundreds of thousands of Northerners of their stereotypes. "Who asks now in doubt and derision, 'Will the Negro fight?'" commented one abolitionist. "The answer is spoken from the cannon's mouth. . . . It comes to us from . . . those graves beneath Fort Wagner's walls, which the American people will surely never forget."[5] "Through the cannon smoke of that black night," said the *Atlantic Monthly*, "the manhood of the colored race shines before many eyes that would not see." For the *New York Tribune*, the assault resolved any lingering doubts: "It made Fort Wagner such a name to the colored race as Bunker Hill had been for ninety years to the white Yankees."[6]

White officers of the Fifty-fourth represented the elite of New England society. Some, including Shaw, were Harvard alumni and sons of prominent families. Several—also including Shaw—were combat veterans of white regiments during the first two years of the war. Antislavery in conviction, they had willingly risked stigma and ridicule to cast their lot with a black regiment. Shaw's death made a deeper impression on Yankee culture than that of any of the other thirty-five thousand men from New England killed in the Civil War. The clergyman Henry Ward Beecher wrote that Shaw's martyrdom had regenerated Boston's past glory as America's cradle of liberty: "Our young men seemed ignoble; the faith of old heroic times had died . . . but the trumpet of this war sounded the call and Oh! how joyful has been the sight of such unexpected nobleness in our young men." Ralph Waldo Emerson and James Russell Lowell extolled Shaw in verse. Lowell wrote:

> *Right in the van,*
> *On the red rampart's slippery swell,*
> *With heart that beat a charge, he fell*

5. *Thirteenth Annual Report of the Philadelphia Female Anti-Slavery Society* (1864), p. 17.

6. *Atlantic Monthly,* quoted in Lawrence Lader, *The Bold Brahmins: New England's War against Slavery* (New York, 1961), p. 290; *New York Tribune,* Sept. 8, 1865.

> Foeward, as fits a man;
> But the high soul burns on to light men's feet
> Where death for noble ends makes dying sweet.[7]

The Confederate defenders of Fort Wagner stripped Shaw's body and dumped it into an unmarked mass grave with the bodies of the men of the regiment who had been killed in the attack. When the Union commander sent a flag of truce across the lines a day later to request the return of Shaw's body (a customary practice for high-ranking officers killed in the Civil War), a Confederate officer replied contemptuously: "We have buried him with his niggers." The report of these words produced anger as well as more poetry in the North, the best of which was perhaps these lines by an obscure bard:

> They buried him with his niggers!
>   A wide grave should it be.
> They buried more in that shallow trench
>   Than human eye could see.
> Ay, all the shames and sorrows
>   of more than a hundred years
> Lie under the weight of that Southern soil
>   Despite those cruel sneers.[8]

Several weeks after the battle, Union forces finally occupied Fort Wagner after a punishing artillery bombardment from land and sea had compelled the Confederates to evacuate it. When a Union officer offered to search for Shaw's grave to recover his body, Shaw's father wrote an eloquent letter to stop the effort: "We hold that a soldier's most appropriate burial-place is on the field where he has fallen."[9]

---

7. Beecher quoted in George M. Fredrickson, *The Inner Civil War: Northern Intellectuals and the Crisis of the Union* (New York, 1965), p. 153; Lowell in Lader, *Bold Brahmins,* p. 291.

8. Quoted in James M. McPherson, *Marching toward Freedom: Blacks in the Civil War 1861–1865* (2nd ed., New York, 1991), p. 78.

9. Quoted in Luis F. Emilio, *A Brave Black Regiment: History of the Fifty-Fourth Regiment of Massachusetts Volunteer Infantry* (Boston, 1894), pp. 102–3.

The most fitting marker for Shaw and the soldiers of the Fifty-fourth is Augustus St. Gaudens's superb bas-relief sculpture on Boston Common showing Shaw in the foreground on his horse while his soldiers march alongside with shouldered rifles and heads held high in pride—surely the noblest of the thousands of Civil War monuments in this country.

The apotheosis of Shaw and his men in July 1863 came just after the terrible four-day draft riot in New York City. The riot had been fueled in part by the hostility of Irish-Americans to being drafted to fight in a war to free the slaves, who they feared would come North to compete for jobs and social space. Black New Yorkers were the chief victims of the rioters. On July 15 the mob beat to death the nephew of one of the Fifty-fourth's sergeants, Robert Simmons; three days later Simmons was mortally wounded in the attack on Fort Wagner.

The draft riot occurred in the context of opposition by Northern Democrats to the Lincoln administration's war policies, including emancipation, black soldiers, and the draft. Democrats had done much to stir up the racial hatreds manifested by the rioters, who chanted the antiwar and antiblack slogans of the "Copperhead" wing of the party. Few Republican commentators failed to juxtapose the draft riot with the heroic conduct of the Fifty-fourth at Fort Wagner, and to point to the moral: Black men who fought for the Union deserved more respect than white men who rioted against it.

Lincoln himself made this point in a public letter to a political meeting in August 1863, which was reprinted in nearly every Northern newspaper. "Some of the commanders of our armies in the field who have given us our most important successes," wrote Lincoln, "believe the emancipation policy, and the use of colored troops, constitute the heaviest blow yet dealt to the rebellion." This was a reference to General Ulysses S. Grant, who in a recent letter to Lincoln had endorsed the value of black regiments. Addressing himself to anti-emancipation Democrats, Lincoln continued: "You say you will not fight to free negroes. Some of them seem willing to fight for you," that is, for the Union. In an obvious reference to the assault of the Fifty-fourth on Fort Wagner, Lincoln concluded with a moving peroration: When final victory brought a new birth of freedom to the re-United States,

> there will be some black men who can remember that, with silent tongue, and clenched teeth, and steady eye, and well-poised bayonet, they have helped mankind on to this great consummation; while, I fear, there will be some white ones, unable to forget that, with malignant heart, and deceitful speech, they have strove to hinder it.[10]

Glory does not go into detail about the impact of the battle of Fort Wagner on Northern opinion; it is sketchy on the political context of the black soldier issue; it does not mention the draft riot. The Fifty-fourth continued to serve through the war, fighting in several more battles and skirmishes. The movie, however, ends with the attack on Fort Wagner. That is appropriate, for Shaw and the black soldiers played by the actors Denzel Washington and Morgan Freeman are killed in that attack. Their deaths make a fitting climax to the drama whose tensions build steadily to that moment of consummation. If the Fifty-fourth had done nothing else in the war, that assault would have elevated it to the deserved status of the most famous of the 166 black regiments in the Union army. If it is not literally true, as the caption appearing on the screen at the end of the movie would have it, that the bravery of the Fifty-fourth at Fort Wagner caused Congress to authorize more black regiments—that had happened months earlier—the example of the Fifty-fourth did help to transform experiment into policy. It also helped to earn a front-line combat role for many other black regiments instead of the rear-area role as service and labor battalions that had been their original purpose.

A central theme of *Glory* is Shaw's determined fight to win a combat assignment for the Fifty-fourth, so it can earn respect for

10. Lincoln to James C. Conkling, Aug. 26, 1863, in Basler et al., eds., *Collected Works of Lincoln*, VI, 408–10.

black manhood and overcome the stereotype of shiftless, cowering, comic darkies. *Glory* portrays this theme with sensitivity and dramatic power—even though many scenes and characters that convey it are fictional. This raises the question posed by the *Times* article "Can Movies Teach History?" It observes that "more people are getting their history, or what they think is history, from the movies these days than from the standard history books." For every person who has read one of the several excellent histories of black soldiers in the Civil War, a hundred or more will have seen this movie. That being true, does "the filmmaker, like the novelist, have license to use the material of history selectively and partially in the goal of entertaining, creating a good dramatic product, even forging what is sometimes called the poetic truth, a truth truer than the literal truth?" asked the *Times* article. In other words, "Does it matter if the details are wrong if the underlying meaning of events is accurate?" [11]

Glory does confront the literal-minded historian with this question on several occasions. Most of the details are right. And when they are wrong, there is often a rational explanation that minimizes the distortion. Knowledgeable viewers will note that in the movie the Fifty-fourth charges *southward* against Fort Wagner, with the Atlantic ocean on its left, when in reality the assault went northward. The reason is the configuration of the Georgia beach where the set of Fort Wagner was built, which required a southward assault. Does it really matter?

Some errors in the film are inexplicable, however, because they seem to serve no purpose. The Fifty-fourth began organizing in February 1863—not three months earlier. In his brief cameo role, black leader Frederick Douglass appears as a venerable sage whose screen image is modeled on a photograph taken two decades later when Douglass was in his sixties instead of the vigorous forty-five he was in 1863. The real Robert Gould Shaw received the offer of command

---

11. *New York Times,* Nov. 26, 1989: Arts and Entertainment section.

of the Fifty-fourth by letter from Governor Andrew borne by his father to Shaw in winter camp with his regiment (the Second Massachusetts) in Virginia. Rob discussed it earnestly with his father, wrestled with his conscience overnight, declined, then changed his mind a day later and accepted. In the movie, Shaw is attending an elegant drawing-room party in Boston while on furlough when Andrew offers the command; without hesitation, Shaw accepts. Literal history in this case would seem to have offered greater dramatic possibilities for getting at a deeper truth than the cinematic version.

Except for Shaw, the principal characters in the film are fictional: There was no real Major Cabot Forbes; no Emerson-quoting black boyhood friend of Shaw's named Thomas Searles; no tough Irish Sergeant Major Mulcahy; no black Sergeant and father figure John Rawlins (Morgan Freeman); no brash, hardened Private Trip (Denzel Washington). Indeed, there is a larger fiction involved here. The movie gives the impression that most of the Fifty-fourth's soldiers were former slaves. But in fact, the regiment was recruited mainly in the North and most of the men had always been free. Some of them came from prominent Northern black families; two of Frederick Douglass's sons were among the first to sign up. The older son, Lewis, was sergeant major of the regiment from the start. The young adjutant of the regiment, wounded in the assault on Fort Wagner, was Garth Wilkinson James, brother of William and Henry James. A dramatic and important story about the relationship of Northern blacks to slavery and the war, and about the wartime ideals of New England culture, could have been constructed from a cast of real, historical figures. That story might also have included Sergeant Simmons, his nephew, and the draft riot.

But the story that producer Freddie Fields, director Edward Zwick, and screenwriter Kevin Jarre chose to tell is equally important—and, in that sense of "the underlying meaning of events," equally true. This is a film not simply about the Fifty-fourth Massachusetts but about blacks in the Civil War. Most of the 179,000 black soldiers (and 10,000 black sailors) were slaves until a few months, even a few days, before they joined up. They fought for their freedom, for the freedom of their families, their people. This was the most revolutionary feature of a war that wrought a revolutionary transformation in America by freeing four million slaves and uprooting the social structure of half the country. Arms in the hands of slaves had been the nightmare of Southern whites for generations. In 1863 the nightmare came true. It achieved a new dignity, self respect, and militancy for the former slaves who fought for the Union. It helped them achieve equal citizenship and political rights—for a time—after the war.

That is the real story told by *Glory*. That is why most of the soldiers are depicted as former slaves. It is a story of their transformation from an oppressed to a proud people. It is a story told skillfully through several of the fictional events in the film—the incident of the racist quartermaster who initially refuses to distribute shoes to Shaw's men; the punishment of Trip by whipping for going AWOL; the regiment's dramatic refusal on principle to accept less pay than white soldiers, which launched an ultimately successful movement to shame Congress into equalizing the pay of black soldiers (this actually happened, but mainly on Shaw's initiative, not Trip's); the religious meeting the night before the assault on Fort Wagner.

It is a story told symbolically in one of the most surreal and, at first glance, irrelevant scenes in the movie, when Shaw (played by Matthew Broderick) gallops his horse along a path flanked by stakes, each with a watermelon (in February in Massachusetts?) jammed on its top. Shaw slashes right and left with his sword slicing and smashing every watermelon. The point becomes clear when we recall the identification of watermelons with the darky stereotype. If the image of smashed watermelons in *Glory* can replace that of moonlight and magnolias in *Gone with the Wind* as America's cinematic version of the Civil War, it will be a great gain for truth.

III

WHY THE
NORTH
WON

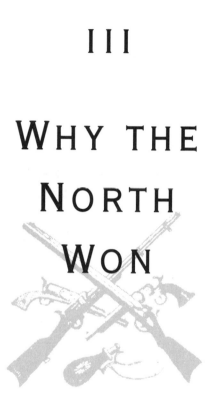

8

WHY DID
THE CONFEDERACY LOSE?

EVER SINCE THE GUNS CEASED FIRING IN 1865, EFFORTS TO EX-
plain the causes of Confederate defeat have generated a great deal
of controversy. The debate began with the publication in 1866 of *The
Lost Cause* by Richmond journalist Edward Pollard, who blamed
Jefferson Davis. Many books and articles since then have addressed
the issue explicitly in their titles, as did the anthology of essays published in 1960, *Why the North Won the Civil War,* and the volume
published in 1986 coauthored by four historians, *Why the South Lost
the Civil War.* Many other books suggest by their titles an answer to
the question of why the Confederacy lost, including Frank Owsley's
State Rights in the Confederacy, Paul Escott's *After Secession: Jefferson
Davis and the Failure of Southern Nationalism,* and Grady McWhiney's and Perry D. Jamieson's *Attack and Die: Civil War Military
Tactics and the Southern Heritage.* Rare is the Civil War historian
who does not have something to say on this subject, at least implicitly.

Yet despite all the efforts to explain Why the North Won or Why
the South Lost—the difference in phraseology is sometimes signifi-

cant—we still do not have a consensus. The books and essays cited in the previous paragraph offer a variety of explanations. In fact, dozens of different interpretations have come forth during the past 130 years. This suggests that a definitive answer is not possible. That will not stop us from trying to come up with one, though—nor should it. If definitive truth were possible in history, historians would soon have nothing left to write about. The following critical review of the literature on the reasons for Confederate defeat will disclose that I do not pretend to have a definitive answer. But this review may shed new light on the question at hand as well as on other important matters central to the meaning of the Civil War.

Most interpretations fall into one of two categories: internal or external. Internal explanations focus mainly or entirely on the Confederacy, and usually phrase the issue as "Why the South Lost." External interpretations look at both the Union and Confederacy, and often phrase it as "Why the North Won." No matter which approach they take, most studies assume, at least implicitly, that Union victory was inevitable. My analysis of these interpretations should make clear that I think an external approach more sensible but that I do *not* regard the outcome to have been inevitable.

To illustrate the difference between an internal and external interpretation, let us look at the battle of Gettysburg as a microcosm of the larger issue. Most of the controversy that has swirled endlessly around this matter has focused on the question of why the Confederates *lost* the battle—an *internal* explanation. Contemporaries and historians have blamed almost every prominent Confederate general at Gettysburg for mistakes that lost the battle: among them Robert E. Lee himself for mismanagement, overconfidence, and poor judgment; Jeb Stuart for riding off on a raid around the Union army and losing contact with his own army, leaving Lee blind in the enemy's country; Richard Ewell and Jubal Early for failing to attack Cemetery Hill on the afternoon of July 1 and again for tardiness in attacking on the second; and above all, James Longstreet for lack of cooperation, promptness, and vigor in the assaults of July 2 and 3. It was left to George Pickett to put his finger on the problem with all of these explanations. When someone asked Pickett after the war who was responsible for Confederate defeat at Gettysburg, he scratched his head, and replied: "I've always thought the Yankees had something to do with it."

Pickett's answer was an external explanation. And, in a larger sense, so has been the most durable and perhaps most popular explanation for Northern victory in the war as a whole. It was advanced by Robert E. Lee himself in his farewell address to his soldiers at Appomattox: "The Army of Northern Virginia has been compelled to yield to overwhelming numbers and resources." This interpretation enabled Southerners to preserve their pride in the courage and skill of Confederate soldiers, to reconcile defeat with their sense of honor, even to maintain faith in the righteousness of their cause while admitting that it had been lost. The Confederacy, in other words, lost the war not because it fought badly, or because its soldiers lacked courage, or because its cause was wrong, but simply because the enemy had more men and guns. As one proud Virginian expressed it: "They never whipped us, Sir, unless they were four to one. If we had had anything like a fair chance, or less disparity of numbers, we should have won our cause and established our independence." [1]

Many Yankees echoed this overwhelming-numbers-and-resources argument. While Northerners believed they had won because they fought for a better cause, many of them were also ready to agree with the maxim of Frederick the Great that "God is always with the strongest battalions." In 1960 the historian Richard Current provided a modern version of this interpretation. After reviewing the statistics of Northern population and economic preponderance—two and one-half times the South's population, three times its railroad capacity,

1. David Donald, ed., *Why the North Won the Civil War* (Baton Rouge, 1960), p. ix. For the persistence of this sentiment, see especially Charles Reagan Wilson, *Baptized in Blood: The Religion of the Lost Cause 1865–1920* (Athens, Ga., 1980).

nine times its industrial production, and so on—Current concluded that "surely, in view of the disparity of resources, it would have taken a miracle . . . to enable the South to win. As usual, God was on the side of the heaviest battalions."[2]

Most recently, Shelby Foote reiterated this thesis in his own inimitable fashion. "The North fought that war with one hand behind its back," he told Ken Burns on camera in the PBS documentary *The Civil War*. If necessary, added Foote, "the North simply would have brought that other arm out from behind its back. I don't think the South ever had a chance to win that war."[3] Here was inevitability in its starkest form.

Some Southerners, however, began to question this "overwhelming numbers and resources" thesis soon after the war; many of them eventually rejected it. For while this explanation did credit to Confederate skill and courage in holding out for so long against such great odds, it seemed to do little credit to their intelligence. After all, Southerners in 1861 were well aware of their disadvantages in numbers and resources. They could read the census returns. Yet they went to war confident of victory. Were they simpleminded? Irrational? Inexcusably arrogant?

As they reflected on these questions, many Southerners—and historians—came to the conclusion that overwhelming numbers and resources were not the cause of Northern victory after all. History offered numerous examples of a society winning a war against greater odds than the Confederacy faced. For Americans the outstanding example, of course, was the war of independence against mighty Britain. Other precedents also came easily to Southern minds in 1861: the Netherlands against Spain in the sixteenth century;

2. Richard N. Current, "God and the Strongest Battalions," *ibid.,* p. 22. Frederick the Great made this statement in a letter to Duchess Luise Dorothea von Gotha, May 8, 1760, quoted in Emily Morison Beck, ed., *Bartlett's Familiar Quotations* (Boston, 1980), p. 358.

3. "Men at War: An Interview with Shelby Foote," in Geoffrey C. Ward with Ric Burns and Ken Burns, *The Civil War* (New York, 1990), p. 272.

Greece against the Ottoman Empire in the 1820s. In our own post-Vietnam generation we are familiar with the truth that victory does not necessarily ride with the biggest battalions.

The Confederacy waged a strategically defensive war to protect its territory from conquest and preserve its armies from annihilation. To "win" that kind of war, Confederate armies did not have to invade and conquer the North: they needed only to hold out long enough to force the North to the conclusion that the price of conquering the South and annihilating its armies was too high, as Britain had concluded in 1781 and as the United States concluded with respect to Vietnam in 1972. Southerners thought in 1861 that their resources were more than sufficient to win on these terms. Most outside observers agreed. The military analyst for the *Times* of London wrote that "no war of independence ever terminated unsuccessfully except where the disparity of force was far greater than it is in this case. . . . Just as England during the revolution had to give up conquering the colonies so the North will have to give up conquering the South."[4]

Even after losing the war, many Southerners continued to insist that this reasoning remained sound. In his memoirs, General Joseph E. Johnston maintained that the Southern people had not been "guilty of the high crime of undertaking a war without the means of waging it successfully." And General Pierre G. T. Beauregard made the same point in 1884: "No people ever warred for independence with more relative advantages than the Confederates."[5] To be sure, Johnston and Beauregard had an axe to grind: They blamed the inept leadership of Jefferson Davis for Confederate defeat, partly in a self-serving effort to divert blame from themselves.

We shall return to that question later; for now it can be said

4. *The Times,* Aug. 29, 1862.

5. Johnston quoted in Current, "God and the Strongest Battalions," in Donald, ed., *Why the North Won,* p. 4; Pierre G. T. Beauregard, "The First Battle of Bull Run," in Robert U. Johnson and Clarence C. Buel, eds., *Battles and Leaders of the Civil War,* 4 vols. (New York, 1888), I, 222.

that the "overwhelming numbers and resources" argument has lost considerable favor among historians. The coauthors of *Why the South Lost the Civil War* maintain that "an invader needs more force than the North possessed to conquer such a large country as the South, even one so limited in logistical resources."[6] This might go a bit too far; if read literally, it seems to say that the North could not have won the war. Perhaps a better way to state it would be: To win the kind of war that the Civil War became by 1863, the North had to conquer vast stretches of Southern territory, cripple Southern resources, and destroy the fighting power of Confederate armies; therefore Northern superiority in manpower and resources was a *necessary* but not a *sufficient* cause of victory—that is, the North could not have won without that superiority, but it alone does not explain Union victory.

Recognizing the defects in the "overwhelming numbers and resources" theory, a number of historians developed internal explanations for Confederate defeat. One such approach focused on what might be termed an "internal conflict" thesis: The Confederacy lost because it was plagued by dissent and divisions that undercut the strong and united effort necessary to win the war. Exponents of this interpretation have emphasized various kinds of internal conflict.

One of the earliest and most persistent themes was spelled out by Frank Owsley in his book *State Rights in the Confederacy,* published in 1925. Owsley maintained that the centrifugal force of state rights fatally handicapped the efforts of the central government and of the army to mobilize men and resources for the war. Owsley singled out Governors Joseph E. Brown of Georgia and Zebulon Vance of North Carolina as guilty of obstructive policies, of withholding men and arms from the Confederate army to build up their state militias, and of debilitating political warfare against the Jefferson Davis adminis-

6. Richard E. Beringer, Herman Hattaway, Archer Jones, and William N. Still, Jr., *Why the South Lost the Civil War* (Athens, Ga., 1986), 430.

tration. On the tombstone of the Confederacy, wrote Owsley, should be carved the epitaph "DIED OF STATE RIGHTS."[7]

A variant on the "state rights" thesis focuses on the resistance by many Southerners, including some national leaders like Vice President Alexander H. Stephens, to such war measures as conscription, certain taxes, suspension of the writ of habeas corpus, and martial law. Opponents based their denunciations of these "despotic" measures on grounds of civil liberty, or state rights, or democratic individualism, or all three combined. This opposition crippled the army's ability to fill its ranks, obtain food and supplies, and stem desertions, according to this interpretation. It hindered the government's capacity to crack down on antiwar activists who divided the Southern people and sapped their will to win. The persistence during the war of the democratic practices of individualism, dissent, and carping criticism of the government caused historian David Donald, writing in 1960, to amend that inscription on the Confederacy's tombstone to "DIED OF DEMOCRACY."[8]

This "internal conflict" thesis suffers from three flaws as an explanation for Confederate defeat. First, recent scholarship has demonstrated that the negative effects on the Confederate war effort of state rights sentiment have been much exaggerated. State leaders like Brown and Vance did indeed feud with the Davis administration and criticize the president's leadership. But at the same time these governors, and others, took the initiative in many areas of mobilization: raising regiments, equipping them with arms and uniforms, providing help for the families of soldiers, organizing war production, supply and transportation, building coastal defenses, and so on. It now seems clear that rather than hindering the efforts of the government in Richmond, the activities of states augmented such efforts. "On balance," concludes one study of this question, "state

7. Frank L. Owsley, *State Rights in the Confederacy* (Chicago, 1925), p. 1.
8. Donald, "Died of Democracy," in Donald, ed., *Why the North Won*, p. 90.

contributions to the war effort far outweighed any unnecessary diversion of resources to local defense." And a recent study of Confederate politics argues that internal disputes took place within a broad consensus of Southern nationalism; these disputes "did not destroy the Southern nation . . . if anything the political culture of national unity, with its patriotic appeals and symbols, was a source of strength."[9]

As for the "died of democracy" thesis, a good case can be made that, to the contrary, the Confederate government enforced the draft, suppressed dissent, and suspended civil liberties and democratic rights at least as thoroughly as did the Union government. The Confederacy enacted conscription a year before the Union, and raised a larger portion of its troops by drafting than did the North. And while Abraham Lincoln possessed more authority to suspend the writ of habeas corpus and used this power more often to arrest antiwar activists than did Jefferson Davis, the Confederate army suppressed Unionists with more ruthlessness, especially in east Tennessee and western North Carolina, than Union forces wielded against Copperheads in the North or Confederate sympathizers in the border states.

This points to a second problem with the "internal conflict" interpretation; we might term this flaw the "fallacy of reversibility." That is, if the North had lost the war—which came close to happening on more than one occasion—the same thesis of internal conflict could be advanced to explain *Northern* defeat. Bitter divisions existed in the North over conscription, taxes, suspension of habeas corpus, martial law—and significantly, in the case of the North, over emancipation of the slaves as a war aim. If anything, the opposition was more powerful and effective in the North than in the South. Lincoln endured greater vilification than Davis during much of the war. And Lincoln had to face a campaign for reelection in the midst of the

---

9. Beringer et al., *Why the South Lost,* p. 429; George C. Rable, *The Confederate Republic: A Revolution against Politics* (Chapel Hill, 1994), p. 300.

most crucial military operations of the war—an election that for a time it appeared he would lose, an outcome that would have constituted a repudiation of his policy of war to victory and might have led to peace negotiations with an independent Confederacy. This did not happen, but its narrow avoidance is evidence of intense conflict within the *Northern* polity—which tended to neutralize the similar but perhaps less divisive conflicts within the South as a cause of Confederate defeat.

Finally, we might ask whether the internal conflicts between state governments and central government or among different factions and leaders were greater in the Confederacy than they had been in the United States during the Revolution. The answer is no. In fact, Americans in the war of 1776 were more divided than Southerners in the war of 1861, yet the United States won its independence and the Confederacy did not. Apparently we must look elsewhere for an explanation of Confederate failure.

Similar criticisms apply to another interpretation that overlaps the "internal conflict" thesis. This one might be termed the "internal alienation" argument. In recent years a great deal of scholarship has focused on two large groups in the Confederacy that were or became alienated from the war effort: nonslaveholding whites, and slaves. The nonslaveholders constituted two-thirds of the Confederacy's white population. Many of them, especially in mountainous and up-country regions of small farms and few slaves, opposed secession in 1861. They formed significant enclaves of Unionism in western Virginia where they created a new Union state; in east Tennessee, where they carried out guerrilla operations against the Confederacy and contributed many soldiers to the Union army; and elsewhere in the upland South. Other yeomen farmers who supported the Confederacy at the outset, and fought for it, became alienated over time because of disastrous inflation, shortages of food and salt, high taxes, and a growing conviction that they were risking their lives and property in a war to defend slavery. Clauses in the conscription law that allowed those who could afford it to buy a substitute and exempted from the draft one white man on every plantation with twenty or more slaves lent force to the bitter cry that it was a rich man's war but a poor man's fight. Many soldiers' families suffered severe hardship and malnutrition as food shortages and inflation worsened. Bread riots occurred in parts of the South during 1863—most notably in Richmond itself. Numerous soldiers deserted from the army to return home and support their families. Several historians have argued that this dissension seriously weakened the Confederate war effort and brought eventual defeat.

The alienation of many Southern whites was matched by the alienation of a large portion of that two-fifths of the Southern population that was black and slave. Slaves were essential to the Confederate war effort. They provided a majority of the labor force. They made it possible for the South to mobilize three-quarters of its white men of military age into the armed forces—compared with about half in the North. Thus slavery was at one level a source of strength to the Confederacy. But at another level it was a source of weakness. Most slaves who reflected on their stake in the war believed that a Northern victory would bring freedom. Tens of thousands escaped to Yankee lines, where the North converted their labor power and eventually their military manpower into a Union asset. This leakage of labor from the Confederacy and the unrest of slaves who remained behind retarded Southern economic efficiency and output. It also drained manpower from the Confederate army by keeping some white men at home to control the increasingly restless slave population.

The alienation of these two large blocs of the Southern people seems therefore a plausible explanation for Confederate defeat.[10] But some caveats are in order. The alienated elements of the American population during the Revolution were probably larger than in the

10. The most recent statement of this thesis is William W. Freehling, "The Divided South, the Causes of Confederate Defeat, and the Reintegration of Narrative History," in Freehling, *The Reintegration of American History: Slavery and the Civil War* (New York, 1994), pp. 220–52.

South during the Civil War. Many slaves ran away to the British, while the Loyalist whites undoubtedly weakened the American cause more than the disaffected nonslaveholders weakened the Confederate cause. Yet the Americans triumphed and the Confederates did not. It is easy to exaggerate the amount of class conflict and yeoman alienation in the Confederacy; some historians have done just that. And while large numbers of slaves ran off to Union lines, this happened only where Union military and naval forces invaded and controlled Confederate territory—which introduces an *external* factor and a possible alternative explanation for Union victory.

But perhaps the most important weakness of the "internal alienation" thesis is that same fallacy of reversibility mentioned earlier. Large blocs of Northern people were bitterly, aggressively alienated from the Lincoln administration's war policies. Their opposition weakened and at times threatened to paralyze the Union war effort. Perhaps one-third of the border-state whites actively supported the Confederacy, while many of the remainder were at best lukewarm Unionists, especially after emancipation became a Republican war aim. Guerrilla warfare behind Union lines in these pro-Confederate regions occurred on a far larger scale than in the Unionist areas behind Confederate lines. In the free states themselves, the Democratic party denounced conscription, emancipation, certain war taxes, suspension of habeas corpus, and other measures to mobilize men and resources for an all-out war effort. Democrats exploited these issues in a relentless attempt to cripple the Lincoln administration. The peace wing of the party, the so-called Copperheads, opposed the war itself as a means of restoring the Union.

If the South had its class conflict over the theme of a rich man's war and poor man's fight, so did the North. If the Confederacy had its bread riots, the Union had its draft riots, which were much more violent and threatening. If many soldiers deserted from Confederate armies, a similarly large percentage deserted from Union armies until the autumn of 1864, when the Confederate rate increased because of a perception that the war was lost and further sacrifice was useless. Note that this rising Southern desertion rate was primarily a *result* of defeat, not a cause. If the South had its slaves who wanted Yankee victory and freedom, the North had its Democrats and border-state Unionists who strongly opposed emancipation and withheld their support from the war because of it. Thus internal alienation provides no more of a sufficient explanation for Confederate defeat than internal conflict because the similar and probably greater alienation within the North neutralized this factor.

Another internal explanation for Confederate defeat can be described as the "lack of will" thesis. It holds that the Confederacy could have won if the Southern people had possessed the determination, the *will* to make the sacrifices and the total effort necessary to achieve victory. The most straightforward, unvarnished expression of this thesis was offered by E. Merton Coulter, a Southerner, in his book *The Confederate States of America,* published in 1950. The South lost the war, said Coulter, because its "people did not will hard enough and long enough to win." In 1986 the four authors of *Why The South Lost the Civil War* echoed this conclusion: "We contend that lack of will constituted the decisive deficiency in the Confederate arsenal."[11]

Three principal themes have emerged in this "lack of will" thesis. First is an argument that the Confederacy lacked a strong sense of nationalism. The Confederate States of America, in this interpretation, did not exist long enough to give its people that mystical faith we call nationalism, or patriotism. Southerners did not have as firm a conviction of fighting for a country, a flag, a deep-rooted political and cultural tradition, as Northerners did. Southerners had been Americans before they became Confederates, and many of them— especially former Whigs—had opposed secession. So when the going

11. E. Merton Coulter, *The Confederate States of America 1861–1865* (Baton Rouge, 1950), p. 566; Beringer et al., *Why the South Lost,* p. 64. This theme remains central in the abridged version of Beringer et al., published in 1988 with the title *The Elements of Confederate Defeat: Nationalism, War Aims, and Religion* (Athens, 1988).

got tough, their residual Americanism reemerged and triumphed over their newly minted glossy Confederate nationalism.

Proponents of this "weak nationalism" theme point to the Confederate Constitution, which in most respects was a verbatim copy of the United States Constitution. The Confederate national flag was red, white, and blue with an arrangement of stars and bars not far different from the stars and stripes of the American flag. The great seal of the Confederacy portrayed George Washington, while Confederate money and postage stamps bore the portraits of Washington, Thomas Jefferson, Andrew Jackson, and other heroes of the American pantheon. Surely this indicates that Confederates were closet Americans subconsciously yearning to return to their old allegiance.

But this argument misses the point. Confederates regarded themselves as the true heirs of American nationalism, custodians of the ideals for which their forefathers of 1776 had fought. It was the *Yankees* who had repudiated these ideals. When the Black Republicans took over the government, Southerners departed to form a new government that would conserve the genuine heritage of the old America. Confederate nationalism was American nationalism purified of malign Yankee domination. That is why Confederate money and stamps portrayed great Americans; that is why the Confederate Constitution retained most provisions of the United States Constitution. The South, said Jefferson Davis in his first message to the Confederate Congress after Fort Sumter, was fighting for the same "sacred right of self-government" that their revolutionary fathers had fought for. "Thank God! we have a country at last," said Mississippian L. Q. C. Lamar in 1861, a country "to live for, to pray for, to fight for, and if necessary, to die for."[12]

It is true that the rhetoric of Confederate nationalism did not contain as many references to abstract symbols or concepts like flag,

12. Dunbar Rowland, ed., *Jefferson Davis, Constitutionalist: His Letters, Papers, and Speeches,* 10 vols. (Jackson, Miss., 1923), V, 84; Lamar quoted in Coulter, *Confederate States,* p. 57.

country, Constitution, and democracy as did Union rhetoric. But Southerners felt a stronger and more visceral commitment—to defense of land, home, and family from invasion by "Yankee vandals." In this sense, Confederate nationalism was if anything stronger than its Union counterpart. In their letters and diaries, Southerners expressed a fiercer patriotism, a more passionate dedication to "the Cause," a greater determination to "die in the last ditch" than Northerners did. As the Confederate War Department clerk John Jones expressed it in his diary in 1863, the Southern people had far more at stake in the war than Northerners. "Our men *must* prevail in combat, or lose their property, country, freedom, everything. . . . On the other hand, the enemy, in yielding the contest, may retire into their own country, and possess everything they enjoyed before the war began." A Union officer who was captured in the battle of Atlanta on July 22, 1864, and spent the rest of the war in Southern prisons, wrote in his diary on October 4 that from what he had seen in the South "the End of the War . . . is some time hence as the Idea of the Rebs giving up until they are completely subdued is all Moonshine they submit to privations that would not be believed unless seen." [13] Without question, the Southern people persisted through far greater hardships and suffering than Northern people experienced. Northerners almost threw in the towel in the summer of 1864 because of casualty rates that Southerners had endured for more than two years. In the light of this, it seems difficult to accept the thesis of lack of will stemming from weak nationalism as a cause of Confederate defeat.

A second theme in the "lack of will" interpretation is what might be termed the "guilt" thesis—the suggestion that many Southern whites felt moral qualms about slavery which undermined their will to win a war fought to preserve slavery. The South, wrote historian

13. John B. Jones, *A Rebel War Clerk's Diary,* ed. Earl Schenck Miers (New York, 1958), p. 181; David M. Smith., ed., "The Civil War Diary of Colonel John Henry Smith," *Iowa Journal of History* 47 (April 1949), p. 164.

Kenneth M. Stampp, suffered from a "weakness of morale" caused by "widespread doubts and apprehensions about the validity of the Confederate cause." Defeat rewarded these guilt-ridden Southerners with "a way to rid themselves of the moral burden of slavery," so a good many of them "perhaps unconsciously, welcomed . . . defeat." Other historians with a bent for social science concepts agree that Confederate morale suffered from the "cognitive dissonance" set up in their psyches by fighting a war to establish their own liberty but at the same time to keep four million black people in slavery.[14]

The evidence for this thesis is thin. To be sure, one can find quotations from Southern whites expressing doubts or qualms about slavery. And one can find statements by Southerners after the war expressing relief that it was gone. But the latter are somewhat suspect in their sincerity. And in any case one can find far more quotations on the other side—assertions that slavery was a positive good, the best labor system and the best system of social relations between a superior and inferior race. Two influential studies maintain that most Southern whites "never abandoned the belief that slavery was a divinely ordained institution. . . . Nothing in the postwar behavior and attitudes of these people suggested that the ownership of slaves had necessarily compromised their values or tortured their consciences."[15]

In any case, most Confederates did not think of themselves as fighting for slavery but for independence. If slavery weakened Southern morale to the point of causing defeat, should it not have weakened American morale in the Revolution of 1776 even more? After all, Americans of that generation felt considerably more guilt

14. Kenneth M. Stampp, *The Imperiled Union: Essays on the Background of the Civil War* (New York, 1980), pp. 247, 251–52, 260; Beringer et al., *Why the South Lost,* chap. 15.

15. Wilson, *Baptized in Blood,* p. 68; Leon Litwack, *Been in the Storm So Long: The Aftermath of Slavery* (New York, 1979), p. 189. See also James L. Roark, *Masters without Slaves: Southern Planters in the Civil War and Reconstruction* (New York, 1977).

about slavery than did Southerners of 1861. And it is hard to see that Robert E. Lee, for example, who did have doubts and reservations about slavery—and about secession for that matter—made a lesser contribution to Confederate victory than, say, Braxton Bragg, who believed firmly in both slavery and secession.

A third theme in the "lack of will" interpretation focuses on religion. Southerners were a religious people; under the stress of suffering and death during the war they became more religious. At the outset, Southern clergymen preached that God was on the side of the Confederacy. But as the war went on and the South suffered so much death and destruction, so much disaster and defeat, some Southerners began to wonder whether God was on their side after all. Perhaps, on the contrary, he was punishing them for their sins. "Can we believe in the justice of Providence," asked one prominent Confederate, "or must we conclude that we are after all wrong?"[16] Several historians have pointed to these religious doubts as a source of defeatism and loss of will that corroded Confederate morale and contributed to Southern defeat.

Notice the phrase "loss of will" in the preceding sentence. Not *lack*, but *loss*. There is a difference—a significant difference. A people at war whose armies are destroyed or captured, whose railroads are wrecked, factories and cities burned, ports seized, countryside occupied, and crops laid waste quite naturally lose their will to continue the fight because they have lost the means to do so. That is what happened to the Confederacy. If one analyzes carefully the "lack of will" thesis as it is spelled out in several studies, it becomes clear that what the authors are really writing about is loss of the will to carry on, not an initial *lack* of will. The book *Why the South Lost the Civil War*, which builds its interpretation around the "*lack* of will" thesis, abounds with "*loss* of will" phraseology: Union naval and military victories

---

16. Josiah Gorgas quoted in Beringer et al., *Why the South Lost*, p. 351.

contributed to the *dissolution* of Confederate power and will . . . *created* war weariness and *destroyed* morale. . . . The loss of Atlanta and Sherman's march, combined with Lincoln's re-election, severely *crippled* Confederate will to win. . . . By 1865 the Confederacy had *lost* its will for sacrifice.[17]

This is the right way to put it. It places the cause-effect relationship in the correct order—military defeat caused loss of will, not vice versa. It introduces external agency as a crucial explanatory factor—the agency of Northern military success, especially in the eight months after August 1864. The main defect of the "*lack* of will" thesis, as well as of the "internal conflict" and "internal alienation" theses discussed earlier, is that they attribute Confederate defeat to factors intrinsic to the South. Like the analysts of Confederate mistakes at Gettysburg, they tend to forget about the Yankees. Thus the four authors of *Why the South Lost* conclude flatly, in the face of much of their own evidence, that "the Confederacy succumbed to internal rather than external causes."[18]

This brings us back to the "overwhelming numbers and resources" interpretation, which at least had the merit of recognizing the large external aspect of Confederate defeat. But the deficiencies of that interpretation remain. Another category of analysis with an external dimension, though, might seem to resolve the dilemma of explanation. This one focuses on leadership. Numerous historians both Northern and Southern—and British as well, for they have paid a lot of attention to the American Civil War—have argued that the North developed superior leadership, which became the main factor in ultimate Union victory. This has produced a large and rich literature, which can only be briefly summarized here. It deals mainly with three levels of leadership.

First, generalship. A fairly broad consensus exists that the Confed-

17. *Ibid.,* pp. 198, 20, 333, 350 (italics added).
18. *Ibid.,* p. 439.

eracy benefited from better generalship in the first half of the war, particularly in the eastern theater and at the tactical level. But by 1864 a group of generals including Grant, Sherman, and Sheridan had emerged to top commands in the North with a firm grasp of the need for coordinated offensives in all theaters, a concept of the "total war" strategy necessary to win this conflict, the skill to carry out the strategy, and the relentless, even ruthless determination to keep pressing it despite a high cost in casualties until the South surrendered unconditionally. In this interpretation the Confederacy had brilliant tactical leaders like Lee, Jackson, Forrest, and others who also showed strategic talent in limited theaters. But the South had no generals who rose to the level of overall strategic genius demonstrated by Grant and Sherman. Lee's strategic vision was limited to the Virginia theater, where his influence concentrated Confederate resources at the expense of the western theaters, where the Confederacy suffered from poor generalship and where it really lost the war.

The second level where a number of historians have identified superior Northern leadership is in management of military supply and logistics. In Secretary of War Edwin M. Stanton, Quartermaster General Montgomery Meigs, Assistant Secretary of the Navy Gustavus Fox, the administrators of military railroads Daniel McCallum and Herman Haupt, and numerous other officials, the North developed by 1862 a group of top- and middle-level managers who organized the Northern economy and the logistical flow of supplies and transportation to Union armies with unprecedented efficiency and abundance. The Confederacy could not match Northern skill in organization and administration. Nor did the South manage its economy as well as the North. While the Union developed a balanced system of taxation, loans, and treasury notes to finance the war without unreasonable inflation, the Confederacy relied mostly on fiat money and suffered a crippling 9,000 percent inflation by war's end. In this interpretation, it was not the North's greater resources but its better management of those resources that won the war.[19]

Third, leadership at the top. Lincoln proved to be a better commander in chief than Davis. On this there has been virtual unanimity among historians of Northern birth, and surprising agreement by many Southerners. A couple of quotations from two historians, one Northern and one Southern, writing sixty years apart, will give the flavor of this interpretation. The Yankee James Ford Rhodes wrote at the beginning of the twentieth century that "the preponderating asset of the North proved to be Lincoln." And in 1960 the Southern-born historian David Potter put it even more strongly: "If the Union and the Confederacy had exchanged presidents with one another, the Confederacy might have won its independence."[20]

This may be carrying a good point too far. In any event, a broad consensus exists that Lincoln was more eloquent than Davis in expressing war aims, more successful in communicating with the people, more skillful as a political leader in keeping factions working together for the war effort, better able to endure criticism and work with his critics to achieve a common goal. Lincoln was flexible, pragmatic, with a sense of humor to smooth relationships and help him survive the stress of his job; Davis was austere, rigid, humorless, with the type of personality that readily made enemies. Lincoln had a strong physical constitution; Davis suffered ill health and was frequently prostrated by sickness. Lincoln picked good administrative subordinates (with some exceptions) and knew how to delegate authority to them; Davis went through five secretaries of war in four years; he spent a great deal of time and energy on petty administrative details that he should have left to subordinates. A disputatious

19. This is the implicit and sometimes explicit thesis of the fullest study of the subject, Herman Hattaway and Archer Jones, *How the North Won: A Military History of the Civil War* (Urbana, Ill., 1983).

20. Rhodes quoted by Donald, *Why the North Won,* p. x; David M. Potter, "Jefferson Davis and the Political Factors in Confederate Defeat," *ibid.,* p. 112.

man, Davis sometimes seemed to prefer winning an argument to winning the war; Lincoln was happy to lose an argument if it would help win the war. Davis's well-known feuds with two of the Confederacy's premier generals, Beauregard and Joseph E. Johnston, undoubtedly hurt the South's war effort.

The thesis of superior Northern leadership seems more convincing than other explanations for Union victory. And yet it should not be accepted uncritically. Some caution is advisable. With respect to generalship, for example, comparisons of Grant and Lee, Sheridan and Forrest, Sherman and Johnston, and so on, are a minefield through which historians had better maneuver carefully. And even if the North did enjoy an advantage in this respect during the last year or two of the war, the Union army had its fainthearts and blunderers, its McClellan and Pope and Burnside and Hooker who nearly lost the war to superior Confederate leadership in the East in 1862–1863, despite what was happening in the West. On more than one occasion the outcome seemed to hang in the balance because of *incompetent* Northern military leadership.

As for Union superiority in the management of supply and logistics, this was probably true in most respects. Northern society was more entrepreneurial and business-oriented than Southern society; the Union war effort could draw on a wider field of talent to mobilize men, resources, technology, industry, and transportation. Yet the Confederacy could boast some brilliant successes in this area of leadership. Ordnance Chief Josiah Gorgas almost literally turned plowshares into swords, building from scratch an arms and ammunition industry that kept Confederate armies better supplied than had seemed possible at the outset. The Rains brothers George and Gabriel accomplished miracles in the establishment of nitrate works, the manufacture of gunpowder, and the development of explosive mines (then called torpedoes), which turned out to be the Confederacy's most potent naval weapon. What seems most significant about Confederate logistics and supply is not the obvious deficiencies in railroads and the commissariat, to cite two notorious examples, but the ability of Southern officials to do so much with so little. Instead of losing the war, their efforts did much to keep the Confederacy fighting for so long.

Finally, what about Lincoln's superiority to Davis as commander in chief? This might seem indisputable. Yet Lincoln made mistakes as a war leader. He went through a half-dozen failures as commanders in the eastern theater before he found the right general. Some of his other military appointments and strategic decisions could justly be criticized. And as late as the summer of 1864, when the war seemed to be going badly for the North, when Grant's forces had suffered horrendous casualties to achieve a stalemate at Petersburg and Sherman seemed equally stymied before Atlanta, Lincoln came under enormous pressure to negotiate peace with the Confederacy. To have done so would have been tantamount to admitting Northern defeat. Lincoln resisted this pressure, but at what appeared to be the cost of his reelection to the presidency. If the election had been held in August 1864 instead of November, Lincoln would have lost. He would thus have gone down in history as a loser, a failure unequal to the challenge of the greatest crisis in the American experience. And Jefferson Davis might have gone down in history as the great leader of a war of independence, the architect of a new nation, the George Washington of the Southern Confederacy.

This did not happen, but only because of events on the battlefield—principally Sherman's capture of Atlanta, and Sheridan's spectacular victories over Jubal Early in the Shenandoah Valley. These turned Northern opinion from deepest despair in the summer to confident determination by November. In July, Horace Greeley had written to Lincoln pleading with him to open peace negotiations with the Confederacy. "Our bleeding, bankrupt, almost dying country," said Greeley, "longs for peace—shudders at the prospect of fresh conscriptions, of further wholesale devastations, and of new rivers of human blood." A month later the veteran Republican politician Thurlow Weed said that "the people are wild for peace. . . . Lincoln's reelection [is] an impossibility."[21] But less than two months later, after the fall of Atlanta and Sheridan's first two victories in the Shenandoah Valley, a British war correspondent expressed astonishment at the "extent and depth" of Northern "determination . . . to fight to the last. . . . They are in earnest in a way the like of which the world never saw before, silently, calmly, but desperately in earnest."[22]

This transformation of Northern will illustrates the point made earlier that the will of both the Northern and Southern people was primarily a result of military victory rather than a cause of it. Events on the battlefield might have gone the other way, on these and other occasions during the war. If they had done so, the course of the war might have been quite different. It is this element of contingency that is missing from generalizations about the cause of Confederate defeat, whether such generalizations focus on external or internal factors. *There was nothing inevitable about Northern victory in the Civil War.* Nor was Sherman's capture of Atlanta any more inevitable than, say, McClellan's capture of Richmond in June 1862 had been. There were several major turning points, points of contingency when events moved in one direction but could well have moved in another. Two have just been mentioned: Sherman's capture of Atlanta and McClellan's failure to capture Richmond. The former, coupled with Sheridan's success in the Shenandoah Valley, proved to be the final decisive turning point toward Union victory. Two earlier moments of contingency that turned in favor of the North were of equal importance.

The first occurred in the fall of 1862. Confederate offensives during the summer had taken Southern armies from their backs to the wall in Mississippi and Virginia almost to the Ohio River and across

21. Greeley to Lincoln, July 7, 1864, Lincoln Papers, Library of Congress; Weed quoted in Edward C. Kirkland, *The Peacemakers of 1864* (New York, 1927), p. 108.
22. *London Daily News,* Sept. 27, 1864.

the Potomac River by September. These invasions were the most ambitious Confederate effort to win European recognition and a victorious peace on Union soil. But in September and October Union armies stopped these Confederate thrusts at Antietam and Perryville. This forestalled European intervention, dissuaded Northern voters from repudiating the Lincoln administration by electing a Democratic House of Representatives in the fall of 1862, and gave Lincoln the occasion to issue the Emancipation Proclamation, which enlarged the scope and purpose of the war.

The other major turning point came in the summer of 1863. Before then, during the months between Union defeats at Fredericksburg and Chancellorsville, a time that also witnessed Union failures in the western theater, Northern morale dropped to its lowest point in the war—except perhaps during August 1864. The usually indomitable Captain Oliver Wendell Holmes, Jr., recovering from the second of three wounds he received in the war, wrote during the winter of 1862–1863 that "the Army is tired with its hard and terrible experience. . . . I've pretty much made up my mind that the South have achieved their independence." Even that staunch patriot Joseph Medill, editor of the *Chicago Tribune,* wrote in early 1863 that an armistice had to come: "The rebs can't be conquered by the present machinery."[23]

But then came the battle of Gettysburg and the capture of Vicksburg. This crucial turning point produced Southern cries of despair. At the end of July, Confederate Ordnance Chief Josiah Gorgas wrote:

> One brief month ago we were apparently at the point of success. Lee was in Pennsylvania. . . . Vicksburgh seemed to laugh all Grant's efforts to scorn. . . . Now the picture is just as sombre as it was

23. Mark DeWolfe Howe, ed., *Touched with Fire: Civil War Letters and Diary of Oliver Wendell Holmes, Jr., 1861–1864* (Cambridge, Mass., 1946), p. 73; Medill to Elihu Washburne, Jan. 16, 1863, quoted in Bruce Catton, *Grant Moves South* (Boston, 1960), pp. 369–70.

bright then. . . . It seems incredible that human power could effect such a change in so brief a space. Yesterday we rode on the pinnacle of success—today absolute ruin seems to be our portion. The Confederacy totters to its destruction.[24]

Predictions in July 1863 of the Confederacy's imminent collapse turned out to be premature. More twists and turns marked the road to the end of the war. That only underscores the point about the importance of contingency. To understand why the South lost, in the end, we must turn from large generalizations that imply inevitability and study instead the contingency that hung over each military campaign, each battle, each election, each decision during the war. When we comprehend what happened in each of these events, how it happened, why it happened, and what its consequences were, then we will be on our way toward answering the question: Why did the Confederacy lose?

24. Frank E. Vandiver, ed., *The Civil War Diary of General Josiah Gorgas* (University, Ala., 1947), p. 55.

9

HOW THE CONFEDERACY
ALMOST WON

MANY AMERICANS READ BOOKS OR WATCH VIDEO DOCUMENTARIES about the Civil War as part of their national history; people south of the Potomac and Ohio rivers still *live* the war. No Southerner can escape the legacy of the Civil War; few white Southerners have escaped its bewitching spell. "Like more than one present-day Southerner," wrote the Tennessee-born novelist and literary historian John Bowers in the preface to his biography of Stonewall Jackson, "I fought [against] knowing more about the Civil War then I needed to know. It was too much around me. . . . It was a dark abyss you might fall into and never be heard from again." But his struggle against temptation was a losing battle. Bowers read classic narratives of the Civil War by Bruce Catton and Shelby Foote: "I myself started to slide into that deep hole of obsession from which few Civil War buffs return. . . . I was lost."[1]

Many white Southerners play the war over and over again in their

1. John Bowers, *Stonewall Jackson: Portrait of a Soldier* (New York, 1989), pp. 11–12.

minds, searching in vain for a way to make it come out differently. William Faulkner best described this phenomenon:

> For every Southern boy fourteen years old, not once but whenever he wants it, there is the instant when it's still not yet two oclock on that July afternoon in 1863, the brigades are in position behind the rail fence, the guns are laid and ready in the woods and the furled flags are already loosened to break out and Pickett himself with his long oiled ringlets and his hat in one hand probably and his sword in the other looking up the hill waiting for Longstreet to give the word and it's all in the balance, it hasn't happened yet . . . and that moment doesn't need even a fourteen-year old boy to think *This time. Maybe this time* with all this much to lose and all this much to gain: Pennsylvania, Maryland, the world, the golden dome of Washington itself to crown with desperate and unbelievable victory the desperate gamble, the cast made two years ago.[2]

This yearning is the subconscious manifestation of the conscious question: Why did we lose that war? This query lies at the heart of many Civil War books, whether or not they address it explicitly. It is the unspoken question that frames the argument in Richard McMurry's cogent, concise *Two Great Rebel Armies.*[3] McMurry starts from a basic fact: Confederate arms nearly won the war by victories in the eastern theater (defined mainly as Virginia) but ultimately lost it by defeats in the western theater (defined as the vast region southwest of Virginia).

The Confederacy's two principal armies were Robert E. Lee's Army of Northern Virginia and the Army of Tennessee, which had six different commanders during its unhappy career. For nearly four years the Army of Northern Virginia (and its predecessor) held off

2. William Faulkner, *Intruder in the Dust* (New York: Signet New American Library edition, 1948), pp. 148–49.

3. Richard M. McMurry, *Two Great Rebel Armies: A Essay in Confederate Military History* (Chapel Hill, 1989).

invading Union forces, achieving a strategic stalemate in Virginia while winning several spectacular tactical victories that undermined Northern morale and more than once came close to causing the North to give up trying to conquer the South. But at the same time, Union arms in the West drove the Army of Tennessee (and its predecessor) from Kentucky into and through Tennessee, Mississippi, Alabama, and Georgia, finally forcing the surrender of the remnants of this army in North Carolina. During four years the Army of Tennessee won only one unequivocal tactical victory (Chickamauga) while yielding thousands of square miles of territory to the invaders, whose morale and resources were augmented by each victory in a process that led eventually to Northern triumph in the war.

What explains this contrast in the fortunes of the two main Confederate armies? Many things, according to McMurry. The first was a political decision: to locate the Confederate capital in Richmond. This meant that the hundred-mile belt of Virginia between Washington and Richmond would become the main field of military operations. Preoccupied with the defense of their capital, Confederate strategists focused efforts and resources on this area to the neglect of the West. McMurry claims that Union leaders, by contrast, recognized early that the war could be won in the West and therefore adopted "a strategy that involved acceptance of a stalemate in Virginia and a concentration of effort and resources in the West."[4] This is dubious. Abraham Lincoln was at least as concerned with the defense of Washington as Jefferson Davis was with the defense of Richmond. Northern manpower and supplies flowed disproportionately to the eastern theater, causing complaints of shortages and neglect in the West. To cite one fact not mentioned by McMurry: When Ulysses S. Grant captured the Mississippi stronghold of Vicksburg and its thirty thousand defenders in July 1863, he also acquired sixty thousand Confederate rifles, mostly Enfields imported through the blockade, that were superior to the weapons carried by many of

4. *Ibid.*, p. 54.

Grant's infantry—and to those carried by some units in the Army of Northern Virginia.[5]

McMurry stands on firmer ground when he points to geography and terrain as factors favoring the Army of Northern Virginia. Western Confederate armies had to defend several hundred thousand square miles, while Robert E. Lee was charged mainly with defense of a narrow front in northern and eastern Virginia. In the West the principal navigable rivers—the Mississippi, Tennessee, and Cumberland—pointed southward into the Confederacy's heartland, giving the Union's superior river navy a line for operations in support of invasions. Most Virginia rivers flowed from west to east athwart the line of Union overland offensives, giving Confederate forces good lines of defense behind a half-dozen rivers between Washington and Richmond. But when the Army of the Potomac changed its base for an offensive from Hampton Roads on the Chesapeake Bay westward up the Virginia Peninsula between the York and James rivers, as George B. McClellan did in 1862 and Grant did partially in 1864, the Confederacy's river asset became something of a liability in Virginia.

The Shenandoah Valley west of the Blue Ridge Mountains, however, remained a Confederate asset throughout the war. Running from southwest to northeast, the Valley offered an avenue for Confederate invasions and raids that pointed toward important Northern cities, including Washington. In the other direction it pointed away from Richmond and the Virginia heartland. Confederates used the Valley for three important offensives that took them to or across the Potomac River—Stonewall Jackson's attacks in 1862, Lee's invasion of Pennsylvania in 1863, and Jubal Early's raid to the very outskirts of Washington in July 1864. A Union army under Philip Sheridan finally cleaned Confederate forces out of the Valley in the fall and winter of 1864–1865, but Sheridan then had to transfer his men by

5. *Personal Memoirs of U. S. Grant,* 2 vols. (New York, 1885–1886), I, 572.

a roundabout route to the Richmond-Petersburg front instead of continuing his invasion from the Valley.

The main reason for Confederate success in the East and failure in the West was the contrast in military leadership. On this question McMurry offers persuasive arguments and convincing evidence. Virginia had the strongest military tradition and best militia organization of any Southern state. Virginia Military Institute and the Citadel (in Charleston, South Carolina) were the best military schools in the South—indeed, next to West Point, the best in the entire country. Nearly all of the VMI alumni and most of those from the Citadel served in the Army of Northern Virginia. They provided a cadre of officers unmatched in any other army, Confederate or Union. The raw material to make fighting men was no better in the Army of Northern Virginia than in the Army of Tennessee, but their leadership was far better. "The chief factor in explaining the different fates of the two major Confederate armies," writes McMurry, "was to be found in the personality, character, intelligence, dedication, and, above all, in the integrity and moral courage of their commanding generals." This was true most of all of Robert E. Lee, who in McMurry's judgment as in that of most historians, stands tall above all other Confederate generals. "The explanation for most of the eastern army's success is to be found in Lee himself."[6]

Lee had an uncanny ability to discern his adversary's weakness and a bold willingness to take risks with his smaller army to exploit it. Lee's right-hand man in these enterprises during the year of his greatest victories (from the spring of 1862 to the spring of 1863) was Stonewall Jackson. Curiously, McMurry has little to say about Jackson. But John Bowers's biography of this dour Presbyterian and daring soldier goes partway to compensate for the deficiency. His is not a typical scholarly biography. It does not rest on any new sources or new research. As a novelist, Bowers felt free to put dialogue and

6. McMurry, *Two Great Rebel Armies,* pp. 118–19, 139.

thoughts into the mouths and minds of his protagonists that, while plausible, are not documented. So long as the reader remains aware of this, it is one way to get at a deeper "truth" than the literal documented truth, which is in any case only a partial and often a distorted truth. Bowers's dialogue occasionally seems a bit gratuitous—particularly the profanity of Jackson's quartermaster, John Harmon, who was, admittedly, notorious for his colorful language. Bowers also has a tendency to repeat anecdotes of dubious authenticity, and his grasp of the details of military operations is sometimes shaky.

Nevertheless, he offers a penetrating portrait of Jackson's character and of the qualities of his leadership. An indifferent teacher at VMI for a decade before the war, Jackson was called (behind his back) "Old Tom Fool" by the cadets. He was noted for his eccentricities. Jackson suffered from numerous maladies, some of them imaginary, and tried various quack cures, some of them of his own devising. He sucked constantly on lemons (no one knew where he got them) to help his delicate digestion. He sat and stood rigidly erect in order, he said, "not to bend his digestive organs." He refused to season his food with pepper because it made his left leg ache. He frequently held his right arm in the air—to enable the blood to drain back into his body, he said, and ease an aching pain.

Jackson was a devout Christian almost to the point of fanaticism. An orthdox predestinarian Calvinist, he attributed his Civil War victories to the Lord. He spent as much time as possible attending church, but regularly fell asleep during the sermon. Even after he became famous during the war, Jackson wore a threadbare tunic left over from the Mexican War and a battered cadet forage cap pulled down over his eyes. When his corps captured Harpers Ferry and its twelve thousand defenders in September 1862, "a Northern newspaperman," writes Bowers, reported that "Jackson wore a hat that looked so disreputable that a Northern beggar would refuse to wear it. Actually it was Jackson's new hat. He had retired the old kepi three days before." Curious Union soldiers crowded around to see the famous Stonewall Jackson. "Boys, he's not much for looks," said one, "but if we had him we wouldn't have been caught in this trap."[7]

That was true enough. Jackson had won his nickname "Stonewall" at the first battle of Manassas on July 21, 1861, when he held his brigade like a stone wall against the apparently victorious Yankees, helping to turn the battle in the Southern favor. But his military trademark became speed and offensive striking power. In his Shenandoah Valley campaign of 1862, Jackson marched his army of seventeen thousand men in zigzag fashion 350 miles in one month, fought and won four battles against three separate Union armies whose combined numbers were twice their own, used mobility and secrecy to achieve numerical superiority at the point of contact each time, and tied up sixty thousand enemy troops for more than a month to prevent them from reinforcing McClellan's army besieging Richmond.

Jackson applied his rule of strategy—"always mystify, mislead, and surprise the enemy"—to his own subordinates as well. Fearful of leaks, he never conferred with his division commanders nor divulged his plans to them. He merely ordered them to do what they considered impossible. Jackson consulted only with Robert E. Lee; together they devised plans to trap enemy forces in surprise attacks or raids in their rear that required Jackson's troops to march twenty-five miles a day whether or not they had food to eat or shoes to wear. Jackson expected them to march and fight on sheer willpower alone. "He classed all who were weak and weary, who fainted by the wayside, as men wanting in patriotism," wrote one of its officers. "If a man's face was as white as cotton and his pulse so low you could scarcely feel it, he looked upon him merely as an inefficient soldier and rode off impatiently."[8]

Many of Jackson's officers and men initially resented his iron dis-

7. Bowers, *Stonewall Jackson,* pp. 297–98.

8. Shelby Foote, *The Civil War: A Narrative, Fort Sumter to Perryville* (New York, 1958), p. 426.

cipline and believed him crazy. But when they perceived the results of his methods they began to take pride in their reputation as "Jackson's foot cavalry." Only once did Jackson's vaunted willpower and mobility break down—in the Seven Days' battles before Richmond from June 25 to July 1, 1862. Lee brought Jackson's force secretly from the Shenandoah Valley to attack the right wing of McClellan's army as part of Lee's counteroffensive to relieve the threat to Richmond. The strategy worked, but no thanks to Jackson, who performed sluggishly and even fell asleep frequently during several days of fighting. Jackson and many of his men were suffering from stress fatigue brought on by seven weeks of constant marching and fighting. But Jackson soon revived to perform brilliantly in the campaigns that culminated in the battles of second Manassas, Antietam, Fredericksburg, and Chancellorsville—in each of which Jackson's genius was a major factor in winning a remarkable victory or staving off a disastrous defeat.

The circumstances of Jackson's death were ironic but perhaps not surprising. After a rapid and stealthy flank march at Chancellorsville on May 2, 1863, Jackson's corps crushed the right wing of the Army of the Potomac. Seeking to press forward with a night attack in the light of a full moon, Jackson rode ahead for a personal reconnaissance and was shot mistakenly by his own troops as he galloped back toward Confederate lines. He survived amputation of an arm, but pneumonia set in and he died a week later. The striking power of Lee's army was never again the same.

Some historians come close to attributing the ultimate Confederate loss of the war to the loss of Jackson. They maintain that if Jackson had been in command of his corps the first day at Gettysburg, he would have followed up the initial successful attack by storming Cemetery Hill instead of holding back, as did his cautious successor Richard Ewell. Perhaps. But Richard McMurry perspicaciously warns us that in this instance as well as in the general matter of comparing the eastern and western Confederate armies, success or failure cannot be explained by factors indigenous to the South alone. The relative fighting qualities and leadership of enemy forces must be taken into account. The Army of the Potomac fought well at Gettysburg. And Union armies in the western theater proved to be more effective in the war's earlier stages than the hard-luck Army of the Potomac.

This was true not because western Union soldiers were better fighters than easterners. Indeed, the Army of the Potomac fought more big battles and inflicted (as well as suffered) more casualties than all of the western Union armies combined. Rather, it was because of superior Union leadership in the western theater. All four of the Union's best generals came out of the West: Ulysses S. Grant, William T. Sherman, Philip Sheridan, and George Thomas. Most of the Confederacy's top generals served in Virginia. In effect, during the first three years of the war the Union's first team of generals fought the Confederacy's second team in the West, with the situation reversed in the East. Not until Grant and Sheridan came east in 1864 did the Army of the Potomac acquire the aggressive, determined leadership that finally carried it to victory.

The letters of George B. McClellan edited by Stephen W. Sears, who also published a superb biography of McClellan in 1988, offer the beginnings of an explanation of why the arrival of Grant and Sheridan made such a difference. McClellan created the Army of the Potomac and commanded it during the first sixteen months of its existence. An efficient organizer and drillmaster, McClellan molded this army into a disciplined fighting machine. Cautious, indecisive, and fearful of risk, however, he continually invented reasons why he could not commit this machine to full power. He stamped his personality on the officer corps, including those who succeeded him in command after Lincoln, disillusioned with McClellan's inaction and defense-mindedness, sacked him in November 1862.

Why did McClellan fail? He seemed to have everything going for him. Born into a well-to-do Philadelphia family, he was educated at the best private schools, entered West Point by special permission at the age of fifteen, graduated second in his class in time to fight in the Mexican War where he won two brevets for distinguished service, and emerged as one of the brightest young officers in the peacetime army of the 1850s. After a brief civilian career in which he became a railroad president at the age of thirty-two, McClellan returned to the army when the Civil War broke out. Winning praise as commander of Union forces that gained control of western Virginia and laid the groundwork for the new state of West Virginia, McClellan received a summons to Washington in July 1861 to take command of the dispirited remnants of the Union army routed at Bull Run in the war's first major battle. Three months later he also became general in chief of the entire United States Army, at the age of thirty-four. Newspapers hailed him as the "Young Napoleon" who would promptly win the war and save the Union.

But with the fine army he created McClellan never seized the initiative, never took the war to the enemy except at Antietam, where his timidity threw away the best opportunity before Appomattox to ruin the Army of Northern Virginia. *The Civil War Papers of George B. McClellan* provides clues to the mystery of McClellan's peculiar case of "the slows," as Lincoln called it. More than half of the 811 documents in this volume are published there for the first time. The most important are McClellan's extraordinarily frank and revealing letters to his wife and to his political confidant Samuel L. M. Barlow, a prominent New York Democrat. They contain details of McClellan's political ambitions, which led him to run for president against Lincoln in 1864, and of his conservatism that caused him to oppose the abolition of slavery as a Northern war policy. But the letters are most valuable as a revelation of McClellan's personality, which lay at the root of his military failure. They make clear that his initial success and fame went to his head. "I receive letter after letter—have conversation after conversation calling on me to save the nation," McClellan wrote to his wife soon after he arrived in Washington. In Congress and at the White House

[I] was quite overwhelmed by the congratulations I received & the respect with which I was treated. . . . They gave me my full way in everything. . . . By some strange operation of magic I seem to have become *the* power of the land. . . . God has placed a great work in my hands. . . . I was called to it, my previous life seems to have been unwittingly directed to this great end.[9]

From the euphoria of this messiah complex there was nowhere to go but down. As the months went by and the press began to criticize McClellan for doing nothing with his army except to hold grand reviews, his private letters became filled with self-pity and peevish complaints about lack of support from the administration. He described Lincoln as a "gorilla," the Cabinet as "geese," Secretary of War Edwin M. Stanton as a "depraved hypocrite and villain," and General in Chief Winfield Scott, who retired on November 1, 1861, to make way for McClellan, as "a perfect imbecile. . . . The people call upon me to save the country—I *must* save it and cannot respect anything that is in the way." [10]

Worst of all, McClellan began inflating his intelligence estimates of the number of enemy troops facing him by a factor of two or three. "I am here in a terrible place," he wrote to his wife on one occasion. "The enemy have from 3 to 4 times my force—the Presdt. is an idiot, the old General in his dotage—they cannot or will not see the true state of affairs." [11] In actual fact, McClellan at that time had twice the enemy's numbers. His repeated distortions of Confederate strength provided McClellan with a pretext for inaction and an excuse for failure when Robert E. Lee drove him away from Richmond in the Seven Days' battles. After those battles Secretary of

9. George B. McClellan to Mary Ellen McClellan, July 27, July 30, August 9, October 30, 1861, in Stephen W. Sears, ed., *The Civil War Papers of George B. McClellan: Selected Correspondence, 1860–1865* (New York, 1989), pp. 70, 71, 82, 113.

10. McClellan to Mary Ellen McClellan, Aug. 8, Aug. 9, Oct. 10, Nov. 17, 1861, *ibid.,* pp. 81–82, 106, 135.

11. McClellan to Mary Ellen McClellan, Aug. 16, 1861, *ibid.,* pp. 85–86.

War Stanton denied McClellan's claim that he was outnumbered. McClellan commented: "Stanton's statement that I outnumbered the rebels is simply false—they had more than two to one against me."[12] Stanton, of course, was right. At Antietam McClellan outnumbered Lee by almost two to one but professed to believe that Lee outnumbered him and therefore kept twenty thousand men out of the battle as a reserve against those phantom Confederate legions from whom he expected a counterattack.

What accounts for this pathology of McClellan's? Some historians have blamed Secret Service Chief Allan Pinkerton for the inflated estimates of enemy numbers. But it seems clear that McClellan believed what he wanted to believe. The truth is that, having experienced nothing but success in his career to 1861, McClellan was afraid to risk failure. He lacked the mental and moral courage to act; he did not have the quality possessed by Lee and Grant and Jackson of willingness to risk defeat as the only way to gain victory. To cover his fears, McClellan shifted the blame to others—to Lincoln and Stanton for not sending him reinforcements, to Republicans in general for politically motivated efforts to undermine him.

McClellan also suffered from what might be described as the Manassas Syndrome—a belief in Confederate martial superiority stemming from the rout of Union forces in the war's first big battle. Though McClellan had not fought there, he arrived in Washington a few days later to find, as he later wrote, "no army to command, [but] a mere collection of regiments cowering on the banks of the Potomac, some perfectly raw, others dispirited by their recent defeat."[13] McClellan could never rid his mind of this image, which each subsequent Confederate victory in Virginia reinforced.

This insight is one of the most important contained in the engaging memoirs of Edward Porter Alexander, chief of artillery in James Longstreet's corps and the best artillerist in the Army of Northern

12. McClellan to Samuel L. M. Barlow, July 23, 1862, *ibid.,* p. 370.
13. McClellan to Edwin M. Stanton, Feb. 3, 1862, *ibid.,* p. 163.

Virginia. Alexander wielded a pen with equal skill; his *Fighting for the Confederacy* offers one of the best accounts of that army by a participant in all of its battles.[14] It is actually the second book of Alexander's memoirs to be published; the first, *Military Memoirs of a Confederate,* came out in 1907 during Alexander's lifetime. It won critical acclaim for its rigorous analysis and exact narrative, but it also evoked expressions of regret that Alexander had put so little of himself into the story.

The fact is that he had done just that in an earlier draft completed in 1899, which the historian Gary Gallagher rescued from Alexander's papers and edited with a skilled hand. *Fighting for the Confederacy* is more personal and less restrained than *Military Memoirs* in its frank judgment of men and measures. It also contains valuable subjective as well as critical insights on the point in question here: the success of the Army of Northern Virginia. Evaluating the Confederate victory at first Manassas, Alexander wrote that "if we got no other very material spoils from the fight we at least brought off a great morale, one to which we afterward added in almost every fight." By second Manassas a year later Lee's army "had acquired that magnificent morale which made them equal to twice their numbers"—especially in McClellan's eyes. At Antietam McClellan "threw away a chance which no other Federal commander ever had," perhaps, as Alexander says of another occasion, because of "the moral oppression of knowing who were his antagonists, & feeling himself outclassed" by Lee and Jackson. "Had it been Grant in command he would not have dreamed of giving up the fight," observed Alexander. "But Grant had been built up by successes in the West, & the Army of the Potomac had never had the luck necessary to properly educate a general."[15]

So Grant had to educate the Army of the Potomac out of its

---

14. *Fighting for the Confederacy: The Personal Recollections of General Edward Porter Alexander,* ed. Gary W. Gallagher (Chapel Hill, 1989).

15. *Ibid.,* pp. 59, 139, 153, 217.

McClellan legacy. In his first battle after coming east as general in chief and strategic commander of the Army of the Potomac, Grant began the educating process. On the second day of the battle of the Wilderness, Lee attacked both flanks of the Union forces with some success. A distraught brigadier rode up to Grant and cried out: "This is a crisis. . . . I know Lee's methods well by past experience; he will throw his whole army between us and the Rapidan, and cut us off completely from our communications." Grant slowly took his cigar from his mouth and fixed the man with a stare: "I am heartily tired of hearing about what Lee is going to do. Some of you always seem to think he is suddenly going to turn a double somersault, and land in our rear and on both of our flanks at the same time. Go back to your command, and try to think what we are going to do ourselves, instead of what Lee is going to do."[16]

Here was the formula for success that explained the contrast between the western and eastern Union and Confederate armies. For the first time the North's first team of commanders faced the Confederacy's first team. And one of the Confederacy's best players— Jackson—was no longer on the team, while the defeatist Union coach—McClellan—had been retired. The four books reviewed in this essay, each representing a genre of Civil War letters—monograph, biography, collected letters, and memoirs—help us to understand how the Union finally won the Civil War after the Confederacy had come close to winning it in the eastern theater.

16. Horace Porter, *Campaigning With Grant* (New York, 1897), pp. 69–70.

10

LEE DISSECTED

IN 1961 ALAN NOLAN PUBLISHED A SUPERB BOOK ABOUT THE IRON Brigade of the Army of the Potomac.[1] Nolan will need the same tough hide possessed by the Union veterans he described in that book to endure the attacks on his book about Robert E. Lee from spiritual descendants of the legions who marched with Lee. For *Lee Considered* is nothing less than a wholesale revision of the heroic image of the white South's favorite icon. Nolan calls his study *Lee Considered* rather than *Reconsidered* because he believes that the image of the legendary Lee has blocked genuine consideration of the historical Lee—apart from Thomas L. Connelly's 1977 book, *The Marble Man,* which was primarily an account of the construction of the Lee myth.[2]

Anticipating the outcry that would greet his interpretation, Nolan disavowed any purpose to defame Lee. "I do not deny Lee's great-

---

1. Alan T. Nolan, *The Iron Brigade: A Military History* (New York, 1961).
2. Alan T. Nolan, *Lee Considered: General Robert E. Lee and Civil War History* (Chapel Hill, 1991), p. 8.

ness," he assures the reader, but "Lee was, after all, one of us, a human being . . . a great man but, indeed, a man," not a god. "Excessive adulation is not the stuff of history."[3] To a historian this is unexceptionable. But Nolan's disclaimer of bias is a bit disingenuous. He is a lawyer by profession. The book has something of the tone of an indictment of Lee in the court of history, with the author as prosecuting attorney. He wants the jury—his readers—to convict Lee of entering willingly into a war to destroy the American nation. Lee did so, he believes, in the interest of perpetuating slavery. Lee pursued a faulty military strategy that ensured Confederate defeat, prolonging the war long after victory was possible at the cost of incalculable and unnecessary death and destruction. There is truth in some of these charges. But it is not the whole truth. Nolan's portrait of Lee may be closer to the real Lee than the flawless marble image promoted by tradition. But the prosecutorial style of his book produces some new distortions.

The Lee hagiography offers Nolan a large target. An early biographer wrote that "the Divinity in [Lee's] bosom shone translucent through the man, and his spirit rose up to the Godlike." *The Oxford Companion to American History* described Lee as "a great and simple person. His character offers historians no moral flaws to probe." The 1989 edition of the *Encyclopedia Americana* pronounced Lee "one of the truly gifted commanders of all time . . . one of the greatest, if not the greatest, soldier who ever spoke the English language." Douglas Southall Freeman, whose four-volume biography of Lee won the Pulitzer prize in 1935 and did more to shape our image of Lee than perhaps any other work, wrote of Lee: "Noble he was; nobler he became." Under the entry "personal characteristics" in his index, Freeman listed: abstemiousness, alertness, amiability, boldness, calmness, charm of manner, cheerfulness, courage, courtesy, dignity, diligence, fairness, faith in God, friendliness, generosity, goodness, good judgment, good looks, grace, heroic character, humility, integ-

3. *Ibid.*, pp. xi–xii.

rity, intelligence, justice, kindness, mercy, modesty, patience, poise, politeness, resourcefulness, sincerity, tact, thoughtfulness, wisdom.[4]

In his determination to cut this godlike icon down to human size, Nolan tackles first Lee's reputation as an opponent of slavery and secession. These matters were important in the white South's construction after the war of a Lost Cause mythology. According to this myth, a heroic people took up arms reluctantly to defend liberty and states' rights against the overweening imperialist pretensions of Lincoln's government in its war of Northern aggression against the South's constitutional rights. In this rendition slavery had nothing to do with secession; the ugly truth that Southern states seceded and fought a war to preserve this institution became an awkward blemish on the image of a war for liberty and rights. Lee's supposed opposition to slavery, therefore, was an essential part of the Lost Cause romanticism of the Confederacy. Lee "had believed steadfastly in gradual emancipation," wrote Freeman; he was "personally opposed to slavery," according to the *Historical Times Illustrated Encyclopedia of the Civil War,* published in 1986; Lee himself told a congressional committee after the war that "I have always been in favor of emancipation."[5]

Like some other Southerners, during the antebellum era Lee privately described slavery as "a moral & political evil." As executor of his father-in-law's will, he carried out its provision for manumission of the slaves inherited by his wife. In the final months of the Civil War he urged the freeing and enlistment of slaves to fight for the Confederacy. But Lee also owned slaves, evidently sold some of them to a trader, and recaptured two slaves who had escaped. He denounced Northern abolitionists, defended the right of Southerners to take their slaves into the western territories (the issue that provoked the sectional conflict leading to secession), and said during the war

---

4. Quotations from *ibid.,* pp. 5, 7, 59; see also Douglas Southall Freeman, *R. E. Lee: A Biography,* 4 vols. (New York, 1934–1935).

5. Quotations from Nolan, *Lee Considered,* pp. 9–10.

that the Confederacy fought to save "our social system [i.e., slavery] from destruction." He did nothing to prevent his army from capturing dozens of blacks in Pennsylvania and sending them South into slavery during the Gettysburg campaign, and countenanced the Confederacy's refusal to exchange captured black Union soldiers who had been slaves. Even as late as January 1865, Lee described slavery not as an evil but "as the best [relation] that can exist between the white and black races while intermingled as at present in this country."[6] The fair-minded reader must agree with Nolan's conclusion:

> Lee *believed* in slavery although, like many Southerners, he at the same time disliked it in the abstract. . . . The historical record flatly contradicts the assertion of Freeman and the Lee tradition that . . . Lee was personally opposed to slavery in any practical sense.[7]

Before Virginia seceded in April 1861, Lee privately denied the right of a state to secede and lamented the breakup of the nation he had served for more than thirty years as an army officer. Yet when Virginia left the Union he promptly resigned from the army and, even before his resignation was accepted, became a general in the Army of Virginia. This quick decision, accompanied by denunciations of "the aggressions of the North," calls into question the legend of Lee the tragic hero forced by circumstances beyond his control to choose between loyalty to nation and loyalty to state. If Lee really opposed secession, why did he not remain loyal to the Union as did George H. Thomas, a Virginian, and David G. Farragut, a Tennessean, who became two of the top commanders in the Union forces? "Surely," writes Nolan, "it is plain that Lee was a Southerner harboring Southern sectional feelings."[8]

6. *Ibid.*, pp. 10–21.
7. *Ibid.*, pp. 29, 23.
8. *Ibid.*, p. 48.

This conclusion may oversimplify the ambivalence of Lee's convictions and the difficulty of his choice. But Nolan's treatment of the slavery and disunion themes provides a healthy corrective to the "virgin birth" theory of secession, which held that the Confederacy was not conceived by any such worldly cause as slavery but by the divine principle—embodied in Robert E. Lee—of states' rights and constitutional liberty.

Nolan's analysis of Lee's generalship, while brilliant in some respects, is dubious in others. The underlying premise of those who regard Lee as the "greatest soldier who ever spoke the English language" is the belief that the Confederacy had no chance to win the war because Northern preponderance in manpower, resources, and industrial might made Union victory inevitable. Thus Lee's stunning victories and the Confederacy's success in holding off the Yankee juggernaut for so long are testimony to Lee's military genius. This image of a gallant welterweight inflicting repeated knockdown blows against a flailing heavyweight before finally succumbing to raw power is central to the romantic image of the Lost Cause. Nolan thoroughly discredits the notion of inevitable Union victory. Such an outcome was no more certain than was British triumph over the American Revolution or American victory in Vietnam. Confederate strength was relatively greater than that of the victors in those conflicts.

Then why did the Confederacy fail? Because, Nolan thinks, of Lee's faulty choice of an offensive strategy. Instead of conserving manpower by a strategy of trading space for time and employing selective counterattacks against targets of opportunity, wearing down the will of the enemy as did George Washington, Lee repeatedly attacked and invaded, sacrificing his limited manpower until forced to surrender. Lee could have lost most of his battles but won the war, Nolan writes; instead he won most of his battles and lost the war. Turning the Lee legend on its head, Nolan asserts that the very qualities his admirers praise are those that ensured Confederate defeat: "devotion to the offensive, daring, combativeness, audacity, eagerness to attack, taking the initiative."[9]

Nolan is not the first to make this point. And at a glance it seems persuasive. Lee's great victories produced a higher proportion of casualties in his own army than in the enemy's. Of all army commanders on both sides in the Civil War, Lee's troops suffered the highest percentage of casualties. Yet it was Grant who acquired the label of "butcher." One comparison will illustrate the power of the Lee legend. Union casualties in the assault at Cold Harbor on June 3, 1864, numbered seven thousand in less than an hour. More than anything else, this attack gave Grant his reputation as a butcher. By a remarkable coincidence, Confederate casualties in Pickett's assault at Gettysburg also totaled seven thousand in less than an hour. This was a 50 percent casualty rate—compared with 15 percent for Union troops at Cold Harbor. Yet Pickett's charge has been celebrated in legend and history as the ultimate act of Southern honor and courage against the Yankee Goliath, while Cold Harbor symbolizes callous stupidity. The Lee legend has indeed romanticized some harsh realities.

But this is not to endorse Nolan's main point that Lee's offensive strategy lost a war he might otherwise have won. It is quite true that the Confederacy had a chance to win the war—not by conquering the North or destroying its armies, but by sapping the Northern will and capacity to conquer the South and destroy Confederate armies. On three occasions the Confederacy came close to winning on these terms. Each time it was Lee who almost pulled it off. His victories at the Seven Days' and second Manassas battles and the invasion of Maryland in the summer of 1862; his triumph at Chancellorsville and the invasion of Pennsylvania in 1863; and the casualties his army inflicted on Grant's forces in the Wilderness-Petersburg campaign in the spring and summer of 1864, plus Jubal Early's raid to the outskirts of Washington itself—these three campaigns each came close

9. *Ibid.*, p. 106.

to sapping the Northern will to continue the war. The battles of Antietam and Gettysburg forced Lee to retreat from Maryland and Pennsylvania; Sherman's capture of Atlanta and Sheridan's victories over Early in the Shenandoah Valley turned Northern morale around in 1864. Thus Lee's strategy in the end failed to win the war. But the point is that of all Confederate commanders, Lee was the only one whose victories had some potential for winning the war. The notion that a more gradual strategy would have done better is speculative at best. The one Confederate general who did adopt such a strategy, Joseph E. Johnston, might well have yielded Richmond in the summer of 1862 had Lee not replaced him; Johnston failed to raise the siege of Vicksburg in 1863; and he probably would have lost Atlanta in July 1864 had Jefferson Davis not relieved him of command.

Whatever the historical jury's decision may be on Nolan's other indictments of Lee, it must declare him innocent of the most serious charge. Nolan's chapter entitled "The Price of Honor" maintains that by August 1863, after Gettysburg and Vicksburg, or at the latest by June 1864, when his army was pinned in the trenches before Petersburg and Richmond, Lee recognized—or should have recognized—that the war was lost. Thus every man killed or maimed, every farm or factory destroyed, every widow and orphan created during the last twenty or ten months of the war was Lee's responsibility. He had the same authority to surrender, writes Nolan, "anywhere from twenty to five months prior to April 9, 1865 . . . as he had on April 9." Yet he fought on "in the absence of any rational purpose" except to salvage the South's honor as well as "Lee's personal sense of honor. . . . There is, of course, a nobility and poignancy, a romance, in the tragic and relentless pursuit of a hopeless cause. But in practical terms" it meant another two or three hundred thousand dead.[10]

Not guilty. The Confederacy's cause was not hopeless after Get-

10. *Ibid.,* pp. 122, 129, 126.

tysburg or at any other time before Lincoln's reelection in November 1864. To suggest otherwise is inconsistent with Nolan's own challenge to the thesis of inevitable Union victory. The idea that Lee should have surrendered a still-potent army seems perverse. Lee's surrender in 1863 or 1864 would not have ended the war, because the Confederate government, most of its people, and indeed most of the soldiers themselves were determined to fight on. As it was, the war continued for seven weeks after Appomattox until Jefferson Davis was captured and other Confederate armies had surrendered.

Although not all of Nolan's arguments are persuasive, his book is one of the most stimulating revisionist studies of the Civil War to have appeared in many years. It is also full of unconscious irony— that is, the themes are ironic, though Nolan's approach is not. We have Lee the professed Unionist and emancipationist fighting for disunion and slavery; Lee the general who won more battles than almost any other but lost the war; Lee the humane Christian who caused untold death and sorrow. But the central irony of Lee's career is missing from the book. When he took command of the Army of Northern Virginia in June 1862, the Confederacy was on the verge of collapse. In the previous four months it had experienced crucial military defeats in Kentucky, Tennessee, Arkansas, Louisiana, and North Carolina; it had lost its largest city, New Orleans, much of the Mississippi Valley, and most of Tennessee; McClellan's Army of the Potomac had moved to within five miles of Richmond, where the Confederate government at one point had packed the archives and treasury on special trains to evacuate the capital. Within three months Lee's offensives had taken the Confederacy off the floor at the count of nine and had driven Union forces onto the ropes. Without Lee the Confederacy might have died in 1862. But slavery would have survived; the South would have suffered only limited death and destruction. Lee's victories prolonged the war until it destroyed slavery, the plantation economy, the wealth and infrastructure of the region, and virtually everything else the Confederacy stood for. That was the profound irony of Lee's military genius.

11

GRANT'S FINAL VICTORY

"WHEN I PUT MY PEN TO PAPER I DID NOT KNOW THE FIRST WORD that I should make use of in writing the terms. I only knew what was in my mind, and I wished to express it clearly, so that there could be no mistaking it."[1] So wrote Ulysses S. Grant in the summer of 1885, a few weeks before he died of throat cancer. He was describing the scene in Wilmer McLean's parlor at Appomattox Court House twenty years earlier, when he had started to write the formal terms for the surrender of the Army of Northern Virginia. But he could have been describing his feelings in July 1884, as he sat down to write the first of three articles for *Century* magazine's "Battles and Leaders" series on the Civil War.

These articles were subsequently incorporated into Grant's *Personal Memoirs,* two volumes totaling nearly three hundred thousand words written in a race against the painful death that the author knew would soon overtake him. The result was a military narrative that Mark Twain in 1885 and Edmund Wilson in 1962 judged to be

1. *Personal Memoirs of U. S. Grant,* 2 vols. (New York, 1885–1886), II, 492.

the best work of its kind since Julius Caesar's *Commentaries,* and that John Keegan in 1987 pronounced "the most revelatory autobiography of high command to exist in any language."[2]

Grant would have been astonished by this praise. He had resisted earlier attempts to persuade him to write his memoirs, declaring that he had little to say and less literary ability to say it. There is no reason to doubt his sincerity in this conviction. Grant had always been loath to speak in public and equally reluctant to consider writing for the public. As president of the United States from 1869 to 1877, he had confined his communications to formal messages, proclamations, and executive orders drafted mainly by subordinates.

In 1880, after a post-presidential trip around the world, Grant bought a brownstone in New York and settled down at age fifty-eight to a comfortable retirement. He invested his life's savings in a brokerage partnership of his son and Frederick Ward, a Wall Street high roller. Ward made a paper fortune in speculative ventures, some of them illegal. In 1884 this house of cards collapsed with a crash that sent Ward to jail and left Grant with $180 in cash and $150,000 in debts.

It was then that he overcame his literary shyness and accepted a commission to write three articles for the *Century.* They revealed a talent for lucid prose, and although the three thousand dollars he earned for them would not begin to pay his debts, it would at least pay the bills.

While working on the articles, however, Grant experienced growing pain in his throat. It was diagnosed in October 1884 as cancer, incurable and fatal. Grant accepted the verdict with the same outward calm and dignity that had marked his response to earlier misfortunes and triumphs alike. To earn more money for his family, he almost accepted an offer from the *Century* of the standard 10 percent

2. Edmund Wilson, *Patriotic Gore: Studies in the Literature of the American Civil War* (New York, 1962), p. 132; John Keegan, *The Mask of Command* (New York, 1987), p. 202.

royalty for his memoirs. But his friend Mark Twain, angry at being exploited by publishers, had formed his own publishing company, and he persuaded Grant to sign up with him for 70 percent of the net proceeds of sales by subscription. It was one of the few good financial decisions Grant ever made. The *Personal Memoirs* earned $450,000 for his family after his death, which came just days after he completed the final chapter.

Grant's indomitability in his battle against this grim deadline attracted almost as much attention and admiration as his victory over rebellion twenty years earlier. Both were triumphs of will and determination, of a clarity of conception and simplicity of execution that made a hard task look easy. To read Grant's memoirs with a knowledge of the circumstances in which he wrote them is to gain insight into the reasons for his military success.

In April 1885, when Grant had written a bit more than half the narrative—through the November 1863 battles of Chattanooga—he suffered a severe hemorrhage that left him apparently dying. But by an act of will, and with the help of cocaine for the pain, he recovered and returned to work. The chapters on the campaign from the Wilderness to Petersburg, written during periods of intense suffering and sleepless nights, bear witness to these conditions. The narrative becomes bogged down in details; digressions and repetition creep into the text. Just as the Union cause had reached a nadir in August 1864, with Grant blocked at Petersburg and Sherman seemingly frustrated before Atlanta while war-weariness and defeatism in the North seemed sure to vanquish Lincoln in the presidential election, so did Grant's narrative flounder in these chapters.

As Grant's health temporarily improved in the late spring of 1885, so did the terse vigor of his prose. He led the reader through Sherman's capture of Atlanta and his marches through Georgia and the Carolinas, Sheridan's victories in the Shenandoah Valley, and the Army of the Potomac's campaign to Appomattox. These final chapters pulsate with the same energy that animated Union armies as they delivered their knockout blows in the winter and spring of

1864–1865. Just as he had controlled the far-flung Union armies by telegraph during those final campaigns, Grant once again had the numerous threads of his narrative under control as he brought the story to its climax in Wilmer McLean's parlor.

Grant's strength of will, his determination to do the best he could with what he had, his refusal to give up or to complain about the cruelty of fate, help explain the success of both his generalship and his memoirs. These qualities were by no means common among Civil War generals. Many of them spent more time and energy clamoring for reinforcements or explaining why they could not do what they were ordered to do than they did in trying to carry out their orders. Their memoirs are full of self-serving excuses for failure, which was always somebody else's fault.

Early in his memoirs Grant described General Zachary Taylor, under whom he had served as a twenty-four-year-old lieutenant in the Mexican War. Taylor's little army won three battles against larger Mexican forces. Fearing that the general was becoming too popular and might win the Whig presidential nomination, Democratic president James K. Polk transferred most of Taylor's troops (including Grant's regiment) to General Winfield Scott's campaign against Mexico City. This left Taylor with only a handful of veterans and a few raw volunteer regiments. Nevertheless, he won the battle of Buena Vista against an army three times larger than his own—and thereby ensured his election as the next president. Grant wrote nearly forty years later:

> General Taylor was not an officer to trouble the administration much with his demands, but was inclined to do the best he could with the means given him. . . . If he had thought that he was sent to perform an impossibility with the means given him, he would probably have informed the authorities of his opinion and . . . have gone on and done the best he could with the means at hand without parading his grievance before the public. No soldier could face either danger or

responsibility more calmly than he. These are qualities more rarely found than genius or physical courage.[3]

Whether subconsciously or not, with these words Grant described himself as much as he described Taylor. Old Zack became a role model for young Ulysses. "General Taylor never made any show or parade either of uniform or retinue." Neither did Grant when he was commanding general. "In dress he was possibly too plain, rarely wearing anything in the field to indicate his rank." Nor did Grant. "But he was known to every soldier in his army, and was respected by all." The same was true of Grant in the next war. "Taylor was not a conversationalist." Neither was Grant. "But on paper he could put his meaning so plainly that there could be no mistaking it. He knew how to express what he wanted to say in the fewest well-chosen words, but would not sacrifice meaning to the construction of high-sounding sentences."[4] This describes Grant's prose perfectly, his memoirs as well as his wartime orders to subordinates.

This question of "plain meaning" is no small matter. There are many Civil War examples of vague, ambiguous, confusing orders that affected the outcome of a campaign or battle in unfortunate ways. Grant's orders, by contrast, were invariably clear and concise. Many of his wartime associates commented on this. George G. Meade's chief of staff wrote that "there is one striking feature of Grant's orders; no matter how hurriedly he may write them on the field, no one ever has the slightest doubt as to their meaning, or even has to read them over a second time to understand them."[5]

Unlike many other generals, Grant did not rely on staff officers to draft his orders and dispatches; he wrote them himself. Horace Porter of General George Thomas's staff first met Grant at Chattanooga in October 1863. After a daylong inspection of the besieged

3. *Personal Memoirs,* I, 99–100.
4. *Ibid.,* 100, 139.
5. Quoted in Keegan, *Mask of Command,* p. 200.

Army of the Cumberland, which was in dire condition, Grant returned to his headquarters and sat down to write. Porter was impressed

> by the manner in which he went to work at his correspondence. . . .
> His work was performed swiftly and uninterruptedly, but without
> any marked display of nervous energy. His thoughts flowed as freely
> from his mind as the ink from his pen; he was never at a loss for an
> expression, and seldom interlined a word or made a material correction.[6]

After a couple of hours, Grant gathered up the dispatches and had them sent by telegraph or courier to every point on the compass from Vicksburg to Washington, giving orders, Porter said, "for the taking of vigorous and comprehensive steps in every direction throughout his new and extensive command." These orders launched the movements that opened a new supply line into Chattanooga, brought in reinforcements, and prepared the Union armies for the campaigns that lifted the sieges of Chattanooga and Knoxville and drove Braxton Bragg's demoralized Army of Tennessee into Georgia after the assault on Missionary Ridge.

Porter, amazed by Grant's "singular mental powers and his rare military qualities," joined Grant's staff and served with him from the Wilderness to Appomattox. His own version of those events, entitled *Campaigning with Grant,* is next in value only to Grant's memoirs as a firsthand account of command decisions in that campaign.

Porter had particularly noticed how Grant never hesitated but wrote steadily, as if the thoughts flowed directly from his mind to the paper. How can this be reconciled with Grant's recollection that when he sat down to write out the surrender terms for Lee's army, he had no idea how to start? How can it be reconciled with his initial reluctance to write his memoirs because he thought he had no

6. Horace Porter, *Campaigning with Grant* (New York, 1897), p. 7.

literary ability? The truth is, as he admitted in his account of writing the surrender terms, "I only knew what was in my mind."

There lies the explanation of Grant's ability as a writer: *He knew what was in his mind.* That is a rare quality in a writer or a general, but a necessary one for literary or military success. Once unlocked by an act of will, the mind poured out the words smoothly.

Grant had another and probably related talent, which might be described as a "topographical memory." He could remember every feature of the terrain over which he traveled, and find his way over it again; he could also look at a map and visualize the features of terrain he had never seen. Horace Porter noted that any map "seemed to become photographed indelibly on his brain, and he could follow its features without referring to it again."[7]

Grant could see in his mind the disposition of troops over thousands of square miles, visualize their relationship to roads and terrain, and know how and where to move them to take advantage of topography. Most important, he could transpose this image into words that could be understood by others—though the modern reader of his memoirs would be well advised to have a set of Civil War maps on hand to match the maps in Grant's head.

During the last stages of his illness, unable to speak, Grant penned a note to his physician: "A verb is anything that signifies to be; to do; to suffer; I signify all three."[8] It is not surprising that he would think of verbs at such a time; they are what give his writing its terse, muscular quality. As agents to translate thought into action, verbs offer a clue to the secret of Grant's military success, which also consisted of translating thought into action. Consider these orders to Sherman early in the Vicksburg campaign:

> You will proceed . . . to Memphis, taking with you one division of your present command. On your arrival at Memphis you will assume

7. *Ibid.,* p. 514; Keegan, *Mask of Command,* p. 213.
8. William S. McFeely, *Grant: A Biography* (New York, 1981), p. 516.

command of all the troops there . . . and organize them into brigades and divisions in your own army. As soon as possible move with them down the river to the vicinity of Vicksburg, and with the cooperation of the gunboat fleet . . . proceed to the reduction of the place.[9]

In the manner of Caesar's *Veni, vidi, vici,* these sentences bristle with verbs of action: "Proceed . . . take . . . assume command . . . organize . . . move . . . proceed to the reduction. . . ." Note also the absence of adverbs and of all but essential adjectives. Grant used these modifiers only when necessary to his meaning. Take, for example, his famous reply to General Simon B. Buckner's request to negotiate terms for the surrender of Fort Donelson: "No terms except an unconditional and immediate surrender can be accepted. I propose to move immediately on your works." Not an excess word here; the three adjectives and single adverb strengthen and clarify the message; the words produce action—they become action.

The will to act, symbolized by the emphasis on active verbs in Grant's writing, illustrates another crucial facet of his generalship— what Grant himself called "moral courage." This was a quality different from and rarer than physical courage. Grant and many other men who became Civil War generals had demonstrated physical courage under fire in the Mexican War as junior officers carrying out the orders of their superiors. Moral courage involved a willingness to make decisions and initiate the orders. Some officers who were physically brave shrank from this responsibility because decision risked error and initiative risked failure.

This was George B. McClellan's defect as a commander; he was afraid to risk his army in an offensive because he might be defeated. He lacked the moral courage to act, to confront that terrible moment of truth, to decide and to risk. Grant, Lee, Jackson, Sheridan, and other victorious Civil War commanders had moral courage; they understood that without risking defeat they could never achieve victory.

Grant describes how he first confronted that moment of truth and

9. *Personal Memoirs,* I, 429.

learned the lesson of moral courage. His initial Civil War command was as colonel of the Twenty-first Illinois. In July 1861 the regiment was ordered to find Tom Harris's rebel guerrilla outfit in Missouri and attack it. Grant recalled:

> My sensations as we approached what I supposed might be "a field of battle" were anything but agreeable. I had been in all the engagements in Mexico that it was possible for one person to be in; but not in command. If some one else had been colonel and I had been lieutenant-colonel I do not think I would have felt any trepidation. . . . As we approached the brow of the hill from which it was expected we could see Harris' camp, and possibly find his men formed ready to meet us, my heart kept getting higher and higher until it felt to me as though it was in my throat.

But when the Twenty-first reached Harris's camp, they found it abandoned. Wrote Grant:

> My heart resumed its place. It occurred to me at once that Harris had been as much afraid of me as I had been of him. This was a view of the question I had never taken before; but it was one I never forgot afterwards. From that event to the close of the war, I never experienced trepidation upon confronting an enemy, though I always felt more or less anxiety. I never forgot that he had as much reason to fear my forces as I had his. The lesson was valuable.[10]

Grant may have taken that lesson too much to heart; he forgot that there were times when he *should* fear the enemy's intentions. This lesson he learned the hard way, at both Fort Donelson and Shiloh. After the failure of the Union gunboats to subdue the Donelson batteries on February 14, 1862, Grant went downriver several miles to consult with Flag Officer Andrew Foote of the gunboat fleet. Grant was therefore absent on the morning of February 15 when the Confederate garrison launched its breakout attack. He con-

10. *Ibid.*, pp. 248–50.

fessed that "when I left the National line to visit Flag-officer Foote, I had no idea that there would be any engagement on land unless I brought it on myself."[11]

It took one more such experience to drive this lesson home. This time it was the Confederate attack at Shiloh on April 6, 1862, when Grant was again absent at his headquarters seven miles downriver. "The fact is," he admitted in the memoirs, "I regarded the campaign we were engaged in as an offensive one and had no idea that the enemy would leave strong intrenchments to take the initiative." Thereafter he had a healthier respect for the enemy's capabilities.[12]

But this attitude never paralyzed him or caused him to yield the initiative. At both Fort Donelson and Shiloh, Grant's recognition that the enemy still had as much reason to fear him as he to fear the enemy enabled him to wrest the initiative away and grasp victory. Upon returning to his troops at Donelson after a fast ride over icy roads, he calmly took charge and re-formed his broken lines. After hearing reports of the morning's fighting, he told a member of his staff: "Some of our men are pretty badly demoralized, but the enemy must be more so, for he has attempted to force his way out, but has fallen back: the one who attacks first now will be victorious and the enemy will have to be in a hurry if he gets ahead of me." Suiting action to words, he ordered a counterattack, drove back and penned in the Confederate forces, and compelled their surrender.[13]

At Shiloh, Grant conducted a fighting fallback until dusk stopped the Confederate advance. His army was crippled, but he knew that the Confederates were just as badly hurt and that he would be reinforced during the night. Thus he replied to one subordinate who advised retreat: "Retreat? No. I propose to attack at daylight and whip them." And he did.[14]

11. *Ibid.,* p. 305.
12. *Ibid.,* p. 333.
13. *Ibid.,* p. 307.
14. Bruce Catton, *Grant Moves South* (Boston, 1960), p. 241.

One of Grant's superstitions, described in the memoirs, was a dread of turning back or retracing his steps once he had set forth on a journey. If he took the wrong road or made a wrong turn, he would go across country or forward to the next turn rather than go back. This superstition reinforced his risk-taking inclination as a military commander. Crucial decisions in the Vicksburg and Wilderness campaigns illustrate this trait.

During the winter of 1862–1863, Grant's river-based campaign against Vicksburg bogged down in the Louisiana and Mississippi swamps. While criticism mounted to an angry crescendo in the North, Grant remained calm and carefully worked out a daring plan: to run the gunboats past Vicksburg, cross his army to the east bank, cut loose from his base and communications, and live off the land while operating in Vicksburg's rear.

This was the highest-risk operation imaginable. Grant's staff and his most trusted subordinates, especially Sherman, opposed the plan. Sherman "expressed his alarm at the move I had ordered," wrote Grant, "saying that I was putting myself in a position voluntarily which an enemy would be glad to manoeuvre a year—or a long time—to get me in." Go back to Memphis, advised Sherman, establish a secure base of supplies, and move against Vicksburg overland, keeping open your communications—in other words, wage an orthodox campaign by the book.

But Grant threw away the book. He was confident his army could live off the land and substitute mobility for secure communications. "The country is already disheartened over the lack of success on the part of our armies," he told Sherman. He went on to explain in the memoirs:

> If we went back as far as Memphis it would discourage the people so much that bases of supplies would be of no use: neither men to hold them nor supplies to put in them would be furnished. The problem for us was to move forward to a decisive victory, or our cause was

lost. No progress was being made in any other field, and we had to go on.[15]

Go on he did, to what military historians almost universally regard as the most brilliant and innovative campaign of the Civil War.

As Grant departed Washington a year later to set forth on what became the campaign from the Wilderness to Appomattox, he told President Lincoln that "whatever happens, there will be no turning back." What happened in the Wilderness, however, might have caused other Northern commanders to turn back; indeed, similar events in the same place had caused Joe Hooker to turn back exactly a year earlier. On May 6, Confederate attacks on both Union flanks drove them back and gave Lee's army the appearance of victory. The next day Grant ordered preparations for a movement. Men in the ranks who had fought the battle of Chancellorsville in these same woods thought it was another retreat. But when they realized that this time they were moving south, the scales fell from their eyes. It was not "another Chancellorsville . . . another skedaddle" after all. "Our spirits rose," wrote a veteran who recalled this moment as a turning point of the war. "We marched free. The men began to sing."[16] When Grant cantered by one corps, the soldiers recognized him and sent up a cheer. For the first time in a Virginia campaign, the Army of the Potomac was staying on the offensive after its initial battle. Nor did it turn back or retrace its steps until Appomattox eleven months later.

Grant did not tell the story of the men cheering him in his memoirs. Though he kept himself at the center of the story, his memoirs exhibit less egotism than is typical of the genre. Grant is generous with praise of other officers (especially Sherman, Sheridan, and

15. *Personal Memoirs,* I, 542–43n.
16. Bruce Catton, *A Stillness at Appomattox* (Garden City, 1957), pp. 91–92; Shelby Foote, *The Civil War: A Narrative. Red River to Appomattox* (New York, 1974), p. 191.

Meade) and sparing with criticism, carping, and backbiting. He is also willing to admit mistakes, most notably: "I have always regretted that the last assault at Cold Harbor was ever made. . . . No advantage whatever was gained to compensate for the heavy loss we sustained."[17]

But Grant did not admit culpability for the heavy Union casualties in the whole campaign of May–June 1864. Nor should he have done so, despite the label of "butcher" and the subsequent analyses of his "campaign of attrition." It did turn out to be a campaign of attrition, but that was by Lee's choice, not Grant's. The Union commander's purpose was to maneuver Lee into an open field for a showdown; Lee's purpose was to prevent this by entrenching an impenetrable line to protect Richmond and his communications. Lee was hoping to hold out long enough and inflict sufficient casualties on attacking Union forces to discourage the people of the North and overturn the Lincoln administration in the 1864 election.

Lee's strategy of attrition almost worked. That it failed in the end was owing mainly to Grant, who stayed the course and turned the attrition factor in his favor. Although Confederates had the advantage of fighting on the defensive most of the time, Grant inflicted almost as high a percentage of casualties on Lee's army as vice versa. Indeed, for the war as a whole, Lee's armies suffered a higher casualty rate than Grant's. Neither commander was a "butcher," but measured by that statistic, Grant deserved the label less than Lee.

On one matter Grant's memoirs are silent: There is not a word about the rumors and speculations concerning his drinking. On this question there continues to be disagreement among historians and biographers. Most of the numerous stories about Grant's drunkenness at one time or another during the war are false. But drinking problems almost certainly underlay his resignation from the army in 1854, and he may have gone on a bender once or twice during the

17. *Personal Memoirs,* II, 276.

war—though never during active military operations. In any event, his silence on the subject probably reflects his sensitivity about it, not his indifference.

That sensitivity is indicated by Grant's curious failure to mention John A. Rawlins in the memoirs except twice in passing and once in a brief paragraph of opaque praise. Yet as his chief of staff, Rawlins was both Grant's alter ego and his conscience. So far as was possible, Rawlins kept him away from the temptations of the bottle. Grant may have been an alcoholic in the modern medical meaning of the term, but that meaning was unknown in his time. Excessive drinking was in those days regarded as a moral defect and was a matter of deep shame among respectable people. Grant himself doubtless so regarded it.

If Grant was an alcoholic, he should have felt pride rather than shame because he overcame his illness to achieve success and fame without the support system of modern medicine and organizations like Alcoholics Anonymous. But lacking our knowledge and perspective, he could not see it that way. His support network consisted mainly of his wife, Julia, and John Rawlins. A happy family man, Grant did not drink when his wife and family were with him. And when they were not, Rawlins guarded him zealously from temptation. Many contemporaries knew this, but to give Rawlins his due in the memoirs would perhaps have seemed a public confession of weakness and shame.

And, of course, the memoirs are about triumph and success—triumph in war, and success in writing the volumes in a race against death. They are military memoirs, which devote only a few pages to Grant's early years and to the years of peace between the Mexican War and the Civil War. Nor do they cover his less than triumphant career after the Civil War. But perhaps this is as it should be. Grant's great contribution to American history was as a Civil War general. In that capacity he did more to shape the future of America than anyone else except Abraham Lincoln. He earned a secure place as one of the great captains of history, an "unheroic" hero, in John Keegan's apt description.[18] Both in their substance and in the circumstances of their writing, the personal memoirs of Ulysses S. Grant offer answers to that perennial question of Civil War historiography: Why did the North win?

18. Keegan, *Mask of Command,* p. 234.

IV

THE
ENDURING
LINCOLN

12

A NEW BIRTH OF FREEDOM

In 1984 I lectured on lincoln's birthday to the lincoln Group of Delaware, one of many similar organizations dedicated to preserving the memory of our sixteenth president. I spoke about Lincoln's leadership in the "Second American Revolution" that abolished slavery and overthrew the power of the planter class. After the talk I agreed to an interview with a Wilmington radio station. The first question the interviewer asked was: "If Lincoln were alive today, what would he do about abortion and the budget deficit?"

This question was my initial encounter with a phenomenon familiar to seasoned Lincoln scholars: the "What Would Lincoln Do" syndrome. I was tempted to answer, as did Senator George Norris when asked in the 1930s what Lincoln would do about the Depression, that "Lincoln would be just like me. He wouldn't know what the hell to do."[1]

More has been written in the English language about Abraham

1. Merrill D. Peterson, *Lincoln in American Memory* (New York, 1994), p. 314.

Lincoln than about anyone else except Jesus of Nazareth and William Shakespeare. Books run the gamut from multivolume biographies to those with titles like *Lincoln Never Smoked a Cigarette* and *Abraham Lincoln on the Coming of the Caterpillar Tractor.* In 1955 the historian David Donald published an astute essay, "Getting Right with Lincoln," which analyzed the compulsion of American public figures to square their own position with what they suppose Lincoln would have done in similar circumstances, or to find a Lincoln quotation that allegedly supports their present view on almost any issue under the sun. And if they cannot find a genuine Lincoln saying, there are plenty of spurious ones to choose from.[2]

Merrill Peterson's *Lincoln in American Memory* provides us with an engaging and encyclopedic chronicle of the numerous ways in which Americans used and misused Lincoln over a period of more than six score years. The book is neither history nor historiography nor cultural criticism, but a combination of all three. Here one can find analyses of serious Lincoln scholarship, popular biographies, novels and plays and movies and inspirational stories for children, Lincoln iconography in sculpture and monuments, Lincoln collectors whose zeal and resources have driven the prices of Lincoln documents to seven figures and forgers who saw their opportunities and took them, partisans ranging from the American Enterprise Institute to Communists and from the Ku Klux Klan to Martin Luther King, Jr., who have conjured up Lincoln's name and blessing.

Peterson does not offer an explicit answer to the big question: Why does Lincoln's image loom so large over our cultural landscape? But he provides a wealth of evidence to help readers tease out answers for themselves. The first—and perhaps most important— clues came in the initial reactions to Lincoln's assassination. That fell deed occurred on Good Friday. Five days earlier, on Palm Sunday, Lincoln had returned in triumph to Washington after a two weeks' visit to the battlefront in Virginia, during which Union forces cap-

2. David Donald, *Lincoln Reconsidered,* 2d ed. (New York, 1961), pp. 3–18.

tured Richmond and caught up with Robert E. Lee's army at Appomattox, forcing its surrender the very day that Lincoln returned to Washington. His supporters did not on that occasion spread palms before him, but on Easter Sunday hundreds of sermons drew the obvious parallel. "Heaven rejoices this Easter morning in the resurrection of our lost leader," said one of New York City's leading clergymen, "dying on the anniversary of our Lord's great sacrifice, a mighty sacrifice himself for the sins of a whole people."[3]

As generations rolled by, the comparisons deepened and broadened. In 1909 Leo Tolstoy called Lincoln "a Christ in miniature, a saint of humanity." Jesus unfolded wisdom for the ages in parables; Lincoln did the same, disguising them as humorous stories. A Muslim leader in the Caucusus said that Lincoln "spoke with a voice of thunder, he laughed like the sunrise and his deeds were as strong as the rock." Rabbi Joseph Silverman of Temple Emanu-El in New York said on Lincoln's birthday in 1910 that "there is no need to preach the precepts of the Bible when we have such a real Messiah, who lived in the flesh and never pretended to be more than a man."[4]

In Walt Whitman's haunting poem *When Lilacs Last in the Dooryard Bloom'd,* the parallel was not to the Messiah but to nature's symbols of the perennial return of springtime and therefore of eternal life: the lilac, the hermit thrush warbling "the carol of death" in spring twilights, and the evening star burning with unusual brightness in the spring sky before falling below the horizon.

> *Ever-returning spring, trinity sure*
> *to me you bring,*
> *Lilac blooming perennial and*
> *drooping star in the west,*
> *And thought of him I love.*

Whatever the image, Lincoln's apotheosis gave him a godlike quality. He became the deity of American civil religion, a Delphic

---

3. Peterson, *Lincoln in American Memory,* p. 8.
4. *Ibid.,* pp. 185, 218.

oracle to whom one can go for a solution to any problem—including abortion and the budget deficit. In 1938 the playwright Robert Sherwood wrote *Abe Lincoln in Illinois,* which opened on Broadway the week of the Munich crisis and became, in Peterson's words, "a tonic to democratic despair." Raymond Massey, who played Lincoln, said in an interview that "if you substitute the word dictatorship for the word slavery throughout Sherwood's script, it becomes electric for our time." A quarter-century later, Jacqueline Kennedy sought comfort in the Lincoln Room of the White House in times of trouble. "The kind of peace I felt in that room was what you feel when going into a church. I used to feel his strength, I'd sort of be talking with him."[5]

Peterson discerns five themes in the apotheosis of Lincoln, themes that occur in serious history as well as in popular culture: Savior of the Union; Great Emancipator; Man of the People; the First American; and the Self-Made Man. "Like the movements of a symphony," writes Peterson, these themes "interpret and reinterpret each other" and all are blended in the grand theme of democratic nationalism, as in Sherwood's play. Peterson does not hammer the themes into the reader's head; rather, he lets them emerge and recur in numerous variations throughout the book, which is organized chronologically beginning with Lincoln's death and culminating in the early 1990s with the publication and translation into Eastern European languages of a collection of Lincoln's writings on democracy sponsored by Governor Mario Cuomo.[6]

The themes of Lincoln as Savior of the Union and as Great Emancipator are of most interest to historians, for they encompass the two great results of Lincoln's leadership in the Civil War. Man of the People and Self-Made Man remain part of popular mythology,

5. *Ibid.,* pp. 322, 324n.
6. *Ibid.,* p. 27; Mario M. Cuomo and Harold Holzer, eds., *Lincoln on Democracy* (New York, 1990); the Polish edition, published in Warsaw, is titled *Lincoln O Demokracji.*

as expressed by the opening sentence of a college student's paper some years ago: "Lincoln was born in a log cabin that he built with his own hands." Essays by high school students in a contest sponsored by the Lincoln Sesquicentennial Commission in 1959 demonstrated a better grasp of chronology, but Lincoln's rise to fame in the face of adversity remained the dominant theme. By 1990, however, the Self-Made Man theme had faded, according to Peterson. He cites a professor at Lincoln Memorial University, founded to help Appalachian youth get ahead, who said that "Lincoln doesn't cut it with these kids any more."[7]

That conclusion may be premature, for the theme appears to be alive and well in essays submitted for another high school contest sponsored by the Farmers' Insurance Group and Huntington Library in connection with the library's 1993–1994 Lincoln exhibit. Lincoln's "accomplishments prove to me that America is the Land of Opportunity if I am willing to work hard and achieve my goals," wrote a student from a tiny town (population 301) in Oklahoma. "I can see by studying Lincoln's life that I should not view my background as an obstacle but as a stepping stone." Another essayist fused the Self-Made Man theme with that of the Great Emancipator in writing of a high school teacher in Bulgaria who learned of Lincoln in the 1950s and inspired his students with a Lincolnian vision of freedom until the government arrested him. One of those students kept the vision alive and escaped to the United States where she became the essayist's mother. "Mr. Lincoln freed my Mother from a slavery to communism; and into this freedom I was born." Both of these essayists are girls.[8]

For black Americans the theme of Great Emancipator has been the most meaningful. Numerous Lincoln sculptures and other kinds of iconography portray the president striking the shackles from a

7. Peterson, *Lincoln in American Memory,* pp. 196, 388.
8. Copies of the essays are in the author's possession.

slave. The Lincoln Memorial in Washington has been the scene of powerful moments in the freedom struggle, most notably Marian Anderson's concert on Easter Sunday 1939 (after the DAR had denied her the use of Constitution Hall) and the March on Washington in 1963. In 1957 Martin Luther King, Jr., led an earlier civil rights pilgrimage to the Lincoln Memorial, where Mahalia Jackson sang "I Been 'Buked and I Been Scorned" with such feeling, wrote Langston Hughes, that "even Abe Lincoln's statue nodded his head." When King stood in front of the crowd of two hundred thousand along the reflecting pool six years later, he began his "I have a dream" speech with the words: "Fivescore years ago, a great American, in whose symbolic shadow we stand today, signed the Emancipation Proclamation. This momentous decree came as a great beacon of hope to millions of Negro slaves who had been scarred in the flame of withering injustice."[9]

But among many African-Americans today, Lincoln's image does not stand tall. They have noted his remarks in the debates with Stephen A. Douglas in 1858 disavowing a belief in racial equality (which white supremacists are wont to quote) and his apparently grudging gradualism on the issue of emancipation during the Civil War. Frederick Douglass had these things in mind when he spoke in 1876 at the dedication of the Freedman's Monument in Washington. "You are the children of Abraham Lincoln," he told whites in the audience. "We are at best his step-children." Douglass, however, had a more realistic appreciation of Lincoln's leadership in the war for the Union than do modern black critics. In the same address, Douglass went on to point out that although Lincoln was "preeminently the white man's President," although "the Union was more to him than our freedom or our future," under "his wise and beneficent rule we saw ourselves gradually lifted from the depths of slavery to the heights of liberty and manhood," we "saw two hundred thousand of our dark and dusky people responding to the call of Abraham

9. Peterson, *Lincoln in American Memory*, pp. 353, 355–56.

Lincoln, and with muskets on their shoulders . . . timing their high footsteps to liberty and union under the national flag." [10]

Lincoln's legacy of positive liberalism went beyond the issue of chattel slavery and its abolition, according to *The Lincoln Persuasion*, by J. David Greenstone. A political scientist who left this study un-completed at his death, Greenstone maintained that Lincoln is the most important figure in the history of American liberalism because he melded its two separate streams, humanistic liberalism and reform liberalism. Humanistic liberalism derived from Thomas Jefferson. It emphasized "the freedom of the individual in forming and attaining individual goals" and sought to mediate "preferences among humans according to a utilitarian calculus." [11] Reform liberalism derived from John Adams and his Puritan forebears. It rejected the moral neutral-ity of humanistic liberalism in favor of policies to encourage and enable human beings to develop their faculties to the highest possi-ble state.

On the issue of temperance, for example, humanistic liberals would mediate competing positions while trying to maximize the broadest possible freedom to drink or not to drink. Reform liberals would seek to discourage drinking in order to free humans from enslavement to alcohol so they could make the most of their faculties.

The touchstone for both kinds of liberalism in the nineteenth cen-tury was slavery. Stephen A. Douglas became the exponent of hu-manistic liberalism with his position of popular sovereignty permit-ting white men in a state or territory to vote slavery up or down. Lincoln, of course, was the spokesman for reform liberalism, which condemned slavery as a moral wrong that must be "placed in the course of ultimate extinction." Liberty was the central tenet of re-form liberalism, Union of humanistic liberalism; Lincoln's great achievement, in Greenstone's view, was to fuse Liberty and Union,

10. *Ibid.*, p. 60; Douglass, *Life and Times of Frederick Douglass* (New York: Collier Books edition, 1962), pp. 484, 486–87.

11. J. David Greenstone, *The Lincoln Persuasion: Remaking American Liberal-ism* (Princeton, 1993), pp. 59, xxv.

giving liberalism a moral imperative that carried into Progressivism, the New Deal, and presumably down to the present.

Greenstone uses the phrases "negative liberty" and "positive liberty" to help clarify his interpretation of the bipolarity of liberalism. Negative liberty can be defined as the absence of restraint, a freedom from interference with individual thought or behavior. A law requiring automobile passengers to wear seat belts is a violation of their negative liberty, which is best described as freedom *from*. Positive liberty can best be understood as freedom *to*—freedom to develop one's faculties because wearing a seat belt has saved one from death or crippling injury.

The analogy of freedom of the press perhaps provides a better illustration. This freedom is generally viewed as a negative liberty— freedom from interference with what a writer writes or a reader reads. But an illiterate person suffers from an absence of positive liberty; he is unable to enjoy the freedom to read or write whatever he pleases not because someone censors it but because he cannot read and write. The remedy lies not in the removal of restraint but in the achievement of capacity. True freedom of the press requires a melding of negative and positive liberty—of humanistic and reform liberalism—through absence of censorship *and* the provision of means for people to achieve literacy.

Negative liberty was the dominant theme in early American history—freedom *from* constraints on individual rights imposed by a powerful state. The Bill of Rights is the classic expression of negative liberty, or Jeffersonian humanistic liberalism. These first ten amendments to the Constitution protect individual liberties by placing a straitjacket of "shall nots" on the federal government. Those strictures, and the corresponding elevation of states' rights into a Southern credo, became a bulwark of slavery—the "liberty of making slaves of other people," as Lincoln once put it sarcastically. In 1861 Southern states invoked the negative liberties of state sovereignty and individual rights of property (i.e., slave property) to break up the United States. Lincoln thereby gained an opportunity to invoke the positive liberty of reform liberalism, exercised through the power of the army and the state, to overthrow the negative liberties of disunion and ownership of slaves. This reform liberalism enabled freed slaves to develop their faculties. If America has not lived up to this promise of reform liberalism, it is not because the foundation is absent from the Constitution. Whereas eleven of the first twelve constitutional amendments severely limited the power of the national government, six of the next seven vastly expanded those powers and contained the significant phrase "Congress *shall have* the power to enforce this article." The first three post–Civil War amendments abolished slavery and extended equal civil and political rights to freed slaves and their descendants. This achievement combined negative and positive liberty by removing slavery's restraints on black people and conferring on them the liberties guaranteed in the Bill of Rights.

The most eloquent expression of the new birth of freedom brought forth by reform liberalism is the Gettysburg Address. This brief speech "remade America," according to Garry Wills's striking and original interpretation of the Gettysburg Address.[12] Many Americans have committed Lincoln's 272-word address to memory during their school days. But like the Apostles' Creed, recited in unison every Sunday morning by millions of Christians, the Gettysburg Address is more often iterated than understood. Whole libraries of theology undergird the meaning of the Apostles' Creed; generations of American political philosophy and experience lay behind the Gettysburg Address. A rich mythology has grown up around this mythic moment in American history; shelves of serious monographs, many of them devoted to puncturing the myths, have also proliferated on every aspect of the Gettysburg Address, from the question of where Lincoln stood when he delivered it to the deepest meaning of each phrase. Of all these studies, Garry Wills's *Lincoln at Gettys-*

12. Garry Wills, *Lincoln at Gettysburg: The Words That Remade America* (New York, 1992).

burg is the best. In precision and economy of language it emulates Lincoln's masterpiece.

Wills dispels some of the curiously persistent myths about the occasion. The invitation to Lincoln to speak at the ceremony dedicating this first cemetery for Union war dead was not an insulting afterthought; Lincoln did not write his speech on the back of an envelope during the train ride to Gettysburg; Edward Everett's two-hour oration did not leave the crowd so bored and restless that it paid no attention to Lincoln; Lincoln's tenor speaking voice had great carrying power, and he could be heard clearly by the ten or fifteen thousand people in the audience (estimates of attendance vary); the speech did not fall flat on the ears and minds of contemporaries, only to be revived and appreciated by later generations.

But all of these matters form the prologue to Wills's thematic chapters, which trace the roots and analyze the meaning of both form and substance of the Gettysburg Address. Two of these chapters in particular are a stunning tour de force. "Oratory of the Greek Revival" compares the occasion at Gettysburg with classical funeral oratory—notably Pericles' famous funeral speech at Athens in 531 B.C. The initial emphasis of this chapter is not on Lincoln but on Edward Everett. The most renowned orator of the age, Everett had been a professor of Greek literature at Harvard, president of that institution, congressman, governor, senator, minister to the Court of St. James, and secretary of state. Everett helped promote the Greek revival in American culture during the first half of the nineteenth century, when American public buildings and private homes sprouted Doric columns and dozens of frontier villages named themselves Athens, Troy, Sparta, or Syracuse. While studying at Göttingen for the first Ph.D. earned there by an American, Everett "went to Greece, to walk over the battlefields where the first democracy of the West won its freedom. He returned to America convinced that a new Athens was rising here."[13]

13. *Ibid.,* p. 44.

Everett modeled *his* Gettysburg Address on the themes of Greek drama as well as funeral orations. By conventional standards he succeeded. In their biography of Lincoln, the president's private secretaries John Nicolay and John Hay praised Everett's oration as "worthy alike of his own fame and the extraordinary occasion. . . . It is not too much to say that for the space of two hours he held his listeners spell-bound by the rare power of his art."[14] But no one today quotes Everett's Gettysburg Address. "As Aeschylus had used the gods to explain Athenian ideals to the Athenians," writes Wills, Everett "would use Greek ideals to explain America to Americans. That he failed is no disgrace, given the height of his aspiration. What is amazing, and can seem almost like a joke of the gods themselves, is that where he failed Lincoln succeeded."[15]

But whence came this "Periclean effect" that made Lincoln's speech "at least as famous as the Athenian's"? Lincoln had no Latin and even less Greek. The sum total of his formal education consisted of fewer than twelve months in the frontier "blab schools" of his day. Wills cannot trace any direct effect of Greek revival culture on Lincoln—except to note, rather vaguely, that the additions he made to his house in Springfield "were in the Greek Revival style." Lincoln studied Euclid's geometry on his own, as he studied grammar in a quest for Euclidean precision and logic in his literary style. Lincoln "was an artist, not just a scholar. Classicism of Everett's sort looks backward; but the classic *artifact* sets standards for the future. . . . Lincoln's Address created a political prose for America, to rank with the vernacular excellence of Twain." Thus it was that Lincoln "sensed, from his own developed artistry, the demands that bring forth classic art—compression, grasp of the essential, balance, ideality."[16]

If Lincoln's artistry was original, the Gettysburg Address never-

14. John G. Nicolay and John Hay, *Abraham Lincoln: A History,* 10 vols. (New York, 1890), VIII, 191–92.

15. Wills, *Lincoln at Gettysburg,* p. 52.

16. *Ibid.*

theless bears striking parallels with the classical model. Greek prose was characterized by antithesis; so was Lincoln's. The following polarities in the Gettysburg Address are also present in Pericles' funeral oration and in other surviving Epitaphioi:

1. *Mortal and immortal.* The soldiers' lives were cut short but their work will live forever: "those who here gave their lives" so that the nation "shall not perish from the earth."

2. *Athenians and others.* America, too, was different: "a new nation, conceived in Liberty, and dedicated to the proposition that all men are created equal."

3. *Word and deed.* The words of an oration cannot match the deeds of fallen heroes: "The world will little note, nor long remember, what we say here, but it can never forget what they did here."

4. *Teachers and taught.* By their deaths, those who fell in the war with Sparta taught the polis to live: "from these honored dead we take increased devotion to that cause for which they gave the last full measure of devotion."

5. *Choice and determination.* The necessity of death for the life of the nation is contrasted to the heroes' choice to risk their lives: "that cause for which they *gave* the last full measure of devotion."

6. *Past and present.* "Four score and seven years ago, our fathers brought forth . . . Now we are engaged in a great civil war. . . . It is rather for us to be here dedicated to the unfinished work remaining before us."

7. *Life and death.* This is the greatest polarity, the principal antithesis that subsumes the others in Lincoln's address as in the Epitaphioi. The antithesis in the Gettysburg Address follows a birth/death/rebirth cycle:

> Four score and seven years ago, our fathers *brought forth* on this continent a new nation, *conceived* in Liberty. . . .
>
> We have come to dedicate a portion of that field, as a final resting place for those who *gave their lives* that the nation might *live.* . . .

> We here highly resolve that these *dead* shall not have *died in vain*—
> that this nation, under God, shall have a *new birth* of freedom.

Thus, according to Wills, "The largest contrasts of existence are focused on one moment of history. . . . The Address does what all great art accomplishes. Like Keats's Grecian urn, it 'tease[s] us out of thought/As doth eternity.'"[17] What is that ultimate meaning? Wills's chapter "The Transcendental Declaration" comes closest to teasing it out. Here the dominant motif is not the classicism of the Greek revival but the romantic idealism of transcendentalism, a philosophy that measured the real by its relationship to the ideal, a product of the mind that transcends reality. In this chapter Theodore Parker, like Everett a Massachusetts intellectual, is Lincoln's unconscious mentor and foil.

Lincoln's law partner William Herndon was a devoted follower of Parker; Herndon persuaded Lincoln to read some of the works of that militant transcendentalist and antislavery leader. Parker's idealism had a distinctly patriotic component; its text was the Declaration of Independence, "the American ideal" by which the reality of history was to be measured. Both Parker and Lincoln regarded the Declaration that all men are created equal as an ideal on which the United States was founded. That ideal was not a reality in Jefferson's time, nor was it in Parker's and Lincoln's time. But for Lincoln that did not diminish its transcendent truth, or the duty of Americans to bring their institutions progressively closer to that truth. The Founders "did not mean to assert the obvious untruth that all were then actually enjoying that equality," said Lincoln in 1857.

> They meant to set up a standard maxim for free society, which should
> be familiar to all, and revered by all, constantly looked to, constantly
> labored for, and even though never perfectly attained, constantly ap-
> proximated, and thereby constantly spreading and deepening its in-

17. *Ibid.*, p. 62.

fluence, and augmenting the happiness and value of life to all people of all colors everywhere.[18]

The Declaration proclaimed equal liberty; the Constitution sanctioned slavery; Lincoln's political philosophy envisioned the convergence of these founding charters until the ideal became real. That is why Stephen A. Douglas's Kansas-Nebraska Act in 1854 propelled Lincoln back into the political maelstrom that elected him president six years later. By legalizing the expansion of slavery, the Kansas-Nebraska Act reversed the promised course of American history, Lincoln said, and defiled the ideal of the Founders. "The spirit of seventy-six and the spirit of [Kansas-]Nebraska, are utter antagonisms," said Lincoln in his remarkable Peoria speech of 1854, which anticipated the central theme of the Gettysburg Address.

> Little by little . . . we have been giving up the OLD for the NEW faith. Near eighty years ago we began by declaring that all men are created equal, but now from that beginning we have run down to the other declaration, that for SOME men to enslave OTHERS is a "sacred right of self-government." These principles can not stand together. . . . Our republican robe is soiled, and trailed in the dust. Let us re-purify it. . . . Let us re-adopt the Declaration of Independence, and with it, the practices, and policy, which harmonize with it. . . . If we do this, we shall not only have saved the Union; but we shall have so saved it, as to make, and to keep it, forever worthy of the saving.[19]

The great achievement of the Gettysburg Address, Wills maintains, was to bring America a giant step closer to the ideal affirmed by the Declaration. It reshaped a Constitution that permitted slavery, squaring it with a Declaration that proclaimed liberty; this was the "new birth of freedom." Thus "the Gettysburg Address has become an authoritative expression of the American spirit," wrote Wills, "as

18. Roy P. Basler et al., eds., *The Collected Works of Abraham Lincoln,* 9 vols. (New Brunswick, N.J., 1952–1955), II, 405–6.

19. *Ibid.,* II, 275–76.

authoritative as the Declaration itself, and perhaps even more influential, since it determines how we read the Declaration. For most people now, the Declaration means what Lincoln told us it means, as a way of correcting the Constitution itself without overthrowing it." That is why Wills subtitled his book *The Words That Remade America*. The thousands who heard Lincoln at Gettysburg

> departed with a new thing in [their] intellectual baggage, that new constitution Lincoln had substituted for the one they brought there with them. They walked off from those curving graves on the hillside, under a changed sky, into a different America.[20]

Different, to be sure, but in some ways not so different after all. A century after the Gettysburg Address, Martin Luther King, Jr., entreated John F. Kennedy to issue "a Second Emancipation Proclamation to free all Negroes from second-class citizenship. . . . We believe you, like Abraham Lincoln before you, stand at a historic crossroads in the life and conscience of our nation."[21] Kennedy's successor and Congress finally took action. The new birth of freedom, the positive liberty invoked by Lincoln in the 1860s, finally reached fruition in the 1960s. But in the 1990s the spirit of negative liberty, stripped of its humanistic liberalism, has forged into renewed prominence. Lincoln's melding of humanistic liberalism and reform liberalism is in danger of being rent in twain by the party he helped to found and which he led to victory in 1860.

20. Wills, *Lincoln at Gettysburg*, pp. 146–47, 38.
21. Peterson, *Lincoln in American Memory*, p. 354.

13

WHO FREED THE SLAVES?

IF WE WERE TO GO OUT ON THE STREETS OF ALMOST ANY TOWN in America and ask the question posed by the title of this essay, probably nine out of ten respondents would answer unhesitatingly, "Abraham Lincoln." Most of them would cite the Emancipation Proclamation as the key document. Some of the more reflective and better informed respondents would add the Thirteenth Amendment and point to Lincoln's important role in its adoption. And a few might qualify their answer by noting that without Union military victory the Emancipation Proclamation and Thirteenth Amendment would never have gone into effect, or at least would not have applied to the states where most of the slaves lived. But, of course, Lincoln was commander in chief of Union armies, so the credit for their victories would belong mainly to him. The answer would still be the same: Lincoln freed the slaves.

In recent years, though, this answer has been challenged as another example of elitist history, of focusing only on the actions of great white males and ignoring the actions of the overwhelming majority of the people, who also make history. If we were to ask our question of professional historians, the reply would be quite different. For one thing, it would not be simple or clear-cut. Many of them would answer along the lines of "On the one hand . . . but on the other. . . ." They would speak of ambivalence, ambiguity, nuances, paradox, irony. They would point to Lincoln's gradualism, his slow and apparently reluctant decision for emancipation, his revocation of emancipation orders by Generals John C. Frémont and David Hunter, his exemption of border states and parts of the Confederacy from the Emancipation Proclamation, his statements seemingly endorsing white supremacy. They would say that the whole issue is more complex than it appears—in other words many historians, as is their wont, would not give a straight answer to the question.

But of those who did, a growing number would reply, as did a historian speaking to the Civil War Institute at Gettysburg College in 1991: "THE SLAVES FREED THEMSELVES."[1] They saw the Civil War as a potential war for abolition well before Lincoln did. By flooding into Union military camps in the South, they forced the issue of emancipation on the Lincoln administration. By creating a situation in which Northern officials would either have to return them to slavery or acknowledge their freedom, these "contrabands," as they came to be called, "acted resolutely to place their freedom—and that of their posterity—on the wartime agenda." Union officers, then Congress, and finally Lincoln decided to confiscate this human property belonging to the enemy and put it to work for the Union in the form of servants, teamsters, laborers, and eventually soldiers in Northern armies. Weighed in the scale of war, these 190,000 black soldiers and sailors (and probably a larger number of black army laborers) tipped the balance in favor of Union victory. Even deep in the Confederate interior remote from the fighting fronts, with the departure of masters and overseers to the army, "leaving women and old men in charge, the balance of power gradually shifted in favor

1. Robert F. Engs, "The Great American Slave Rebellion," lecture delivered to the Civil War Institute at Gettysburg College, June 27, 1991, p. 3.

of slaves, undermining slavery on farms and plantations far from the line of battle."[2]

One of the leading exponents of the black self-emancipation thesis is the historian and theologian Vincent Harding, whose book *There Is a River: The Black Struggle for Freedom in America* has become almost a Bible for the argument. "While Lincoln continued to hesitate about the legal, constitutional, moral, and military aspects of the matter," Harding writes, "the relentless movement of the self-liberated fugitives into the Union lines" soon "approached and surpassed every level of force previously known. . . . Making themselves an unavoidable military and political issue . . . this overwhelming human movement . . . of self-freed men and women . . . took their freedom into their own hands." The Emancipation Proclamation, when it finally and belatedly came, merely "confirmed and gave ambiguous legal standing to the freedom which black people had already claimed through their own surging, living proclamations."[3]

During the 1980s this self-emancipation theme achieved the status of orthodoxy among social historians. The largest scholarly enterprise on the history of emancipation and the transition from a slave to a free society during the Civil War era, the Freedmen and Southern Society project at the University of Maryland, stamped its imprimatur on the interpretation. The slaves, wrote the editors of this project, were "the prime movers in securing their own liberty." The Columbia University historian Barbara J. Fields gave wide publicity to this thesis. On camera in the PBS television documentary *The Civil War* and in an essay in the lavishly illustrated volume accompanying the series, she insisted that "freedom did not come to the slaves from words on paper, either the words of Congress or those of the Presi-

2. Ira Berlin, Barbara J. Fields, Thavolia Glymph, Joseph P. Reidy, and Leslie S. Rowland, eds., *Freedom: A Documentary History of Emancipation 1861–1867*, Ser. I, Vol. I, *The Destruction of Slavery* (Cambridge, 1985), pp. 2, 10.

3. Vincent Harding, *There Is a River: The Black Struggle for Freedom in America* (New York, 1981), pp. 231, 230, 225, 226, 228, 235.

dent," but "from the initiative of the slaves" themselves. "It was they who taught the nation that it must place the abolition of slavery at the head of its agenda. . . . The slaves themselves had to make their freedom real."[4]

Two important corollaries of the self-emancipation thesis are the arguments, first, that Lincoln hindered more than he helped the cause, and second, that the image of him as the Great Emancipator is a myth created by whites to deprive blacks of credit for achieving their own freedom. This "reluctant ally of black freedom," wrote Vincent Harding, "played an actively conservative role in a situation which . . . needed to be pushed toward its most profound revolutionary implications." Lincoln repeatedly "placed the preservation of the white Union above the death of black slavery"; even as late as August 1862, when he wrote his famous letter to Horace Greeley stating that "if I could save the Union without freeing *any* slave, I would do it," he was "still trapped in his own obsession with saving the white Union at all costs, even the cost of continued black slavery." By exempting one-third of the South from the Emancipation Proclamation, wrote Barbara Fields, "Lincoln was more determined to retain the goodwill of the slaveowners than to secure the liberty of the slaves." Despite Lincoln, though, "no human being alive could have held back the tide that swept toward freedom" by 1863.[5]

Nevertheless, lamented Vincent Harding, "while the concrete historical realities of the time testified to the costly, daring, courageous activities of hundreds of thousands of black people breaking loose from slavery and setting themselves free, the myth gave the credit for this freedom to a white Republican president." University of Pennsylvania historian Robert Engs goes even farther; he thinks the "fiction" that " 'Massa Lincoln' freed the slaves" was a sort of tacit

4. Berlin et al., eds., *The Destruction of Slavery*, p. 3; Barbara J. Fields, "Who Freed the Slaves?" in Geoffrey C. Ward with Ric Burns and Ken Burns, *The Civil War: An Illustrated History* (New York, 1990), pp. 181, 179.

5. Harding, *There Is a River*, pp. 254, 216, 223; Fields, "Who Freed the Slaves?" in Ward et al., *The Civil War*, pp. 179, 181.

conspiracy among whites to convince blacks that "white America, personified by Abraham Lincoln, had *given* them their freedom [rather] than allow them to realize the *empowerment* that their taking of it implied. The poor, uneducated freedman fell for that masterful propaganda stroke. But so have most of the rest of us, black and white, for over a century!"[6]

How valid are these statements? First, we must recognize the considerable degree of truth in the main thesis. By coming into Union lines, by withdrawing their labor from Confederate owners, by working for the Union army and fighting as soldiers in it, slaves did play an active part in achieving their own freedom and, for that matter, in preserving the Union. Like workers, immigrants, women, and other nonelites, slaves were neither passive victims nor pawns of powerful white males who loom so large in our traditional image of American history. They too played a part in determining their own destiny; they too made a history that historians have finally discovered. That is all to the good. But by challenging the "myth" that Lincoln freed the slaves, proponents of the self-emancipation thesis are in danger of creating another myth—that he had little to do with it. It may turn out, upon close examination, that the traditional answer to the question "Who Freed the Slaves?" is closer to being the right answer than is the new and currently more fashionable answer.

First, one must ask what was the sine qua non of emancipation in the 1860s—the essential condition, the one thing without which it would not have happened. The clear answer is the war. Without the Civil War there would have been no confiscation act, no Emancipation Proclamation, no Thirteenth Amendment (not to mention the Fourteenth and Fifteenth), certainly no self-emancipation, and almost certainly no end of slavery for several more decades at least. Slavery had existed in North America for more than two centuries before 1861, but except for a tiny fraction of slaves who fought in

6. Harding, *There Is a River,* p. 236; Engs, "The Great American Slave Rebellion," p. 13.

the Revolution, or escaped, or bought their freedom, there had been no self-emancipation during that time. Every slave insurrection or insurrection conspiracy failed in the end. On the eve of the Civil War, plantation agriculture was more profitable, slavery more entrenched, slave owners more prosperous, and the "slave power" more dominant within the South if not in the nation at large than it had ever been. Without the war, the door to freedom would have remained closed for an indeterminate length of time.

What brought the war and opened that door? The answer, of course, is complex as well as controversial. A short and simplified summary is that secession and the refusal of the United States government to recognize the legitimacy of secession brought on the war. In both of these matters Abraham Lincoln moves to center stage. Seven states seceded and formed the Confederacy because he won election to the presidency on an antislavery platform; four more seceded after shooting broke out when he refused to evacuate Fort Sumter; the shooting escalated to full-scale war because he called out the troops to suppress rebellion. The common denominator in all of the steps that opened the door to freedom was the active agency of Abraham Lincoln as antislavery political leader, president-elect, president, and commander in chief.

The statement quoted above, that Lincoln "placed the preservation of the white Union above the death of black slavery," while true in a narrow sense, is highly misleading when shorn of its context. From 1854, when he returned to politics, until nominated for president in 1860, the dominant, unifying theme of Lincoln's career was opposition to the expansion of slavery as the vital first step toward placing it in the course of ultimate extinction. A student of Lincoln's oratory has estimated that he gave 175 political speeches during those six years. The "central message" of these speeches showed Lincoln to be a "one-issue" man—the issue being slavery. Over and over again, Lincoln denounced slavery as a "monstrous injustice," "an unqualified evil to the negro, to the white man, to the soil, and to the State." He attacked his main political rival, Stephen A. Douglas, for his "*declared* indifference" to the moral wrong of slavery. Douglas "*looks to no end of the institution of slavery,*" said Lincoln.

> That is the real issue. That is the issue that will continue in this country when these poor tongues of Judge Douglas and myself shall be silent. It is the eternal struggle between these two principles—right and wrong—throughout the world. . . . One is the common right of humanity and the other the divine right of kings. . . . No matter in what shape it comes, whether from the mouth of a king who seeks to bestride the people of his own nation and live by the fruit of their labor, or from one race of men as an apology for enslaving another race, it is the same tyrannical principle.[7]

Southerners read Lincoln's speeches; they knew by heart his words about the house divided and the ultimate extinction of slavery. Lincoln's election in 1860 was a sign that they had lost control of the national government; if they remained in the Union, they feared that ultimate extinction of their way of life would be their destiny. That is why they seceded. It was not merely Lincoln's election but his election as a *principled opponent of slavery on moral grounds* that precipitated secession. Militant abolitionists critical of Lincoln for falling short of their own standard nevertheless recognized this truth. No longer would the slave power rule the nation, said Frederick Douglass. "Lincoln's election has vitiated their authority, and broken their power."[8] Without Lincoln's election, Southern states would not have seceded in 1861, the war would not have come when and as it did, the door of emancipation would not have been opened as it was. Here was an event that qualifies as a sine qua non, and it proceeded more from the ideas and agency of Abraham Lincoln than from any other single cause.

But, we must ask, would not the election of *any* Republican in

7. Waldo W. Braden, *Abraham Lincoln: Public Speaker* (Baton Rouge, 1988), pp. 35–36; Roy P. Basler, ed., *The Collected Works of Abraham Lincoln,* 9 vols. (New Brunswick, N.J., 1953–1955), II, 255, III, 92, 315.

8. *Douglass' Monthly,* Dec. 1860.

1860 have provoked secession? Probably not, if the candidate had been Edward Bates—who might conceivably have won the election but had no chance of winning the nomination. Yes, almost certainly, if William H. Seward had been the nominee. Seward's earlier talk of a "higher law" and an "irrepressible conflict" had given him a more radical reputation than Lincoln. But Seward might not have won the election. More to the point, if he had won, seven states would undoubtedly have seceded but Seward would have favored compromises and concessions to keep others from going out and perhaps to lure those seven back in. Most important of all, he would have evacuated Fort Sumter and thereby extinguished the spark that threatened to flame into war.

As it was, Seward did his best to compel Lincoln into concessions and evacuation of the fort. But Lincoln stood firm. When Seward flirted with the notion of supporting the Crittenden Compromise, which would have repudiated the Republican platform by permitting the expansion of slavery, Lincoln stiffened the backbones of Seward and other key Republican leaders. "Entertain no proposition for a compromise in regard to the *extension* of slavery," he wrote to them. "The tug has to come, & better now, than any time hereafter." Crittenden's compromise "would lose us everything we gained by the election." It "acknowledges that slavery has equal rights with liberty, and surrenders all we have contended for. . . . We have just carried an election on principles fairly stated to the people. Now we are told in advance, the government shall be broken up, unless we surrender to those we have beaten. . . . If we surrender, it is the end of us. They will repeat the experiment upon us *ad libitum*. A year will not pass, till we shall have to take Cuba as a condition upon which they will stay in the Union."[9]

It is worth emphasizing here that the common denominator in these letters from Lincoln to Republican leaders was slavery. To be

9. Basler et al., eds., *Collected Works of Lincoln*, IV, 149–51, 154, 183, 155, 172.

sure, on the matters of slavery where it already existed and enforcement of the fugitive slave provision of the Constitution, Lincoln was
willing to reassure the South. But on the crucial issue of 1860, slavery
in the territories, he refused to compromise, and this refusal kept his
party in line. Seward, or any other person who might conceivably
have been elected president in 1860, would have pursued a different
course. This sheds a different light on the assertion that Lincoln
"placed the preservation of the white Union above the death of black
slavery." The Crittenden Compromise did indeed place preservation
of the Union above the death of slavery. So did Seward; so did most
white Americans during the secession crisis. But that assertion does
not describe Lincoln. He refused to yield the core of his antislavery
position to stay the breakup of the Union. As Lincoln expressed it in
a private letter to his old friend Alexander Stephens, "You think
slavery is *right* and ought to be extended; while we think it is *wrong*
and ought to be restricted. That I suppose is the rub." [10]

It was indeed the rub. Even more than in his election to the presidency, Lincoln's refusal to compromise on the expansion of slavery
or on Fort Sumter proved decisive. If another person had been in
his place, the course of history—and of emancipation—would have
been different. Here again we have without question a sine qua non.

It is quite true that once the war started, Lincoln moved more
slowly and apparently more reluctantly toward making it a war for
emancipation than black leaders, abolitionists, radical Republicans,
and the slaves themselves wanted him to move. He did reassure
Southern whites that he had no intention and no constitutional
power to interfere with slavery in the states. In September 1861 and
May 1862 he revoked orders by Generals Frémont and Hunter freeing the slaves of Confederates in their military districts. In December
1861 he forced Secretary of War Simon Cameron to delete from his
annual report a paragraph recommending the freeing and arming of
slaves. And though Lincoln signed the confiscation acts of August

10. Lincoln to Stephens, Dec. 22, 1860, *ibid.,* 160.

1861 and July 1862 that freed some slaves owned by Confederates, this legislation did not come from his initiative. Out in the field it was the slaves who escaped to Union lines and officers like General Benjamin Butler who accepted them as "contraband of war" that took the initiative.

All of this appears to support the thesis that slaves emancipated themselves and that Lincoln's image as emancipator is a myth. But let us take a closer look. It seems clear today, as it did in 1861, that no matter how many thousands of slaves came into Union lines, the ultimate fate of the millions who did not, as well as the fate of the institution of slavery itself, depended on the outcome of the war. If the North won, slavery would be weakened if not destroyed; if the Confederacy won, slavery would survive and perhaps grow stronger from the postwar territorial expansion of an independent and confident slave power. Thus Lincoln's emphasis on the priority of Union had positive implications for emancipation, while precipitate or premature actions against slavery might jeopardize the cause of Union and therefore boomerang in favor of slavery.

Lincoln's chief concern in 1861 was to maintain a united coalition of War Democrats and border-state Unionists as well as Republicans in support of the war effort. To do this he considered it essential to define the war as being waged solely for Union, which united this coalition, and not a war against slavery, which would fragment it. When General Frémont issued his emancipation edict in Missouri on August 30, 1861, the political and military efforts to prevent Kentucky, Maryland, and Missouri from seceding and to cultivate Unionists in western Virginia and eastern Tennessee were at a crucial stage, balancing on a knife edge. To keep his fragile coalition from falling apart, therefore, Lincoln rescinded Frémont's order.

Almost certainly this was the right decision at the time. Lincoln's greatest skills as a political leader were his sensitivity to public opinion and his sense of timing. Within six months of his revocation of Frémont's order, he began moving toward a stronger antislavery position. During the spring and early summer of 1862 he alternately coaxed and prodded border-state Unionists toward recognition of the inevitable escalation of the conflict into a war against slavery and toward acceptance of his plan for compensated emancipation in their states. He warned them that the "friction and abrasion" of a war that had by this time swept every institution into its maelstrom could not leave slavery untouched. But the border states remained deaf to Lincoln's warnings and refused to consider his offer of federally compensated emancipation.

By July 1862, Lincoln turned a decisive corner toward abolition. He made up his mind to issue an emancipation proclamation. Whereas a year earlier, even three months earlier, Lincoln had believed that avoidance of such a drastic step was necessary to maintain that knife-edge balance in the Union coalition, things had now changed. The escalation of the war in scope and fury had mobilized all the resources of both sides, including the slave labor force of the Confederacy. The imminent prospect of Union victory in the spring had been shredded by Robert E. Lee's successful counteroffensives in the Seven Days. The risks of alienating the border states and Northern Democrats, Lincoln now believed, were outweighed by the opportunity to energize the Republican majority and to mobilize part of the slave population for the cause of Union—and freedom. When Lincoln told his cabinet on July 22, 1862, that he had decided to issue an emancipation proclamation, Montgomery Blair, speaking for the forces of conservatism in the North and border states, warned of the consequences among these groups if he did so. But Lincoln was done conciliating them. He had tried to make the border states see reason; now "we must make the forward movement" without them. "They [will] acquiesce, if not immediately, soon." As for the Northern Democrats, "their clubs would be used against us take what course we might." [11]

Two years later, speaking to a visiting delegation of abolitionists,

11. John G. Nicolay and John Hay, *Abraham Lincoln: A History,* 10 vols. (New York, 1890), VI, 158–63.

Lincoln explained why he had moved more slowly against slavery than they had urged. Having taken an oath to preserve and defend the Constitution, which protected slavery, "I did not consider that I had a *right* to touch the 'State' institution of 'Slavery' until all other measures for restoring the Union had failed. . . . The moment came when I felt that slavery must die that the nation might live! . . . Many of my strongest supporters urged *Emancipation* before I thought it indispensable, and, I may say, before I thought the country ready for it. It is my conviction that, had the proclamation been issued even six months earlier than it was, public sentiment would not have sustained it."[12]

Lincoln actually could have made a case that the country had not been ready for the Emancipation Proclamation in Septemper 1862, even in January 1863. Democratic gains in the Northern congressional elections of 1862 resulted in part from a voter backlash against the preliminary Emancipation Proclamation. The morale crisis in Union armies and swelling Copperhead strength during the winter of 1863 grew in part from a resentful conviction that Lincoln had unconstitutionally transformed the purpose of the war from restoring the Union to freeing the slaves. Without question, this issue bitterly divided the Northern people and threatened fatally to erode support for the war effort—the very consequence Lincoln had feared in 1861 and Montgomery Blair had warned against in 1862. Not until after the twin military victories at Gettysburg and Vicksburg did this divisiveness diminish and emancipation gain a clear mandate in the off-year elections of 1863. In his annual message of December 1863, Lincoln conceded that the Emancipation Proclamation a year earlier had been "followed by dark and doubtful days." But now, he added, "the crisis which threatened to divide the friends of the Union is past."[13]

Even that statement turned out to be premature and overoptimis-

12. Francis B. Carpenter, *Six Months at the White House with Abraham Lincoln* (New York, 1866), pp. 76–77.
13. Basler et al., eds., *Collected Works of Lincoln,* VII, 49–50.

tic. In the summer of 1864, Northern morale again plummeted and the emancipation issue once more threatened to undermine the war effort. By August, Grant's campaign in Virginia had bogged down in the trenches after enormous casualties. Sherman seemed similarly thwarted before Atlanta and smaller Union armies elsewhere appeared to be accomplishing nothing. War weariness and defeatism corroded the will of Northerners as they contemplated the staggering cost of this conflict in the lives of their young men. Lincoln came under enormous pressure to open peace negotiations to end the slaughter. Even though Jefferson Davis insisted that Confederate independence was his essential condition for peace, Northern Democrats managed to convince many Northern people that only Lincoln's insistence on emancipation blocked peace. A typical Democratic newspaper editorial declared that "tens of thousands of white men must yet bite the dust to allay the negro mania of the President." [14]

Even Republicans like Horace Greeley, who had criticized Lincoln two years earlier for slowness to embrace emancipation, now criticized him for refusing to abandon it as a precondition for negotiations. The Democratic national convention adopted a platform for the 1864 presidential election calling for peace negotiations to restore the Union with slavery. Every political observer, including Lincoln himself, believed in August that the Republicans would lose the election. The *New York Times* editor and Republican national chairman Henry Raymond told Lincoln that "two special causes are assigned [for] this great reaction in public sentiment,—the want of military success, and the impression . . . that we *can* have peace with Union if we would . . . [but that you are] fighting not for Union but for the abolition of slavery." [15]

The pressure on Lincoln to back down on emancipation caused him to waver temporarily but not to buckle. Instead, he told weak-

14. *Columbus Crisis,* Aug. 3, 1864.
15. Raymond to Lincoln, Aug. 22, 1864, in Basler, ed., *Collected Works of Lincoln,* VII, 518.

kneed Republicans that "no human power can subdue this rebellion without using the Emancipation lever as I have done." More than one hundred thousand black soldiers and sailors were fighting for the Union, said Lincoln. They would not do so if they thought the North intended to "betray them. . . . If they stake their lives for us they must be prompted by the strongest motive . . . the promise of freedom. And the promise being made, must be kept. . . . There have been men who proposed to me to return to slavery the black warriors" who had fought for the Union. "I should be damned in time & in eternity for so doing. The world shall know that I will keep my faith to friends and enemies, come what will."[16]

When Lincoln said this, he fully expected to lose the election. In effect, he was saying that he would rather be right than president. In many ways this was his finest hour. As matters turned out, of course, he was both right and president. Sherman's capture of Atlanta, Sheridan's victories in the Shenandoah Valley, and military success elsewhere transformed the Northern mood from deepest despair in August 1864 to determined confidence by November, and Lincoln was triumphantly reelected. He won without compromising one inch on the emancipation question.

It is instructive to consider two possible alternatives to this outcome. If the Democrats had won, at best the Union would have been restored without a Thirteenth Amendment; at worst the Confederacy would have achieved its independence. In either case the institution of slavery would have survived. That this did not happen was owing more to the steadfast purpose of Abraham Lincoln than to any other single factor.

The proponents of the self-emancipation thesis, however, would avow that all of this is irrelevant. If it is true, as Barbara Fields maintains, that by the time of the Emancipation Proclamation "no

---

16. Lincoln to Charles D. Robinson, Aug. 17, 1864; interview of Lincoln with Alexander W. Randall and Joseph T. Mills, Aug. 19, 1864, both in *ibid.,* 500, 506–7.

human being alive could have held back the tide that swept toward freedom," that tide must have been even stronger by the fall of 1864. But I disagree. The tide of freedom could have been swept back. On numerous occasions during the war, it was. When Union forces moved through or were compelled to retreat from areas of the Confederacy where their presence had attracted and liberated contrabands, the tide of slavery closed in behind them and reenslaved those who could not keep up with the advancing or retreating armies. Many of the thousands who did keep up with the Army of the Ohio when it was forced out of Alabama and Tennessee by the Confederate invasion of Kentucky in the fall of 1862 were seized and sold as slaves by Kentuckians. Lee's army captured dozens of black people in Pennsylvania in June 1863 and sent them back South into slavery. Hundreds of black Union soldiers captured by Confederate forces were reenslaved. Lincoln took note of this phenomenon when he warned that if "the pressure of the war should call off our forces from New Orleans to defend some other point, what is to prevent the masters from reducing the blacks to slavery again; for I am told that whenever the rebels take any black prisoners, free or slave, they immediately auction them off!" [17] The editors of the Freedmen's and Southern Society project, the most scholarly advocates of the self-emancipation thesis, acknowledge that "Southern armies could recapture black people who had already reached Union lines. . . . Indeed, any Union retreat could reverse the process of liberation and throw men and women who had tasted freedom back into bondage. . . . Their travail testified to the link between the military success of the Northern armies and the liberty of Southern slaves." [18]

Precisely. That is the crucial point. Slaves did not emancipate themselves; they were liberated by Union armies. Freedom quite literally came from the barrel of a gun. And who was the commander in chief that called these armies into being, appointed their generals,

17. *Ibid.,* V, 421.
18. Berlin et al., eds., *The Destruction of Slavery,* pp. 35–36.

and gave them direction and purpose? There, indubitably, is our sine qua non.

But let us grant that once the war was carried into slave territory, no matter how it came out the ensuing "friction and abrasion" would have enabled thousands of slaves to escape to freedom. In that respect, a degree of self-emancipation did occur. But even on a large scale, such emancipation was very different from *the abolition of the institution of slavery*. During the American Revolution almost as large a percentage of the slaves won freedom by coming within British lines as achieved liberation by coming within Union lines during the Civil War. Yet slavery survived the Revolution. Ending the institution of bondage required Union victory; it required Lincoln's reelection in 1864; it required the Thirteenth Amendment. Lincoln played a vital role, indeed the central role, in all of these achievements. It was also his policies and his skillful political leadership that set in motion the processes by which the reconstructed or Unionist states of Louisiana, Arkansas, Tennessee, Maryland, and Missouri abolished the institution in those states during the war itself.

Regrettably, Lincoln did not live to see the final ratification of the Thirteenth Amendment. But if he had never lived, it seems safe to say that we would not have had a Thirteenth Amendment in 1865. In that sense, the traditional answer to the question "Who Freed the Slaves?" is the right answer. Lincoln did not accomplish this in the manner sometimes symbolically portrayed, breaking the chains of helpless and passive bondsmen with the stroke of a pen by signing the Emancipation Proclamation. But by pronouncing slavery a moral evil that must come to an end and then winning the presidency in 1860, provoking the South to secede, by refusing to compromise on the issue of slavery's expansion or on Fort Sumter, by careful leadership and timing that kept a fragile Unionist coalition together in the first year of war and committed it to emancipation in the second, by refusing to compromise this policy once he had adopted it, and by prosecuting the war to unconditional victory as commander in chief of an army of liberation, Abraham Lincoln freed the slaves.

14

"THE WHOLE FAMILY OF MAN"

Lincoln and the Last Best Hope Abroad

On december 1, 1862, abraham lincoln delivered his second annual message to Congress. Today we would call it the State of the Union Address. The state of the Union in December 1862 was perilous in the extreme. The Confederate States of America stood proud and defiant as an independent nation whose existence mocked the pretense of union. Most European statesmen assumed that it was merely a matter of time until Lincoln would recognize the inevitable truth that the Union had ceased to exist and give up his bloody, quixotic effort to cobble it together again by force. At home, political opposition menaced the administration's ability to continue the war. That opposition focused particularly on the Emancipation Proclamation, announced the preceding September and scheduled to go into effect on January 1, 1863. Lincoln had embraced emancipation both as a way to weaken the Confederacy by depriving it of slave labor and as a sweeping expansion of Union war aims. Many in the North did not approve this expansion. Nevertheless, Lincoln forged ahead. No longer would the North fight merely for restoration of the old Union—a Union where slavery flouted American ideals of liberty.

Now the North would fight to give that Union "a new birth of freedom," as Lincoln put it almost a year later at Gettysburg.

By then the prospects of Union victory appeared much better than they had a year earlier. Even so, Lincoln's eloquence in December 1862 shone almost as brightly as it did at Gettysburg. "Fellow-citizens, *we* cannot escape history," he told Congress—and the American people. "The fiery trial through which we pass, will light us down, in honor or dishonor, to the latest generation. . . . In *giving* freedom to the *slave,* we *assure* freedom to the free." For America, Lincoln insisted, this was the crossroads of history; this was where "we shall nobly save, or meanly lose, the last best, hope of earth."[1]

What did Lincoln mean? Why did he consider the Union—by which he meant the United States as one nation indivisible—to be the last best hope of earth? The last best hope for what?

Like other political leaders of his generation, Lincoln was painfully aware of the fate of most republics through history. The United States stood almost alone as a democratic republic in the nineteenth century. The hopes of 1848 for the triumph of popular governments in Europe had been shattered by the counterrevolutions that brought a conservative reaction in the Old World. The brave experiment launched in Philadelphia four score and six years before Lincoln delivered his second annual message seemed fragile indeed in a world dominated by kings, emperors, a czar, and theories of aristocracy and inequality. Would the American experiment also succumb to the fate of most republics and collapse into tyranny or fall to pieces?

Not if Lincoln could help it. The central vision that guided him was preservation of the United States as a republic governed by popular suffrage, majority rule, and the Constitution. If the Confederate rebellion succeeded in its effort to sever the United States in twain,

1. Roy P. Basler et al., eds., *The Collected Works of Abraham Lincoln,* 9 vols. (New Brunswick, N.J., 1953–1955), V, 537.

popular government would be swept into the dustbin of history. The next time a disaffected minority lost a presidential election, as Southern Rights Democrats had in 1860, that minority might invoke the Confederate precedent to proclaim secession. *United* States would become an oxymoron. "We must settle this question now," said Lincoln in 1861, "whether in a free government the minority have the right to break up the government whenever they choose. If we fail it will go far to prove the incapability of the people to govern themselves." Nor was this struggle "altogether for today," Lincoln told Congress. "It is for a vast future also." It "embraces more than the fate of these United States. It presents to the whole family of man, the question, whether a constitutional republic, or a democracy . . . can, or cannot maintain its territorial integrity." If it could not, the forces of reaction in Europe would smile in smug satisfaction at this proof of their contention that the upstart republic launched in 1776 could never survive—that government of, by, and for the people had indeed perished from the earth.[2]

The American sense of mission invoked by Lincoln—the idea that this New World experiment was a beacon of freedom for oppressed peoples everywhere—is as old as the Mayflower Compact and as new as apparent American victory in the cold war. "We shall be as a City upon a hill," said John Winthrop to his fellow Puritans as their ship approached Massachusetts Bay in 1630. "The eyes of all people are upon us." Thomas Jefferson addressed the Declaration of Independence to "the opinions of mankind." In 1783 George Washington congratulated his compatriots on the achievement of independence but warned them that "the eyes of the whole World are turned upon them." Like Lincoln four-score years later, Washington declared that the impact of the American Revolution would not be confined "to

---

2. Tyler Dennett, ed., *Lincoln and the Civil War in the Diaries and Letters of John Hay* (New York, 1939), pp. 19–20; Basler, ed., *Collected Works of Lincoln,* V, 53, IV, 426.

the present age alone, for with our fate will the destiny of unborn Millions be involved."[3]

Most Northern people in 1861 shared Lincoln's conviction that the fate of democratic government hung on the outcome of the Civil War. That passion sustained them through four years of the bloodiest war in the Western world between 1815 and 1914. "We must fight," insisted an Indianapolis newspaper two weeks after the firing on Fort Sumter,

> because we *must*. The National Government has been assailed. The Nation has been defied. If either can be done with impunity neither Nation nor Government is worth a cent. . . . War is self preservation, if our form of Government is worth preserving. If monarchy would be better, it might be wise to quit fighting, admit that a Republic is too weak to take care of itself, and invite some deposed Duke or Prince of Europe to come over here and rule us. But otherwise, *we must fight*.[4]

None felt this sense of democratic mission more strongly than Union soldiers, who periled their lives for it. "I do feel that the liberty of the world is placed in our hands to defend," wrote a Massachusetts private to his wife in 1862, "and if we are overcome then farewell to freedom." In 1863 on the second anniversary of his enlistment, an Ohio private wrote in his diary that he had not expected the war to last so long, but no matter how much longer it took it must be carried on "for the great principles of liberty and self government at stake, for should we fail, the onward march of Liberty in the Old World will be retarded at least a century, and Monarchs,

3. Quoted in Richard N. Current, "Lincoln, the Civil War, and the American Mission," in Cullom Davis et al., eds., *The Public and Private Lincoln: Contemporary Perspectives* (Carbondale, Ill., 1979), pp. 140, 141.

4. *Indianapolis Daily Journal,* April 27, 1861.

Kings, and Aristocrats will be more powerful against their subjects than ever."[5]

Some foreign-born soldiers expressed such convictions with even greater intensity. In 1863 an Irish-born carpenter, a private in the Twenty-eighth Massachusetts Infantry of the famous Irish Brigade, rebuked both his wife in Boston and his father-in-law in Ireland for questioning his judgment in risking his life for the Lincoln administration's war aims. "This is the first test of a modern free government in the act of sustaining itself against internal enemies," he wrote almost in echo of Lincoln. "If it fail then the hopes of milions fall and the designs and wishes of all tyrants will succeed the old cry will be sent forth from the aristocrats of europe that such is the common lot of all republics. . . . Irishmen and their descendants have . . . a stake in [this] nation. . . . America is Irlands refuge Irlands last hope destroy this republic and her hopes are blasted." In 1864 a forty-year-old Ohio corporal who had immigrated from England wrote to his wife explaining his decision to reenlist for a second three-year hitch: "If I do get hurt I want you to remember that it will be not only for my Country and my Children but for Liberty all over the World that I risked my life, for if Liberty should be crushed here, what hope would there be for the cause of Human Progress anywhere else?" Later that summer, in the Atlanta campaign, he gave his life for these convictions.[6]

Perhaps it is not surprising that Americans both native and adopted felt this way. They had never hidden their self-proclaimed

5. Josiah Perry to Phebe Perry, Oct. 3, 1862, Josiah Perry Papers, Illinois State Historical Library, Springfield; Robert T. McMahan diary, entry of Sept. 3, 1863, State Historical Society of Missouri, Columbia.

6. Peter Welsh to Mary Welsh, Feb. 3, 1863, Peter Welsh to Patrick Prendergast, June 1, 1863, in *Irish Green and Union Blue: The Civil War Letters of Peter Welsh*, ed. Laurence Frederick Kohl and Margaret Cosee Richard (New York, 1986), pp. 65–66, 102; George H. Cadman to Esther Cadman, March 6, 1864, Cadman Papers, Southern Historical Collection, University of North Carolina, Chapel Hill.

beacon light of freedom under a bushel. But did peoples of other lands share the belief in America's mission to show them the path upward from autocracy and oppression? For liberals, radicals, progressives, reformers, and revolutionaries of all stripes, the answer was yes. During the first century of its history as a nation, the United States did serve as a model for the European and Latin American "Left" that sought to reform or overthrow the anciens régimes in their own countries. During the debate that produced the British Reform Act of 1832, the London Working Men's Association pronounced "the Republic of America" to be a "beacon of freedom" for all mankind, while a British newspaper named the *Poor Man's Guardian* pointed to American institutions as "the best precedent and guide to the oppressed and enslaved people of England in *their* struggle for the RIGHT OF REPRESENTATION FOR EVERY MAN." In the 1840s, English Chartists praised "the bright luminary of the western hemisphere whose radiance will . . . light the whole world to freedom . . . [and triumph] over the dark fiends of despotism, vice, and wretchedness."[7]

In the preface to the twelfth edition of his monumental *Democracy in America,* written during the heady days of the 1848 uprisings in Europe, Alexis de Tocqueville urged the leaders of France's newly created Second Republic to study American institutions as a guide to "the approaching irresistible and universal spread of democracy throughout the world." When instead of democracy France got the Second Empire under Napoleon III, the liberal opposition to his régime looked to the United States for inspiration. "Many of the suggested reforms," wrote the historian of the French opposition, "would have remained utopic had it not been for the demonstrable existence of the United States and its republican institutions." Napoleon's interior minister noted sourly that "one would almost be

7. Quoted in G. D. Lillibridge, *Beacon of Freedom: The Impact of American Democracy upon Great Britain 1830–1870* (Philadelphia, 1955), pp. 5, 28, 40, 43.

tempted to think that there was a fixed determination or combination to offer the United States always as an example for everything."[8]

Anti-Americanism was the hobby of the European "Right" in those years, particularly in England. As a British radical newspaper expressed it in 1856, "to the oppressors of Europe, especially those of England, the [United States] is a constant terror, and an everlasting menace" because it stood as "a practical and triumphant refutation of the lying and servile sophists who maintain that without kings and aristocrats, civilized communities cannot exist."[9] This rhetoric undoubtedly overstated the case. But the sentiments it described certainly existed among high Tories—and some not so high. Many of them expressed delight, at least in private, at the "immortal smash" of the dis-United States in 1861, which demonstrated "the failure of republican institutions in time of pressure." The Earl of Shrewsbury looked upon "the trial of Democracy and its failure" with pleasure. "I believe that the dissolution of the Union is inevitable, and that men before me will live to see an aristocracy established in America." The voice of the British Establishment, the *Times* of London, considered the downfall of "the American colossus" a good "riddance of a nightmare. . . . Excepting a few gentlemen of republican tendencies, we all expect, we nearly all wish, success to the Confederate cause."[10]

We should not overgeneralize from such examples. A simple dichotomy between British liberals who admired American democracy and supported the Union and conservatives who detested both does

8. Tocqueville, *Democracy in America,* 12th ed., new translation by George Lawrence, ed. J. P. Mayer (New York, 1969), p. xiii; Serge Gavronsky, *The French Liberal Opposition and the American Civil War* (New York, 1968), pp. 11, 12.

9. Lillibridge, *Beacon of Freedom,* p. 80.

10. William H. Russell to John Bigelow, April 14, 1861, in John Bigelow, *Retrospections of an Active Life,* 2 vols. (New York, 1909), I, 347; Earl of Shrewsbury quoted in Ephraim D. Adams, *Great Britain and the American Civil War,* 2 vols. (New York, 1925), II, 282; *Times* quoted in Frank L. Owsley, *King Cotton Diplomacy: Foreign Relations of the Confederate States of America,* 2d ed., revised by Harriet C. Owsley (Chicago, 1959), p. 186.

considerable violence to historical reality. Several prominent members of the nobility and gentry sympathized with the Union. And the Conservative party, out of power during the years of the American Civil War, did not press for recognition of the Confederacy despite the presence of many Southern sympathizers in its ranks.

Nevertheless, most members of that minority of Englishmen who owned enough property to vote—and who were therefore represented in Parliament—probably would have welcomed the dissolution of the American republic. The foremost British champion of the Union, John Bright, explained to an American friend that "Our Govt is made up of men drawn from the aristocratic families . . . and from a natural instinct, it must be hostile to your greatness & to the permanence of your institutions." Bright's pro-Union colleague, Richard Cobden, may have exaggerated only slightly when he wrote in December 1861, at the time of the furor over the Union navy's seizure of Confederate envoys James Mason and John Slidell from the British ship *Trent,* that "three fourths of the House [of Commons] will be glad to find an excuse for voting for the dismemberment of the Great Republic."[11] When Sir John Ramsden, a Tory member of the House, expressed satisfaction that "the great republican bubble had burst," loud cheers broke forth from the back benches. The American minister to the Court of St. James's, Charles Francis Adams, was not too far off the mark when he wrote in December 1862 that "the great body of the aristocracy and the commercial classes are anxious to see the United States go to pieces."[12]

11. Bright to John Bigelow, Jan. 3, 1862, in Belle Becker Sideman and Lillian Friedman, eds., *Europe Looks at the Civil War* (New York, 1960), p. 129; Cobden to "Mr. Paulton," Dec. ?, 1861, in *ibid.,* p. 91.

12. Ramsden quoted in Jay Monaghan, *Diplomat in Carpet Slippers: Abraham Lincoln Deals with Foreign Affairs* (Indianapolis, 1945), 116; Charles Francis Adams to Charles Francis Adams, Jr., Dec. 25, 1862, in Worthington C. Ford, ed., *A Cycle of Adams Letters, 1861–1865,* 2 vols. (Boston, 1920), I, 220–21. See also Donald Bellows, "A Study of British Conservative Reaction to the American Civil War," *Journal of Southern History* 51 (1985), 505–26; and Sheldon Va-

We know less about conservative attitudes toward the Civil War in other countries. What little we do know, however, finds conservatives outside of Britain expressing the same kind of satisfaction with the failure of democracy. The leading English-language newspaper in South Africa concluded in June 1861 that the "boasted republic" had "fallen asunder at the first touch, and added another to the many examples of the inefficiency of large republics to stand against popular passions." A year later, a royalist Spanish journal, the *Pensamiento Español,* found it scarcely surprising that Americans were butchering each other, for that nation "was populated by the dregs of all the nations of the world. . . . Such is the real history of the one and only state in the world which has succeeded in constituting itself according to the flaming theories of democracy. The example is too horrible to stir any desire for emulation." [13]

In Paris *La Patrie,* a semi-official organ for Napoleon III, stated with ill-concealed relish in August 1861 that "the work of George Washington has come to an end." Napoleon's foreign policy was the most pro-Confederate of any European power. If the emperor had been able to persuade Britain or Russia to go along, France would have offered mediation and diplomatic recognition of the Confederacy. The French liberal Edgar Quinet exaggerated only slightly when he wrote from exile in Switzerland in 1862 that Napoleon's purpose was "to weaken or destroy Democracy in the United States . . . because in order for Napoleonic ideas to succeed, it is absolutely indispensable that this vast republic disappear from the face of the earth." [14]

Whether or not Napoleon thought he could destroy republicanism in the United States, he undertook to do so in Mexico. That unhappy

nauken, *The Glittering Illusion: English Sympathy for the Southern Confederacy* (Worthing, England, 1988).

13. *Cape Argus,* June 11, 1861; *Pensamiento Español,* Sept. 1862, quoted in Sideman and Friedman, eds., *Europe Looks at the Civil War,* pp. 173–74.

14. *La Patrie* and Quinet quoted in Gavronsky, *The French Liberal Opposition,* pp. 58, 167.

country experienced its own civil war in the 1860s between a reactionary alliance of the church and large landowners against followers of the republican liberal Benito Juárez. Under the pretext of collecting debts owed to French citizens, Napoleon sent an army of thirty-five thousand men to Mexico to overthrow Juárez. Napoleon's main motive was to reestablish the French presence in the New World yielded by his uncle sixty years earlier when he had sold Louisiana to the United States. Napoleon was also quite willing to go along with his fellow emperor, Franz Joseph of Austria, whose younger brother Ferdinand Maximilian was at loose ends with little to do. Why not set him up as emperor of Mexico, thereby reclaiming at least part of the vast Spanish domain once ruled by the Hapsburgs? King Leopold of Belgium, Maximilian's father-in-law, had an additional purpose in mind. Describing the Lincoln administration as being characterized by "the most rank Radicalism," Leopold feared that if the North won the war, "America, in collaboration with Europe's revolutionaries, might undermine the very basis of the traditional social order of Europe." Therefore he strongly supported the installation of Maximilian as emperor of Mexico in 1864 "to raise a barrier against the United States and provide a support for the monarchical-aristocratic principle in the Southern states." [15]

While these emperors were fishing in troubled New World waters, the most autocratic of them all, Czar Alexander of Russia, proved to be the Union's most steadfast friend. This friendship did not result from reasons of sentiment or ideology. Quite the contrary; no two regimes could have been farther apart in political philosophy and cultural values. Russo-American relations during the Civil War were a marriage of convenience founded on the self-interest of both parties: the Russian interest in a strong United States as a counterweight to Britain, and the American dependence on Russia as a

15. Leopold quoted in Sideman and Friedman, eds., *Europe Looks at the Civil War,* p. 98; and in A. R. Tyrner-Tyrnauer, *Lincoln and the Emperors* (New York, 1962), pp. 69, 109.

counterweight to French and British flirtation with recognition of the Confederacy. Russian opposition to mediation of the American conflict by the great powers gave the coup de grâce to that effort in November 1862. A year later the Russian fleet visited American ports, staying for months, ostensibly as a goodwill gesture but in reality as a way to prevent the British navy from bottling up Russian ships in their home ports during a period of tension over Russian suppression of an uprising of Polish nationalists.

Although ideology did not inhibit the strange-bedfellow comity between Russia and the United States, that does not mean ideology was absent from Russian perceptions of the war's meaning for democracy. The confidential dispatches of the Russian minister to the United States, Edouard de Stoeckl, to the Russian foreign minister, Prince Alexander Gorchakov, provide a fascinating glimpse of the crosscurrents and contradictions of realpolitik and ideology. Stoeckl had lived in the United States for twenty years before the war. He liked Americans and married one in 1856. But he fancied himself an aristocrat and enjoyed being addressed as "Baron" though he had no title of nobility. He supported the Union cause but considered it hopeless until almost the end of the war. He disliked democracy and regarded the Civil War as proof of its failure. "The republican form of government, so much talked about by the Europeans and so much praised by the Americans, is breaking down," he wrote to Prince Gorchakov with apparent satisfaction in December 1863. "What can be expected from a country where men of humble origin are elevated to the highest positions?" He meant Lincoln, whose abilities Stoeckl held in low regard. "This is democracy in practice, the democracy that European theorists rave about," continued Stoeckl. "If they could only see it at work they would cease their agitation and thank God for the government which they are enjoying." [16]

Those theorists whom Stoeckl sneered at—that is, European liber-

---

16. Albert A. Woldman, *Lincoln and the Russians* (Cleveland, 1952), pp. 216–17.

als and radicals—viewed the American Civil War with alarm. Perhaps the reactionaries were right after all and the downfall of Lincoln's last best hope of earth would prove the absurdity of everything they believed in. French liberals, wrote one of them in 1861, "feel somehow humbled and certainly very distressed by this deplorable Civil War" because "it may very well bring about the failure of a society" held up by liberals as the "defenders of right and humanity."[17]

In England John Bright described "that free country and that free government [which] has had a prodigious influence upon freedom in Europe and in England" and was now fighting with backs to the wall as the "advocates and defenders of freedom and civilization." The famous economist and political philosopher John Stuart Mill, who favored the Union cause, believed that Confederate success "would be a victory for the powers of evil which would give courage to the enemies of progress and damp the spirits of its friends all over the civilized world. . . . [The American war] is destined to be a turning point, for good and evil, of the course of human affairs."[18]

Slavery was a sticking point for both Union and Confederacy in their quest for European sympathy and support. Having abolished the institution in their colonies, European countries now prided themselves on their antislavery stance. Even autocratic Russia had ended serfdom in 1861. Britain regarded itself as the world's policeman against the slave trade. Even Tories professed distaste for the South's peculiar institution. Confederate envoys in Britain seeking diplomatic recognition in 1861 acknowledged ruefully that "the public mind here is entirely opposed to the Government of the Confederate States of America on the question of slavery. . . . The sincerity

17. *Revue des Deux Mondes,* Aug. 15, 1861, quoted in Sideman and Friedman, eds., *Europe Looks at the Civil War,* p. 81.

18. Bright quoted in H. C. Allen, "Civil War, Reconstruction, and Great Britain," in Harold M. Hyman, ed., *Heard Round the World: The Impact Abroad of the Civil War* (New York, 1969), pp. 96, 75; Mill quoted in Sideman and Friedman, eds., *Europe Looks at the Civil War,* pp. 117–18.

and universality of this feeling embarrass the Government in dealing with the question of our recognition." Lincoln recognized this truth when he said privately in January 1862: "I cannot imagine that any European power would dare to recognize and aid the Southern Confederacy if it became clear that the Confederacy stands for slavery and the Union for freedom." [19]

The problem was that in the first seventeen months of the war, the Union did not stand for freedom. This perplexed and even embittered some Europeans, who failed to understand the constitutional and political constraints that hindered Lincoln from turning the war for Union into a war against slavery. Since "the North does not proclaim abolition and never pretended to fight for anti-slavery," asked perturbed Englishmen in September 1861, how "can we be fairly called upon to sympathize so warmly with the Federal cause?" [20]

This attitude helps explain the ambivalent attitude of British workingmen toward the American war. On the one hand, most of them sympathized with the Union as the great symbol of progressivism and equal rights—the last best hope of earth for democracy—even though the livelihood of workers in Britain's largest industry depended on slave-grown cotton. By 1862 workers in the textile industry were suffering grievous unemployment and hardships because of the blockade of Southern ports. Some of their spokesmen, therefore, urged recognition of the Confederacy and British intervention to break the Union blockade and get cotton. So long as the North fought merely for restoration of the Union—a Union with slavery—

19. William L. Yancey and A. Dudley Mann to Robert Toombs, May 21, 1861, in James D. Richardson, comp., *A Compilation of the Messages and Papers of the Confederacy,* 2 vols. (Nashville, 1906), II, 37; Lincoln quoted in *The Reminiscences of Carl Schurz,* 3 vols. (New York, 1907–1908), II, 309.

20. *Saturday Review,* Sept. 14, 1861, quoted in Adams, *Great Britain and the American Civil War,* I, 181; *Economist,* Sept. 1861, quoted in Karl Marx and Friedrich Engels, *The Civil War in the United States,* ed. Richard Enmale (New York, 1937), p. 12.

many labor leaders saw little moral difference between North and South. In a typical editorial a British labor newspaper declared in October 1861:

> Now that it is clear that the Northerners in America are not fighting for the emancipation of the slaves, we are relieved from any moral consideration in their favor, and as the Southerners are not worse than they are, why should we not get cotton? . . . If the North, in blockading the Southern ports, had had emancipation in view, we might have seen the sacred cause of free labour was on their side.

Since this is not the case, "why should we starve any longer?"[21]

Lincoln recognized the force of this question. Years earlier he had noted that the existence of slavery "deprives our republican example of its just influence in the world—enables the enemies of free institutions, with plausibility, to taunt us as hypocrites." In September 1861 Lincoln agreed with a delegation of antislavery clergymen that "emancipation would help us in Europe, and convince them that we are incited by something more than ambition." When he said this, Lincoln had already decided to issue an Emancipation Proclamation and was only awaiting a Union military victory to announce it.[22]

That victory came a few days later, at Antietam. But to Lincoln's disappointment, the Emancipation Proclamation did not immediately transform critical European opinion. The preliminary nature of the edict that Lincoln issued on September 22, 1862, to go into effect the following January 1, the exemption of Unionist areas from its application, and the justification of the proclamation on grounds of military necessity, not morality and justice, gave European cynics a field day. Many regarded it as a Yankee trick to encourage a slave insurrection, undertaken not from moral conviction but as a desperate measure to destroy the Confederacy from within because Union

21. *The Working Man,* Oct. 5, 1861, quoted in Philip S. Foner, *British Labor and the American Civil War* (New York, 1981), pp. 27–28.
22. Basler, ed., *Collected Works of Lincoln,* II, 255, V, 423.

armies could not defeat it from without. The British chargé d'affaires in Washington branded the proclamation as "cold, vindictive, and entirely political." Foreign Secretary Lord John Russell, who had previously withheld sympathy from the Union because it did *not* act against slavery, now perversely pronounced the Emancipation Proclamation a vile encouragement to "acts of plunder, of incendiarism, and of revenge."[23] Choosing not to understand why Lincoln, under the Constitution, had to exempt the loyal border states and Union-occupied portions of the Confederacy, the London *Spectator* sneered that "the principle asserted is not that a human being cannot own another, but that he cannot own him unless he is loyal to the United States." Even the most radical British labor newspaper lamented that "Lincoln offers freedom to the negroes over whom he has no control, and keeps in slavery those other negroes within his power. Thus he associates his Government with slavery by making slaveholding the reward to the planters of rejoining the old Union."[24]

But in the end all of this sound and fury signified little. Most British liberals understood the great portent of the Emancipation Proclamation. A friendly London newspaper pronounced it "a gigantic stride in the paths of Christian and civilized progress—the turning point in the history of the American commonwealth—an act only second in courage and probable results to the Declaration of Independence." When Lincoln, contrary to the prediction of European cynics, followed through with the final Emancipation Proclamation on January 1, 1863, many former skeptics became believers. Implicitly responding to criticisms of the preliminary proclamation, Lincoln this time pronounced emancipation to be "an act of justice"

23. Chargé d'affaires quoted in Brian Jenkins, *Britain & the War for the Union,* 2 vols. (Montreal, 1974–1980), II, 141; Russell quoted in Howard Jones, *Union in Peril: The Crisis over British Intervention in the Civil War* (Chapel Hill, 1992), p. 187.

24. *Spectator,* Oct. 11, 1862, quoted in Jenkins, *Britain & the War for the Union,* II, 153; *Bee-Hive,* Oct. 11, 1862, quoted in Foner, *British Labor and the American Civil War,* p. 29.

as well as of military necessity, and enjoined freed slaves to refrain from violence.[25]

Even though the final proclamation exempted one-quarter of the slaves, Lincoln had nevertheless announced a new war aim. Thenceforth the Union army became officially an army of liberation. If the North won the war, slavery would exist no more. As recognition of this truth began to dawn across the Atlantic during January and February 1863, a powerful pro-Union reaction set in, especially in England. Huge meetings roared their approval of emancipation and endorsement of the Union cause. Young Henry Adams, secretary to his father at the American legation in London, reported that "the Emancipation Proclamation has done more for us here than all our former victories and all our diplomacy. It has created an almost convulsive reaction in our favor."[26]

Many of these mass meetings were organized by workingmen. The Emancipation Proclamation ended their ambivalence toward the Union cause. The speech of a worker at a rally in Manchester on February 24, 1863, offered a typical sentiment. The people of the North, he said in the paraphrased words of a reporter, were

> not merely contending for themselves, but for the rights of the unenfranchised of this and every other country. If the North succeed, liberty [will] be stimulated and encouraged in every country on the face of the earth; if they fail, despotism, like a great pall, [will] envelop all our political and social institutions.[27]

This upswelling of public support for the Union quenched any lingering chance that existed for British recognition of the Confederacy. Richard Cobden reported in February 1863 that one of the largest of the pro-Union mass meetings, at Exeter Hall in London,

25. *Morning Star,* Oct. 6, 1862, quoted in Allan Nevins, *War Becomes Revolution* (New York, 1960), p. 270; Basler, ed., *Collected Works of Lincoln,* VI, 30.

26. Henry Adams to Charles Francis Adams, Jr., in Ford, ed., *Cycle of Adams Letters,* I, 243.

27. Quoted in Foner, *British Labor and the American Civil War,* p. 52.

"has had a powerful effect on our newspapers and politicians. It has closed the mouths of those who have been advocating the side of the South. Recognition of the South, by England, whilst it bases itself on Negro slavery, is an impossibility." In France a year later, at a time when Napoleon was toying with the idea of recognizing the Confederacy in return for Confederate recognition of his puppet Maximilian in Mexico, twelve prominent French citizens of Tours addressed a public letter to Confederate envoy John Slidell, telling him bluntly: "It is useless to make any appeal to the people of France. It may be to our interest to support you. There may be strong material and political reasons for a close alliance between us, but as long as you maintain and are maintained by slavery, we cannot offer you our alliance. On the contrary, we believe and expect you will fail!"[28]

The Confederacy did fail. The last best hope of earth for democracy did not perish from the earth but experienced a new birth of freedom whose impact was felt abroad with telling effect. From Spanish republicans in 1865 came congratulations to "a people democratically governed" who have "carried to its close the greatest enterprise in history." The Italian patriot and revolutionary Guiseppe Mazzini blessed the Northern people, who "have done more for us in four years than fifty years of teaching, preaching and writing from all your European brothers have been able to do." None other than Karl Marx declared that "as in the eighteenth century the American War of Independence sounded the tocsin for the European middle class, so in the nineteenth century, the American Civil War sounded it for the working class."[29]

It is scarcely surprising that European liberals and radicals expressed relief and delight at the news of Union victory. Perhaps even

28. Cobden to Charles Sumner, Feb. 13, 1863, in Sideman and Friedman, eds., *Europe Looks at the Civil War,* p. 222; citizens of Tours quoted in *ibid.,* pp. 261–62.

29. Spanish republicans and Mazzini quoted in *ibid.,* pp. 274, 282; Marx quoted in R. Laurence Moore, *European Socialists and the American Promised Land* (New York, 1970), p. 7.

more illustrative of the impact of that victory were the responses of conservatives. A British Tory in the House of Commons, a critic of American culture and democracy, remarked sourly to an American acquaintance that he considered Union success a misfortune. "I had indulged the hope that your country might break up into two or perhaps more fragments. I regard the United States as a menace to the whole civilized world." A Tory colleague spelled out the menace as "the beginning of an Americanizing process in England. The new Democratic ideas are gradually to find embodiment."[30]

Most remarkable of all was the reaction of Edouard de Stoeckl, the Russian minister who disliked democracy, had considered the Civil War proof of its failure, and had predicted Confederate victory until almost the eve of Appomattox. When the outcome proved him wrong, he ate humble pie in a dispatch to Prince Gorchakov. By "an irresistible strength of the nation at large," wrote Stoeckl, "this exceptional people has given the lie to all predictions and calculations. They have passed through one of the greatest revolutions of a century . . . and they have come out of it with their resources unexhausted, their energy renewed . . . and the prestige of their power greater than ever."[31]

The consequences of this triumph of democracy were more than symbolic. It encouraged liberals in Britain who wanted to expand voting rights there. For almost four years they had endured the taunts and jibes of Tories who pointed to the American "smashup" as evidence of democracy's failure. "Our opponents told us that Republicanism was on trial," recalled Edward Beesly, a liberal professor of political economy at University College London, in 1865. "They insisted on our watching what they called its breakdown. They told us that it was for ever discredited in England. Well, we accepted the

30. Sir Edward Bulwer-Lytton to John Bigelow, April ?, 1865, quoted in Sideman and Friedman, eds., *Europe Looks at the Civil War,* p. 282; Hyman, ed., *Heard Round the World,* xi.

31. Stoeckl to Gorchakov, April 14, 1865, quoted in Woldman, *Lincoln and the Russians,* pp. 256–59.

challenge. We staked our hopes boldly on the result. . . . Under a strain such as no aristocracy, no monarchy, no empire could have supported, Republican institutions have stood firm. It is we, now, who call upon the privileged classes to mark the result. . . . A vast impetus has been given to Republican sentiments in England."[32]

A two-year debate in Parliament, in which the American example figured prominently, led to enactment of the Reform Bill of 1867, which nearly doubled the eligible electorate and enfranchised a large part of the British working class for the first time. With this act the world's most powerful nation took a long stride toward democracy. It is an oversimplification to attribute this achievement mainly to Union victory in the Civil War. But it is probably no exaggeration to say that if the North had lost the war, thereby confirming Tory opinions of democracy and confounding the liberals, the Reform Bill would have been delayed for years.[33]

If the triumph of democracy in Britain was an indirect result of the American Civil War, the triumph of Benito Juárez and republicanism in Mexico was in part a direct result. The United States sent fifty thousand veteran troops to Texas after Appomattox, while Secretary of State William H. Seward pressed the French to pull their troops out of Mexico. Napoleon did so in 1866, whereupon the republican forces under Juárez regained control of the country, captured Maximilian, and executed him in 1867, leaving his widow, Carlotta, to wander insane over the face of Europe for sixty years. Three years after the fall of Maximilian, Napoleon himself lost his throne, an event attributed by the historian of his liberal opposition in part to the example of triumphant republicanism in the United States five years earlier.[34]

This is pushing things too far; the birth of France's third republic was a consequence of French defeat in the Franco-Prussian War, not

---

32. Quoted in H. C. Allen, "Civil War, Reconstruction, and Great Britain," in Hyman, ed., *Heard Round the World*, p. 73.
33. See the discussion in *ibid.*, pp. 49–83.
34. Gavronsky, *The French Liberal Opposition*, p. 13.

of Union victory in the American Civil War. But perhaps it was more than coincidence that within five years of that Union victory, the forces of liberalism had expanded the suffrage in Britain and toppled emperors in Mexico and France. And it is also more than coincidence that after the abolition of slavery in the United States the abolitionist forces in the two remaining slave societies in the Western Hemisphere, Brazil and Cuba, stepped up their campaign for emancipation, which culminated in success two decades later. If he had lived, Lincoln would have been gratified by the statement of a Brazilian intellectual in 1871, referring to his government's commitment to emancipation, that he rejoiced "to see Brazil receive so quickly the moral of the Civil War in the United States."[35]

Lincoln would applaud even more the essay written in 1993 by a seventeen-year-old girl from Texas in a contest sponsored by the Huntington Library in connection with its 1993–1994 exhibit on Lincoln. This girl, whose forebears immigrated from India in the 1960s, wrote that "if the United States was not in existence today, I would not have the opportunity to excel in life and education. The Union was preserved, not only for the people yesterday, but also for the lives of today."[36]

In 1861 Lincoln said that the struggle for the Union involved not just "the fate of these United States" but of "the whole family of man." It was a struggle "not altogether for today" but "for a vast future" as well. Lincoln's words resonate today with as much relevance as they did nearly seven-score years ago.

35. Harry Bernstein, "The Civil War and Latin America," in Hyman, ed., *Heard Round the World,* p. 323.

36. Reena Mathew, "One Set of Footprints," essay in author's possession.

V

HISTORIANS AND THEIR AUDIENCES

15

WHAT'S THE MATTER
WITH HISTORY?

AT LEAST ONCE EVERY GENERATION SINCE HISTORIANS IN THE United States acquired standing as a profession more than a century ago, they have publicly lamented their inability to reach a broad general audience. "Professional" historians are defined here as those who have earned a graduate degree, normally the Ph.D., who teach in colleges or universities or are employed in other educational institutions such as museums, and who belong to one or more of the professional organizations that have proliferated since the founding of the American Historical Association in 1884. Professionals hold themselves to rigorous standards of scholarship and write learned articles and books that are read mainly by other professionals or assigned to students by fellow academics. "Amateurs" write articles and books that reach a larger audience but do not always adhere to the technical standards of professional scholarship. Despite much raising of eyebrows and looking down noses at such "popular" history, professionals periodically wring their hands at their own failure to reach that audience of educated laypeople who hunger for history and need to know it if they are to be informed citizens.

From the 1930s until his death in 1970, Allan Nevins was the foremost proponent of a greater effort by professional historians to reach that audience. Nevins was ideally situated to advocate this cause. He did not have a Ph.D. and he had worked in journalism for twenty years, writing history on the side, before joining the faculty of Columbia University in 1931. There the professor who did not have a Ph.D. trained a hundred Ph.D.s while continuing to write books that sold widely and earned (sometimes grudging) respect within the academy as well. Under Nevins's leadership, several prominent members of the American Historical Association (hereafter AHA) hoped to "revitalize" the profession in the late 1930s by establishing a popular magazine of history under AHA auspices. Professionals had abdicated their responsibility to the public, Nevins insisted, leaving it to the amateurs to fill the void. It was time to remedy that failure. But at its annual meeting in 1938, the AHA voted by a narrow margin after a rancorous debate to reject sponsorship of a popular magazine. The taint of commercialism, said opponents, would fatally infect sound scholarship.[1]

An angry Nevins went public with his contempt for "Professor Dryasdust," as he caricatured academics who wrote unreadable monographs. "The pedant," wrote Nevins in a widely reprinted article entitled "What's the Matter with History?" that first appeared in the *Saturday Review of Literature,* "is chiefly responsible for the present crippled gait of history in America."

> His touch is death. He destroys the public for historical work by convincing it that history is synonymous with heavy, stolid prosing. Indeed, he is responsible for the fact that today a host of intelligent and highly literate Americans will open a book of history only with reluctant dread. . . . It is against this entrenched pedantry

1. John Higham with Leonard Krieger and Felix Gilbert, *History* (Englewood Cliffs, N.J., 1965), pp. 80–81.

that the war of true history will have to be most determined and implacable.[2]

Nevins and his remaining friends in the profession went ahead on their own. They founded the Society of American Historians, which eventually established the Parkman Prize and Nevins Prize to reward books and dissertations that possessed literary excellence. By 1954 they had raised enough money to launch their popular magazine, *American Heritage.* Within a few years its circulation climbed to over three hundred thousand—many times greater than that of all professional historical journals combined. Some academics wrote for *American Heritage,* but most had nothing to do with it. Nevertheless, the AHA gave belated recognition to Nevins by electing him president in 1959. In a conciliatory presidential address entitled "Not Capulets, Not Montagus," Nevins sought to heal old wounds: "We are all amateurs, we are all professionals." It was not true, said Nevins, that "history must be either authoritative and dull or interesting and untrustworthy." In the hands of those who researched like professionals and wrote like amateurs it could be both authoritative and interesting.

Underneath this placatory tone, however, lurked Nevins's real message, which he framed as rhetorical questions: Why "do historians no longer speak of instructing the nation, and why do so few aspire to a general democratic public" as they did in the age of George Bancroft and Francis Parkman? Why were professionals still "writing dull books and abusing bright ones"? A year later Alfred A. Knopf, a leading publisher of works of history, echoed Nevins's criticism of the narrowness of professional historians: "They have abdicated their whole position in our culture."[3]

2. Allan Nevins, "What's the Matter with History?" *Saturday Review of Literature* 19 (Feb. 4, 1939), 4, 16.

3. Allan Nevins, "Not Capulets, Not Montagus," *American Historical Review* 65 (1960), 253–70; Knopf quoted in Higham et al., *History,* p. 68.

During the next two decades, however, few academic historians took notice of such jeremiads. The profession enjoyed a period of explosive growth and creativity. Dozens of new professional associations and journals came into existence. The rapid expansion of higher education, fueled by the demographics of the baby boom, multiplied the number of graduate programs and Ph.D.s. The advent of the computer made new techniques of research and analysis possible. New kinds of historical questions inspired by a spirit of inclusiveness made all people and all aspects of their lives, not just the public activities of elite white males, the legitimate subjects of historical inquiry. A host of new historical fields generated an outpouring of challenging, provocative scholarship: the new social history with its subfields of working-class history, women's history, black history, and ethnic history; the new political history; cliometrics; cultural history; the history of mentalité; and so on. Quantification and the influence of the *Annales* school, with its emphasis on social structure and the *longue dureé* rather than *histoire événementielle,* caused narrative history, the story of "mere events," to fall even further out of favor among academic historians. If these developments caused the increasingly technical and specialized writings of professionals to become inaccessible to a nonprofessional audience, it hardly seemed to matter because the expanding universities and generous foundation support for innovative research seemed unending.

But all good things come to an end. In the later 1970s undergraduate history enrollments declined, higher education retrenched, foundations became less generous, and hundreds of recently minted Ph.D.s could not find jobs. The new social, political, quantitative, and other kinds of "new" history lost vitality. Professional history seemed increasingly irrelevant to the public and fell into a crisis of self-confidence. Out of this turmoil came another round of hand-wringing that produced a call for a revival of narrative history, sometimes phrased as "narrative synthesis" of the compartmentalized, specialized parts. The debate of these matters within the profession during the 1980s focused mainly on the question of audience.

Two giants of the profession launched the debate. In 1979 Lawrence Stone detected a revival of the "once despised narrative mode." An important reason for this revival, said Stone, was the desire of historians "to make their findings accessible once more to an intelligent but not expert reading public, which is eager to learn . . . but cannot stomach indigestible statistical tables, dry analytical argument, and jargon-ridden prose." Two years later Bernard Bailyn took up the cudgels in his AHA presidential address. Deploring the fragmentation and lack of coherence among specializations, Bailyn declared that the critical need of the profession was "to bring order into large areas of history and thus to reintroduce history in a sophisticated form to a wider reading public, through synthetic works narrative in structure, on major themes, works that explain some significant part of how the present world came to be the way it is."[4]

By the mid-1980s this issue had become the subject of numerous articles and forums. They reflected a "growing unease," in the words of Thomas Bender, about "the declining significance of history in the general intellectual culture of our time." To reengage this culture, Bender urged historians to undertake what he termed a "narrative synthesis"—an incorporation of the findings and interpretations of specialized subfields into a new synthesis written in a narrative format that would be accessible and interesting to a lay public.[5]

Bender struck a sympathetic chord. A poll of members of the Organization of American Historians in 1985 revealed that the "central problem" of the profession, as perceived by participants in this poll, was the need for "reorientation of scholarship away from specialization and toward big questions and broader audiences." As one respondent expressed it: "Our discipline is excessively com-

4. Lawrence Stone, "The Revival of Narrative: Reflections on a New Old History," *Past and Present,* no. 85 (1979), 3–24, quotation from p. 15; Bernard Bailyn, "The Challenge of Modern Historiography," *American Historical Review* 87 (1982), 1–24, quotation from pp. 7–8.

5. Thomas Bender, "Wholes and Parts: The Need for Synthesis in American History," *Journal of American History* 73 (1986), 120–36, quotation from p. 120.

partmentalized and irrelevant except to our own diminishing numbers."[6]

But not everyone agreed with the call for a narrative synthesis. Some worried that because traditional narrative history had chronicled only the public activities of elite white males, the history of workers, women, racial and ethnic minorities, and other nonelites would be rendered invisible again by the revival of narrative. Proponents of a new narrative synthesis dismissed these fears as a red herring. They did not advocate a restoration of *traditional* narrative, they said, but rather the incorporation of all those separate parts—race, class, gender, and ethnicity—into a new whole. As Bailyn put it, the "greatest challenge" facing the profession "is not how to deepen and further sophisticate their technical probes of life in the past (that effort will, and of course should, continue in any case) but how to put the story together again, now with a complexity and an analytic dimension never envisioned before . . . into readable accounts of major developments."[7]

The advocates of narrative synthesis seemed to carry the day, at least judging from widespread lip service in the profession support-

6. David Thelen, "The Profession and the *Journal of American History*," in *ibid.*, 9–10.

7. Bailyn, "The Challenge of Modern Historiography," 23–24. See also C. Vann Woodward, "A Short History of American History," in Woodward, *The Future of the Past* (New York, 1989), pp. 315–21; Eric H. Monkkenen, "The Dangers of Synthesis," *American Historical Review* 91 (1986), 1146–57; Susan Porter Benson, Stephen Brier, and Roy Rosenzweig, eds., *Presenting the Past: Essays on History and the Public* (Philadelphia, 1986), pp. 21–49; essays by David Thelen, Nell Irvin Painter, Roy Rosenzweig, and Thomas Bender in "A Round Table: Synthesis in American History," *Journal of American History* 74 (June 1987), pp. 107–30; Gertrude Himmelfarb, *The Old History and the New* (Cambridge, Mass., 1987); Peter Novick, *That Noble Dream: The "Objectivity Question" and the American Historical Profession* (Cambridge, 1988), chap. 16, esp. pp. 622–24; and Allen Megill, "Recounting the Past: 'Description,' Explanation, and Narrative in Historiography," *American Historical Review* 94 (1989), 627–53.

ing this notion. But did it produce anything more than lip service? Apparently not, if the responses by a thousand members of the Organization of American Historians to a survey in 1994 are an accurate indication. On the survey questionnaire, one of the items checked by an overwhelming majority—74 percent—stated that "the academic reward system encourages historians to write for academic audiences and discourages historians from reaching out to multiple audiences." Numerous respondents added their own gloss to this statement. "The profession is imploding. Historians write for one another while journalists grow increasingly popular as writers of history." "We have given history—public history—to popularizers because of our fear of writing clear, dramatic, interesting narrative, which may be interpreted by colleagues as unsophisticated or lacking theoretical understanding." Professional preferments in the form of academic promotions, grants, prizes, favorable reviews in the journals go to "elite monographs . . . not accessible to educated lay persons." "Written by incredibly boring academics. No one reads it. Who can blame them?"[8]

Apprentice historians pick up signals early in their careers about how the "academic reward system" works. Four graduate students at Indiana University wrote in 1994 that

> despite avowals to the contrary by a profession whose democratizing impulses led to "people's history," our professional culture still contains an undercurrent of disdain for works written by amateurs or for public audiences. . . . As graduate students, we hear this in the classroom, where popular works may be credited as "good narratives" but ultimately derided as lacking "sufficient rigor." We absorb it through hallway conversations and professional newsletters. . . . We rehearse it by learning to write . . . in a style that favors subtle distinction and academic jargon at the expense of accessibility.

8. Quotations in David Thelen, "The Practice of American History," *Journal of American History* 81 (1994), 939–43.

"The result?" queried one of their elders, who answered his own question: "Americans get their history from Ken Burns, not the JAH" *(Journal of American History).*[9]

Ken Burns, whose eleven-hour television documentary on the American Civil War has been seen by at least forty million viewers, had something to say on this matter in an interview with the editor of the *Journal of American History.* Speaking with blunt candor to professional historians, he said: "I believe you have failed and lost touch absolutely in the communication of history to the public and that it has fallen to the amateur historians, if you will, to try to rescue that history; I would hope that the academy could change course and join a swelling chorus of interest in history for everyone." Burns also complained that in college "I was never taught what happened in the Civil War. I was taught causes, and then I was taught effects. And [yet] this happens to be a war in which the outcome of battles mattered . . . and the only people who seemed to know something about it were the military historians"—that is, the amateurs like Bruce Catton and Shelby Foote.[10]

Burns's complaint was precisely the opposite of one uttered more than a century earlier, in 1885, by Albion W. Tourgée, a novelist, lawyer, and crusader for black civil rights. Although he was a twice-wounded veteran of the Union army, Tourgée expressed vexation with the flood of books and articles beginning to appear in the 1880s that focused on the battles and military leaders of the Civil War but said little about its causes and effects. What really mattered, said Tourgée, was *"not* the courage, the suffering, the blood, but

9. Chad Berry, Patrick Ettinger, Dot McCullough, and Meg Meneghel, "History from the Bottom Up: On Reproducing Professional Culture in Graduate Education," *ibid.,* 1144; second quotation from Thelen, "The Practice of American History," *ibid.,* 943.

10. "The Movie Maker as Historian: Conversations with Ken Burns," *ibid.,* 1050, 1042.

only the causes that underlay the struggle and the results that followed from it." [11]

The contrasting viewpoints of Burns and Tourgée frame a dichotomy that has affected historical writing about the Civil War for more than a century. This bifurcation reflects a more general polarization between amateur and professional historians. The particular case of the Civil War may therefore shed light on the question of audiences for historical writing.

There are actually three audiences for Civil War history. The degree of overlap among them is the point at issue. The first consists of professional historians and their constituency—other historians and their captive audience of students. They focus on the big questions mentioned by Tourgée: the causes and results of the war. In looking at the South they examine slavery and the socioeconomic structure in which it was embedded, the ideology it generated, the political order that reflected and expressed this structure and ideology, the trauma of transformation from a slave to a free-labor society, the process of class formation and social relations among three principal groups in the South that were profoundly affected by these experiences—the planters, yeomen whites, and blacks—the changes in racial status, relations, and perceptions brought about by these changes, and the impact of all these developments on women and gender roles among both whites and blacks. In looking at the North or the nation as a whole, professional historians focus on many of the same issues of social structure, ideology, political behavior, class formation, racial attitudes and relations, and gender roles. A dominant theme in academic professional analyses of the Civil War era is America's "great transformation" from an agricultural and artisan economy with its attendant social relations and ideology, sometimes defined as pre-capitalist, to a wage-labor industrial capitalist econ-

11. Albion W. Tourgée, "The Veteran and His Pipe," *Chicago Inter Ocean,* April 25, 1885.

omy—a transformation in which the Civil War marked an important punctuation point as a triumph of Northern wage-labor capitalism over Southern plantation slavery.

In their teaching as well as writing about the Civil War, many academic historians virtually ignore what Walt Whitman called "the real war"—the experiences of the three million soldiers and the vicarious extensions of those experiences to their families and friends back home, who constituted almost the whole of the American people. Fought entirely on American soil (except for some naval actions on the high seas), the Civil War killed almost as many American soldiers as all the rest of the wars fought by this country combined. It laid waste millions of acres of farm and forest in the South, destroyed two-thirds of Southern wealth, slaughtered two-fifths of the region's livestock, and killed one-quarter of the South's white males of military age. It left nearly two hundred thousand widows and perhaps twice that number of fatherless children. These facts alone had an enormous impact on the demographic, social, and economic structure of the country, on gender relations, and on the physical environment.

Yet until recently, professional historians in the fields of social, gender, demographic, and environmental history neglected the military dimensions of the Civil War. Some ignored the war altogether. A survey of 603 doctoral dissertations in American women's history completed from 1980 to 1987 found that fewer than 2 percent dealt in any way with the Civil War. Two anthologies of essays on the Civil War and Reconstruction published in the 1970s and intended for college courses contained almost nothing on military events.[12] Anecdotal evidence of college courses in American history that skip over the events of 1861 to 1865 confirms that Ken Burns's experience was not unique. A pamphlet on recent historiography of the Civil

12. Gerda Lerner, "Priorities and Challenges in Women's History Research," *Perspectives* 26 (April 1988), 18; Irwin Unger, ed., *Essays on the Civil War and Reconstruction* (New York, 1970); Charles Crowe, ed., *The Age of the Civil War and Reconstruction,* rev. ed. (Homewood, Ill., 1975).

War era published by the American Historical Association in 1990 virtually ignored the fighting and dying. Stephan Thernstrom's classic study of Newburyport from 1850 to 1880, which in many ways launched the modern boom in American social history, did not even mention the Civil War much less analyze the significant demographic and social impact it had on that very community.[13]

This neglect of the real war is not faithful to the lived experience of Americans of that generation. "The war," wrote Ralph Waldo Emerson in 1861, "has assumed such huge proportions that it threatens to engulf us all—no preoccupation can exclude it, & no hermitage hide us." Three years later, during the titanic battles of the Wilderness and Spotsylvania in Virginia, the New York lawyer George Templeton Strong wrote in his diary: "These are fearfully critical, anxious days, in which the destiny of the continent for centuries will be decided." The destiny of the continent did indeed hinge on these battles—and on others. As Abraham Lincoln noted in his second inaugural address: On "the progress of our arms . . . all else chiefly depends."[14]

"All else" included most of the things that professional historians consider important during that era—the fate of slavery, the structure of society and social relations in both North and South, the direction of the American economy, the destiny of competing nationalisms in Union and Confederacy, the very survival of the United States—all rested on the shoulders of those three million men in blue and gray

13. Eric Foner, *Slavery, the Civil War, and Reconstruction* (Washington, 1990); Stephan Thernstrom, *Poverty and Progress: Social Mobility in a Nineteenth Century City* (Cambridge, Mass., 1964). For the war's impact on Newburyport, see Maris A. Vinovskis, "Have Social Historians Lost the Civil War? Some Preliminary Demographic Speculations," *Journal of American History* 76 (June 1989), 43–50.

14. Ralph L. Lusk, ed., *The Letters of Ralph Waldo Emerson* (New York, 1939), V, 251; *The Diary of George Templeton Strong,* vol. 3, *The Civil War 1860– 1865,* ed. Allan Nevins and Milton Halsey Thomas (New York, 1952), p. 449; Roy P. Basler, ed., *The Collected Works of Abraham Lincoln,* 9 vols. (New Brunswick, N.J., 1953–1955), VIII, 332.

who fought it out during four years of violence unmatched in the Western world between 1815 and 1914. That experience would seem to deserve at least a nod from the academy.

In recent years it has finally gotten at least a small nod. In 1989 Maris Vinovskis published a now-famous article with the double-entendre title, "Have Social Historians Lost the Civil War?"[15] He concluded that they had. But since then, partly because of that article, they are finding it. Numerous recent studies by professional historians have analyzed the impact of the war on American society at all levels and the impact of the society on the way the war was waged.[16] But most of these studies are thematic, analytical, and monographic; they do not meet the felt need for a "narrative synthe-

15. Vinovskis, "Have Social Historians Lost the Civil War? Some Preliminary Demographic Speculations," 34–58.

16. Maris A. Vinovskis, ed., *Toward a Social History of the American Civil War: Exploratory Essays* (Cambridge, 1990); Catherine Clinton and Nina Silber, eds., *Divided Houses: Gender and the Civil War* (New York, 1992); Reid Mitchell, *The Vacant Chair: The Northern Soldier Leaves Home* (New York, 1993); Larry J. Daniel, *Soldiering in the Army of Tennessee* (Chapel Hill, 1991); Joseph T. Glatthaar, *Forged in Battle: The Civil War Alliance of Black Soldiers and White Officers* (New York, 1990); Michael Fellman, *Inside War: The Guerrilla Conflict in Missouri during the American Civil War* (New York, 1989); Charles Royster, *The Destructive War: William Tecumseh Sherman, Stonewall Jackson, and the Americans* (New York, 1991); Mark Grimsley, *The Hard Hand of War: Union Military Policy toward Southern Civilians, 1861–1865* (Cambridge, 1996); Wayne K. Durrill, *War of Another Kind: A Southern Community in the Great Rebellion* (New York, 1990); Grace Palladino, *Another Civil War: Labor, Capital, and the State in the Anthracite Regions of Pennsylvania* (Urbana, 1990); Iver Bernstein, *The New York City Draft Riots: Their Significance for American Society and Politics in the Age of the Civil War* (New York, 1990); J. Matthew Gallman, *The North Fights the Civil War: The Home Front* (Chicago, 1994); George C. Rable, *The Confederate Republic: A Revolution against Politics* (Chapel Hill, 1994); David E. Long, *The Jewel of Liberty: Abraham Lincoln's Re-election and the End of Slavery* (Mechanicsburg, Pa., 1994); George C. Rable, *Civil Wars: Women and the Crisis of Southern Nationalism* (Urbana, 1989); Elizabeth D. Leonard, *Yankee Women: Gender Battles in the Civil War* (New York, 1994); and Anne C. Rose, *Victorian America and the Civil War* (Cambridge, 1992).

sis"; and with some exceptions they have limited appeal to an audience beyond the academy.

If professional historians deserve censure for ignoring the military dimension of the Civil War, the second "audience" for the history of that era deserves censure for the opposite reason. In numbers this is a larger audience than the first. It consists of people who are loosely described as "Civil War buffs." They are a remarkable phenomenon in American life. Indeed, they are unique, for no other facet of American history—not even the Old West—has attracted such a large constituency. They include the members of more than two hundred Civil War Round Tables in all parts of the country, an estimated 40,000 reenactors who don their replica blue or gray uniforms and take up their replica Springfield rifled muskets several weekends each year to reenact Civil War battles, the more than 250,000 subscribers to four popular monthly or bimonthly Civil War magazines, many of whom also buy millions of dollars of Civil War books each year, providing the most faithful customers of the History Book Club and sustaining several publishing houses that specialize in reprinted and new Civil War books, and the network of collectors of everything from brass buttons and minié balls to Civil War paintings and prints.

Some members of this large audience pay occasional attention to the political and social issues at stake in the war. But most are interested mainly, often exclusively, in the military campaigns and battles. Those are what sell the books and magazines and prints, furnish the topics of round table lectures, and of course provide the raison d'être of the reenactors. This focus on military events helps explain why the constituency of Civil War buffs is overwhelmingly male. Indeed, at first the membership of many round tables was entirely male. When the oldest and largest round table, in Chicago, debated the admission of women in 1976, one opponent declared: "To admit the ladies would . . . inevitably lead to an erosion of the purpose of this organization. With all due respect to those few serious female students of the Civil War, the undeniable truth is that most women could [not] care less about the Battle of Antietam or Jackson's strategy in the Valley."[17]

Some things have changed since 1976. All round tables now admit women. The man who made that statement has long since recanted, and he now expresses interest in the nonmilitary issues of the war. But for many buffs things have not changed very much in this latter respect. While most of them would probably concede—in theory—that the battle of Antietam or Jackson's Valley campaign cannot be fully understood apart from the political as well as military purposes they intended to accomplish, the issues of slavery and emancipation that hinged in particular on the Antietam campaign, and the societies from which the soldiers came in this war fought mainly by volunteers, these buffs remain interested mainly in the battles and not in their larger context.

Most authors of books written for this audience are nonacademics. They are skilled in narrative but not in synthesis. Indeed, the trend in recent years has been to write more and more about less and less. We have several books about individual battles ranging from 400 to 650 pages each. For Gettysburg we have an 800-page tome on the first day alone plus two volumes by a single author on the second day totaling 725 pages. Only the most dedicated buff can wade through all of this prose.[18]

There is a third audience for Civil War history. It is the same as for other kinds of history. It consists of that oft-described but seldom-defined category called "general readers" or "lay public"—

17. Quoted in Barbara Hughett, *The Civil War Round Table: Fifty Years of Scholarship and Fellowship* (Chicago, 1990), p. 114.

18. John H. Hennessy, *Return to Bull Run: The Campaign and Battle of Second Manassas* (New York, 1993); Ernest B. Furgurson, *Chancellorsville 1863: The Souls of the Brave* (New York, 1991); Peter Cozzens, *This Terrible Sound: The Battle of Chickamauga* (Urbana, 1992); Gordon C. Rhea, *The Battle of the Wilderness May 5–6, 1864* (Baton Rouge, 1994); David G. Martin, *Gettysburg July 1* (Conchocken, Pa., 1995); Harry Pfanz, *Gettysburg: The Second Day* (Chapel Hill, 1987); and Pfanz, *Gettysburg: Culp's Hill and Cemetery Hill* (Chapel Hill, 1993).

the audience that professional historians ritually wring their hands about failing to reach. Allan Nevins did reach a portion of this audience with his eight volumes on *Ordeal of the Union* and *War for the Union*. But amateurs like Douglas Southall Freeman, Bruce Catton, Shelby Foote, and Ken Burns have been more successful in this regard. The Burns series was in a class by itself with its mega-audience of forty million. Burns consciously set out to provide the kind of narrative synthesis that neither the "old school" (as he termed it) nor the "new history" offered—the old school because while narrative in approach, it did not incorporate material on "women, labor, minorities, and the social transformation" accomplished by the war; the new history because it "often abandoned narrative completely."[19]

Whether or not Burns succeeded in creating a good narrative synthesis—I think he did—he certainly reached the lay public. He also demonstrated how the medium of television can present history in an exciting, intelligent, responsible manner. Professional historians have also explored this medium, and more will doubtless do so in the future. Other new technologies such as CD-ROM are being used to teach history. But most of us will continue to write about the past in the traditional manner, and our audience will consist of readers rather than viewers. In that respect, what more can be said about the historian and his audience? At the risk of appearing egotistical (which is contrary to my intention), I offer my own experience as a case study to suggest some answers to this question. In the process perhaps I can provide a face for that faceless persona, the general reader.

In 1988 my book *Battle Cry of Freedom: The Civil War Era,* a nine-hundred-page volume with fifteen hundred footnotes at the bottom of the pages, was published by Oxford University Press as part of its series *The Oxford History of the United States.* Although the purpose of this series is to present to that legendary general reader

---

19. "The Movie Maker as Historian: Conversations with Ken Burns," 1039–40.

"the scholarship of this generation" in "a readable and coherent narrative framework," the publisher was as astonished as I was by the book's commercial success. It spent sixteen weeks on the *New York Times* best-seller list in hardcover and another twelve weeks in paperback, selling nearly six hundred thousand copies to date in its various cloth, paperback, book club, and foreign editions. Whatever else may explain this phenomenon, it seems to confirm two things: the extraordinary popularity of the American Civil War, and the existence of a lay readership eager for a narrative synthesis—at least of the 1848–1865 era of American history.

During the past seven years I have talked with several hundred people who have read the book and have received 521 letters from individual readers. I made no record of the conversations. But I do have that historian's godsend, written documentation, for the 521 letter writers, which enables me to say something about the nature of that audience. First, some quantitative dimensions: 85 percent are male, only 15 percent female. This fits the expected profile of readers interested in the Civil War and also conforms to the pattern of membership in the History Book Club, which is 80 percent male.[20] The letters came from forty-three states and nine foreign countries; 5 percent of them came from abroad.

Surprisingly, given the high intensity of interest in the Civil War in the South, only 18 percent of the letters came from the eleven states that formed the Confederacy. One explanation of this fact may be that the book challenges the moonlight-and-magnolias *Gone with the Wind* image of the Confederacy. Several of the Southern letters I did receive support this explanation. A Florida lawyer wrote of *Battle Cry of Freedom* that "I enjoyed it very much" but he took offense at my "one sided and biased views of the causes and conduct of that terrible war" and at the " 'cheap shots' at the South and Southerners.

20. Information supplied to the author by Nancy Whitin of the History Book Club, which has 250,000 members, 200,000 of whom are males. About 90 percent of the members have college degrees. The Civil War is the best-selling topic for the club.

. . . You are obviously a 'liberal' on civil rights, particularly for black people. You are certainly entitled to sprinkle your book liberally with personal opinion & argument." But "you should admit as much, and not pass your book off as a politically & racially neutral factual account of the times. . . . Southerners were on the whole much more honorable and noble than you choose to believe. Thanks for a good book anyway."[21]

With respect to the three audiences for Civil War books mentioned earlier, 16 percent of the letters are from academic professional historians, 20 percent are from people whom I can more or less identify as Civil War buffs, and the remaining 64 percent from a generic public. From here on the data become imprecise because exact information on education, age, or occupation is not clear in many of the letters. But it is evident that the overwhelming majority of the 84 percent in the two categories of Civil War buffs and general readers are college-educated. At least one-fourth of them appear to be retired, and consequently have more time for reading. Some 10 percent were students when they wrote. Of those whose occupation I could identify, including some of the retirees, 15 to 18 percent are secondary school teachers; 10 to 12 percent lawyers; about the same percentage are editors, writers, or publishers; 6 percent are in the military; about the same percentage are business people of some sort; about the same number are in the clergy; some 3 or 4 percent are physicians and a similar number are in the hard sciences, mathematics, or engineering; 2 or 3 percent are journalists; and the remainder are scattered among several occupations including two United States senators, two state governors, one congressman, one labor leader, one assistant football coach (of the Philadelphia Eagles), two prison inmates, and one mental patient.

This listing makes no pretense to be a representative sample of

---

21. E. A. to author, September (no day), 1989. All letters from readers cited herein are in the author's possession. I use initials to protect the privacy of the letter writers.

those outside the profession who read history or even of those who read Civil War history. But it is a useful surrogate for such a sample. One notable fact stands out: Among the 84 percent who are not professional historians, a majority are professionals of some sort— teachers, lawyers, editors and writers, military officers, physicians, clergy, and scientists. Most of them appear to be old enough to have grown up before the era when they could have been hooked as teen- agers on television or computer games.

What are these people looking for when they pick up a book of history? (One caveat: readers generally write to authors only when they like a book, so this sample is biased toward favorable opinions of *Battle Cry*). First and foremost, they are looking for that elusive narrative synthesis. "I do not normally read histories," began one letter. "This book, however, was worth every moment I was able to spend with it. It is history but reads like a narrative work of fiction that captures one's interest and keeps it." A World War II veteran from Omaha thought that *Battle Cry* "pleases the learned and the ignorant simultaneously and that's no mean writing accomplishment. You blend narrative and scholarship and often those two elements get in each other's way and the book becomes a mish-mash. Not in this case." A lecturer in history at Christ Church, Oxford, decided to add the Civil War to the American history he teaches there, having previously refused to do so because "the literature is too vast and the issues too complex. Your book has destroyed that excuse. . . . You have provided a model of how to combine narrative and analysis, explanation of causes as well as a vivid presentation of events. Above all, you give the English reader what has long been wanted, a single- volume survey of a most difficult and baffling conflict."[22]

These expressions of appreciation for the narrative framework re- paid me for the endless hours spent trying to resolve the problems

---

22. A. C. to author, Oct. 10, 1989; R. M. to author, Nov. 7, 1990; W. T. to author, March 22, 1990.

of organizing the material to create such a framework. I know now why so many historians choose a topical or thematic format rather than the basically chronological approach that narrative requires. A topical structure is much, *much* easier to create than a chronological one. That is especially true in writing about a war, say the Civil War, in which all events are important and take place on several planes simultaneously: military, political, economic, social, diplomatic, in both Union and Confederacy and in Europe as well. The easy way to organize all of this is to write separate chapters on each topic—military campaigns and battles, diplomacy, politics in the Union, politics in the Confederacy, slavery and emancipation, economic mobilization, and so on. Such a format is neat, clean, compartmentalized; it is also static, dull, and fails to give the reader a sense of the dynamism of change over time or the cause-effect relationships among all of these events interacting with each other within a diachronic framework.

Letters from readers made all of the headaches involved in constructing a diachronic narrative seem worthwhile. An older woman in Santa Rosa, California, who led her reading group in a discussion of the book wrote to me: "By showing the relationships of all that happened, whether social, political, economic, or military, you made everything come alive for me." A Ph.D. candidate in electrical engineering at Stanford wrote that reading *Battle Cry* had "gotten me much more interested in our country's history. . . . Your ability to stitch together so many pieces of the story into a (very easily) readable whole made the reading fun, too." A man from Northampton, Massachusetts, evidently an academic in another field, wrote:

> I really felt I was going *through* your writing into the events themselves. . . . You gave all the events a context . . . relating all the occurrences to one another, how everything affected everything else. . . . Your scholarship augmented this by making me realize that there ARE historical questions, that there are controversies, and made

it great fun for me to glimpse into the realm of the professional historian.[23]

Does writing a narrative synthesis mean refocusing the spotlight on white male elites acting in the public sphere? The danger of doing so is perhaps greater in writing about a war than about other historical subjects. I was gratified that a professional historian at a West Coast university did not think I had committed that sin. "I recently attended a meeting of the American Studies Association," he wrote to me in the fall of 1989.

> Many of the sessions were on "The New History" and were centered on "race, class, ethnicity, and gender." I happen to believe that these are some of the most important topics that we deal with in history. But I didn't think that I learned much about these questions from the papers that I heard. I liked the approach you used in *Battle Cry of Freedom*: to tell the basic story, to seek out the underlying issues. In the end and in a very unself-conscious way, these issues tell us something about race, class, ethnicity, and gender relations.[24]

One of the things that pleased me most in the response by Civil War buffs to the book was the remark many of them made to the effect that it opened their eyes to the connections between military events and the sociopolitical context of the war. I suspect that I was less successful in persuading professional colleagues of the importance of military operations in propelling the social and political changes that interest them. In any case, I was brought up short by a letter from a Ph.D. candidate in English at the University of Michigan who was writing his dissertation on rhetoric with a special interest in the problem of audience. Two of the questions he asked me go to the heart of the concerns voiced by many of the respondents to the Organization of American Historians survey in 1994: "Do you

23. E. H. W. to author, Sept. 22, 1994; B. F. to author, April 9, 1989; A. A. to author, Dec. 3, 1988.
24. W. M. E. to author, Sept. 18, 1989.

think the culture of professional academic historians in America does, to a significant degree, hinder the development of talent for reaching public readerships?" and "Have you had occasion to feel that your public success has diminished your achievement in the eyes of fellow professionals?"[25]

At first I was inclined to answer no to the second question. I could not recall any direct or overt expression of such a sentiment by professional colleagues. But a pause for reflection brought a couple of items to mind. Although *Battle Cry of Freedom* won a few prizes, including the Pulitzer prize, it did not win any of the prizes for which it was eligible that were sponsored by professional associations or awarded by committees of professional historians. I recalled also a puzzling experience that, in thinking about the question asked by the Ph.D. candidate, appeared in a new light. Soon after *Battle Cry* was published, a member of the program committee of a professional association formally invited me to participate in a session about the book at the 1989 meeting of the association. Such sessions have become common features of professional meetings; I was flattered by the invitation and of course I said yes. Six months later I received an apologetic letter from the same committee member calling the whole thing off. No coherent explanation was given, but in my rereading of the correspondence it seemed clear that a majority of the program committee felt that a book which had reached a large audience of nonprofessionals was not sufficiently weighty to merit a session at a professional meeting.

More important to me than these incidents are the many letters I have received stating that *Battle Cry* awakened a dormant or previously nonexistent interest in history. One reader wrote: "I didn't remember a thing from my High School History classes. . . . I just finished reading *Battle Cry of Freedom* and wanted to thank you for filling up the hole. Your book read like a novel . . . bringing out the tiny details and the big picture all in one book." A high school

25. W. C. R. to author, Nov. 21, 1990.

student in New Jersey said she had "always loved history, and reading your book has helped confirm my plans of continuing an extensive study of American history throughout college." A Massachusetts man informed me that he had gotten the book from a book club because he forgot to send in the rejection slip. "I hadn't read a history book since high school," he explained,

> and little expected to read it. . . . But something prompted me to at least give the book a chance. From the very first sentence I was interested. By the end of the first section I was hooked. . . . I don't think it would be an overstatement to say that your book has changed my life—such a large topic, namely HISTORY, has suddenly opened up to me. . . . You have grounded my existence, my PRESENT, into a past. . . . You have made a convert of me, and I can't tell you how happy I am that a subject that previously left me cold . . . has suddenly come alive.[26]

In April 1989 I received a letter from a third-year law student at Duke University who said that reading *Battle Cry* "has had a very important impact on my life. . . . I will practice law as a career but one of my most memorable law school experiences will be the time spent reading your book and the love for history it rekindled in me." Almost three years later I received another letter from the same person. "Following our correspondence," he said, "I went on a voracious History reading binge that continued into my first year as an attorney in New York. I began to agonize over the fact that I had gone to law school instead of to a graduate History program." After a year as an attorney he took the plunge and went to graduate school in history. "My reading your book, it turns out, was an important turning point in my life. It helped launch me on a career in History."[27] One hopes that his enthusiasm will not be dimmed by expe-

---

26. D. K. to author, Aug. 24, 1990; C. M. C. to author, April 5, 1989; A. A. to author, Dec. 3, 1988.

27. M. R. to author, April (no day), 1989, Jan. 9, 1992.

riences similar to those of the four graduate students at Indiana University who heard "popular works . . . credited as 'good narratives' but ultimately derided as lacking 'sufficient rigor.' "

A colleague at a California university recently remarked to me that I would be forced to choose between becoming a "popular historian" or a "historian's historian." He strongly hinted that I was in mortal danger of becoming the former. Why couldn't I be both? I responded. Surely it is possible to say something of value to fellow professionals while at the same time engaging a wider audience. My colleague only smiled sadly at my naïveté. Maybe that is what's the matter with history.

INDEX